IMAGES OF WOMEN

The Portrayal of Women in Photography
of the Middle East 1860–1950

IMAGES OF WOMEN

SARAH GRAHAM-BROWN

New York
Columbia University Press
1988

Library of Congress Cataloging-in-Publication Data available
on request
ISBN 0-231-06826-3

Contents

Acknowledgements

A large number of people have contributed to this book, in a variety of ways. In the two and a half years it took to complete the work, I made a number of trips abroad, which, in most cases, were too brief for the amount of research I had to do, and I have to express my appreciation to all the people who, either in their professional or personal capacities, helped me at short notice, I'm sure sometimes at some inconvenience to themselves.

Much of the photographic material for the book came from archives in Britain and abroad and I would like to thank all the archivists who assisted me in finding photographs and helped with the associated research, and those who made special efforts to help on my usually rushed visits to libraries: George Hobart, Curator of Documentary Photographs, Prints and Photographs Division, Library of Congress, Washington DC; Elizabeth Edwards of the Pitt Rivers Museum, Oxford University; Lyn Ritchie, in charge of the Gertrude Bell archive in the Department of Archaeology, University of Newcastle upon Tyne; Miss P.A. Winker, in charge of the photographic collections in the School of Archaeology and Oriental Studies, University of Liverpool; May Financi, archivist of Robert College, Istanbul; the archive staff of *Ruz al-Yusuf* magazine, Cairo; Mr Karim Helmy, head of archives at the American University in Cairo; George Hintlian, in charge of the photographic collections at the Armenian Patriarchate, Jerusalem. My special thanks go to Gillian Grant, archivist of the Private Papers Collection, Middle East Centre, St Antony's College, Oxford, for giving many hours of her time to searching out and processing photographic orders for me, and for sharing her enthusiasm for and considerable knowledge of Middle Eastern photography and of archival sources.

For arranging for me to use particular photographic collections, I wish to thank especially Shelagh Weir, Assistant Keeper at the Museum of Mankind, for access to the Hilma Granqvist photographic collection; and to Professor Nurhan Atasoy of Istanbul University for giving me access, at short notice, to the Abdul Hamid photographic collection, and also to Muhammad Issa Waley for access to the British Library's collection of photographs from the Abdul Hamid collections. I also appreciate the help of Russell Harris in New York for arranging on my behalf the copying of photographs in the New York Public Library. A number of collectors and historians of Middle Eastern photography have generously allowed me to use pictures from their collections as well as sharing their ideas with me: Badr al-Hajj in London, Nadim Shehadi in Oxford, Engin Çizgen in Istanbul and Malek Alloula and Fouad Debbas in Paris. Other collectors and photographers I would like to thank for their advice are Stephen Wachlin and Wim Heynen in Amsterdam and Barry Iverson in Cairo, and for his help in copying photographs from family collections in Cairo, Bourkan Qawaqji.

Special thanks are also due to photographer Alan Urruty who dealt with a constant stream of orders for prints and succeeded in enhancing even my least successful efforts at photographic copying. Many people also helped in providing comments and criticism of the project in its embryonic stages, supplied, or gave me leads to new visual and written sources, advised on particular aspects of social history and women's studies or helped to contact women in the Middle East. Among these I would particularly like to thank: Zafer Toprak of Boğaziçi University, Istanbul; Hasna Mikdashi, Arab Lutfi, Virginia Danielson, Marilyn Booth and Cynthia Nelson in Cairo; Elias Sanbar in Paris; Iraj Afshar in Tehran; in the United States: Mary Harper, Professor Edward Said, Julia Ballerini, Mervat Hatem, Molly Nolan, Azar Tabari, Judith Tucker, Margaret Meriwether and Barbara Harlow (who also made my brief stay at Cornell University fruitful and enjoyable); in Britain: Floreeda Safiri, Hanan al-Shaykh, Kitty Warnock, Ali Razavi, Nermin Menemencioğlu and Mayam Poya. Thanks also to the numerous friends who provided hospitality and encouragement during my travels.

To all the individual women and families who so generously allowed me to use their photographs and their reminiscences, as well as giving their time and hospitality, I am most grateful – in Istanbul, Süreya Ağaoğlu, Berna Tunali, Mehmet and Nouran Isvan, Tomris Uyar and Engin Gargar; in Cairo, Saad Kamil and his family, Samia Mehrez and her family, particularly Aziza Galal, Lilli Doss, Bahija Rashid and the Huda Shaarawi Association, and Reem Saad; in Beirut, Amira al-Asad; in the West Bank, Hilweh Giacaman and Rita Giacaman; in Britain, Serene and Leila Shahid, the Tashjian family, Nada Andraous, Cecil and Furugh Hourani, Tarif al-Khalidi, Aziz al-Azmeh and Nada Taher.

I had a good deal of help with translation of texts from several languages, and special thanks go to Jana Gough and Fiona Symon.

I am very much indebted to those who read the manuscript in its various drafts for their incisive criticisms, helpful comments and general encouragement. Margot Badran generously shared her insights on women's history in Egypt which are the result of her many years of research on the Egyptian feminist movement. Joanna de Groot, Deniz Kandiyoti and Nels Johnson gave me valuable comment, new ideas and helped to strengthen the theoretical framework of the book. They also gave me a good deal of moral support, as did Barbara Smith, whose rigorous proofreading was also much appreciated. Albert Hourani's great knowledge of modern Middle Eastern history and his meticulous reading of the manuscript rescued me from a number of historical errors and misunderstandings. Zelfa Hourani, the commissioning editor at Quartet Books, has dealt with the slow and laborious progress of production with a combination of patience, firmness and sympathy which I greatly appreciated. My thanks also to designer Ruth Hope and other members of Quartet's staff involved in the production of the book.

Note

The term 'Middle East' is used to describe the area from Iran in the east to Morocco in the west, Turkey and the whole Arab world including Sudan.

Modern geographical names are used except in the following cases: Palestine refers to the boundaries of British Mandate Palestine; Istanbul is used instead of Constantinople; and Iran is used rather than Persia.

The numerals in the margin alongside the main text refer to illustrations which do not appear adjacent to the text.

Chronology

The following chronology of events is not comprehensive: it covers only events relevant to this book.

1830	Beginning of French occupation of Algeria.
1848	Beginning of reign of Nasir al-Din Shah in Iran.
1859/60	Uprisings and civil disturbances in Lebanon; riots in Damascus.
1860s	Establishment of first state-run girls' schools in Turkey as part of *Tanzimat* reforms.
1869	Law passed in Turkey making elementary education compulsory for children of both sexes up to the age of twelve.
1869	Opening of the Suez Canal.
1876	Beginning of reign of Sultan Abdul Hamid II in Ottoman Empire.
1881	French establish a protectorate in Tunisia.
1882	British occupation of Egypt. Defeat of the Urabi Pasha revolt.
1895	Establishment of first state-run primary schools for girls in Egypt.
1906	Constitutional revolution in Iran.
1908	'Young Turk' revolution in Turkey.
1909	Sultan Abdul Hamid II deposed.
1912	Italian occupation of Libya after defeat of Ottoman army.
1912	French establish a protectorate in Morocco.
1912–13	Balkan wars against Ottomans.
1914	Outbreak of World War I. British unilaterally declare a protectorate over Egypt.
1915/16	Deportations and massacres of Armenians in Turkey.
1916	Arab rebellion in the Hijaz (Arabia) against the Ottomans, which received British backing.
1917	British occupy Baghdad and Jerusalem.
1917	Balfour Declaration promises the Zionists a 'homeland' for the Jews in Palestine.
1918	The British and allied armies along with Arab forces occupy Damascus (taken over by the French in 1920).
1919–22	Egyptian nationalist uprising and campaign against British rule.
1920–2	Greek–Turkish war.
1920–1	Anti-Zionist riots in Palestine.
1920	Anti-British uprising in Iraq.
1921	Reza Khan stages coup in Iran.
1922	Egypt becomes formally independent, though British political influence continues to predominate.

1923	Mustafa Kemal (Atatürk) declares Turkey a republic.
1923	League of Nations mandates formally assigned under the Treaty of Lausanne: to Britain for Palestine, Transjordan and Iraq; to France for Syria and Lebanon.
1925	Reza Khan is declared Reza Shah Pahlavi, ruler of Iran.
1925–6	Atatürk announces a series of reforms of the Turkish legal system, including changes in the personal-status law and women's legal position.
1925–6	Druze uprising in Syria.
1929	Major disturbances in Palestine. 'Wailing Wall riots'. Attacks on Jews in Hebron.
1936	Nine-month general strike in Palestine organized by the Palestinian nationalist movement. British retaliate with a wave of arrests and deportations of Palestinian activists and nationalist leaders.
1936–9	Large-scale rebellion in Palestine against British rule and against Zionist settlement.
1941	British and Free French armies invade Lebanon, taking over from Vichy French administration. Lebanese and Syrian nationalist campaigns for independence ensue.
1941	Abdication of Reza Shah and exile at behest of Anglo-Soviet forces in Iran. Succeeded by his son Muhammad Reza Pahlavi.
1943/4	Syria and Lebanon gain independence from France.
1945–52	Egyptian nationalist campaign for withdrawal of British troops from Egypt, including from the Suez Canal Zone.
1948–9	Declaration of the State of Israel; the first Arab–Israeli war results in the expulsion from Palestine of some 800,000 Palestinians.

Introduction

Photography and Social History

[Photography's] perfection is unapproachable by human hand and its truth raises it above all language, painting or poetry. It is the first universal language addressing itself to all who possess vision, and in characters alike understood in the courts of civilization and the hut of the savage. The pictorial language of Mexico, the hieroglyphics of Egypt are now superseded by reality.
('The Daguerreolite' in the *Daily Chronicle* [Cincinnati] Vol. I, No. 38, 17 January 1840)[1]

This triumphant announcement of photography as the universal language of the future was the first of many grandiose claims made for photographic realism. The notion of a documentary form which would supersede the frailties of human observation fitted well with the positivism which characterized much Western thought in the second half of the nineteenth century. Exploration, colonization and the rapid development of science and technology provided the first generations of photographers with ample scope to use their new skills. Although many doubts have since been raised about the veracity of photographic images, there is still a lingering sense that a photograph has a documentary value different from, and perhaps superior to, other forms of representation.

Yet the rise of photography to a position of dominance in the pantheon of visual imagery was not dictated solely by the laws of scientific positivism. Although it was essentially an invention of chemistry, it became entangled in aesthetic and ideological codes of representation. As Alan Sekula suggests, echoing Roland Barthes:

Photography is haunted by two chattering ghosts: that of bourgeois science and that of bourgeois art. The first goes on about the truth of appearances, about the world reduced to a positive ensemble of facts, to a constellation of knowable and possessable *objects*. The second spectre has the historical mission of apologizing for and redeeming the atrocities committed by the subservient – and more than spectral – hand of science.[2]

The rapid growth in the popularity of photography and, from the 1870s onwards, the relative ease of reproduction, has left us today with an enormous array of still photographs from the late nineteenth and early twentieth centuries. But in what way can they be considered as historical evidence? The charm of these faded sepia portraits and the postcards from

1

places far away in time and space is undeniable, but unless anchored to a context, these photographs remain, as Susan Sontag has suggested, fragments, 'frozen moments' of little significance.

For some contemporary analysts – for example, Roland Barthes in his later writings – most photographs can be little more than fragments. Barthes came to the conclusion that the meaning of photographs is determined more by the gaze of the individual viewer than by their wider historical and social context. But it can be argued that this wider context is in fact crucial to an understanding of how particular kinds of photographic images are created, and the impact they have.[3]

The invention of photography and, towards the end of the nineteenth century, the possibility of reproducing photographs on the printed page, contributed to the creation of a new visual mass culture. Photographic images and graphics became part of the fabric of daily life, no longer the province of the connoisseur. They became publicly visible in magazines, newspapers, books, postcards and on advertising billboards. Yet the assumptions which lie behind this multiplicity of images are seldom challenged or questioned. We absorb and internalize these visual clichés almost without being aware of it.

None the less, these photographic images do not exist in a vacuum. They have various layers of significance, contained within the images themselves and in the context in which they appear. One layer of meaning is provided by the immediate context: the form in which the photograph is presented and the use to which it is put – for example, to illustrate an article; to advertise a product; as a postcard souvenir of a holiday; or as a snapshot which preserves a private memory. The form in which the photograph is presented also dictates what we expect of it: for instance, we expect a 'news' photograph to convey 'facts', while a portrait should show us what a person 'looks like'.

The context and intention of the photograph can also be indicated by a caption. Walter Benjamin commented on the way captions in magazine and newspaper photographs were used to shape the viewer's interpretation of what he or she saw:

> . . . At the same time [around the turn of the century] picture magazines began to put up signposts for him [the viewer], right ones or wrong ones, no matter. For the first time captions have become obligatory. And it is clear that they have an altogether different character than the title of a painting. The directives which the captions give to those looking at pictures in illustrated magazines soon become even more explicit and more imperative in the film where the meaning of each single picture appears to be prescribed by the sequence of all preceding ones.[4]

When looking at photographs in the context of social history, a number of other forms of meaning have to be taken into consideration. These include the context in which the photograph was taken; the relationships of power and authority between photographer and subject; the aesthetic and ideological considerations which affected the photographer's choice of subject and the way the photograph might be interpreted by its viewers in a particular historical period. In many cases, photographs come down to us without these vital clues and attempts to discern their meaning can be only a matter of informed guesswork.

Furthermore, when historical photographs are used in a book such as this, they acquire another layer of meaning ascribed to them by the author and, whatever care is taken in the selection of photographs, the power of the images as well as conceptual considerations make the choice a personal one. Even if it is possible to resist the beguiling sense which these photographs often give the viewer of gazing into the past like Alice through the looking-glass, there is still what Barthes describes as the 'punctum' – the unpredictable arresting of the eye, and the emotions – by a detail in a photograph. Sometimes it is a look, when the subject seems to gaze directly at you out of the photograph; sometimes it is an incongruous detail, or an item of clothing which makes the photograph memorable and appealing, demanding to be chosen in preference to other photographs 'showing' the same scene or theme.

There is, in my view, no single formula for understanding the whole range of photographic imagery. Particularly when considered as historical documents, photographs rarely yield an unambiguous meaning. Victor Burgin has remarked that prolonged scrutiny of photographs often courts frustration – that they will not yield up further layers of meaning whatever attention they are given.[5]

All these considerations make the reading of historical photographs a complex task with frequently ambivalent conclusions. But viewed within the wider context of the cultural ideas and visual imagery of their era, they can sometimes provide clues to the way people saw each other – and the way they wished to see themselves. This is of particular importance in understanding the cultural impact of the unequal power relations between the West and the societies under its domination in the century between 1850 and 1950.

Visions of the Orient and Its Women in Nineteenth-century Europe

Meanings of all kinds flow through the figures of women, and they often do not include who she is herself.
(Marina Warner, *Monuments and Maidens*, London, 1985, p. 331)

1 Semi-nude woman lying on a divan. Stereoscopic daguerrotype, c.1852.

The photograph here seeks to imitate art, adopting the pose and style common to so many paintings of women, clothed or unclothed, produced in Europe in the eighteenth and nineteenth centuries. At the same time the interest of the picture is enhanced by the addition of 'Oriental' touches – the water pipe or *narghileh* in the foreground and the decor of palm trees in the background, evoking the figure of the 'odalisque'.

Three themes are intertwined in the development of Western photographic imagery of women in the Middle East. The first reflects the fact that the invention of photography coincided with a period of European imperialism on a global scale. The second is the particular and uneven cultural relationship between European cultures and those of the Middle East, embodied in what has become known as Orientalism. This was a set of assumptions about the Middle East which differed in some respects from Western images of other parts of the non-European world. The third theme is the tension between the Orientalist images of women in the Middle East, and changing attitudes to women's social, cultural and economic role in Europe. Underlying all themes are unequal power relationships: between colonizer and colonized, the creators of Orientalist fantasies and their subjects, male and female.

In this age of exploration and colonization, Western

images of regions of the world as far apart as Latin America and Polynesia shared many of the same notions about the inferiority and picturesqueness of 'native cultures', while the women of these cultures were frequently regarded as exotic sexual objects. The idea of the exotic had two dimensions: one of space – the lure of far-distant lands and peoples; and of time – the pursuit of the historical 'other'. Théophile Gautier summed this up in humorous style:

> The exotic can take one of two forms. The first gives you a taste for the Americas, a penchant for yellow women, for green women and so on . . . The most refined taste, however, the height of decadence, is the taste for an exoticism reaching back through time. Flaubert would aspire to fornicate [among the ruins of] Carthage, for example . . . As for me, nothing would excite me more than an [Egyptian] mummy.[6]

Nowhere were both kinds of exoticism more evident than in the Orientalists' vision of women in the Middle East. But the Orientalists approached the subject with an unusually heavy burden of historical, moral and cultural preconceptions. The nineteenth century saw the height of European fascination with the Orient which, as Edward Said has shown in his study *Orientalism*, manifested itself in a variety of forms from linguistic scholarship to popular novels. On a visual plane it affected everything from the Orientalist school of painting in the French Academy to the picture postcards tourists sent home to their families. In the preface to his book of poems, *Les Orientales*, published in 1829, Victor Hugo was already aware of the Orientalist craze in Europe:

> . . . people are now more taken up with the Orient than they have ever been. Oriental studies have never been so advanced. In the days of Louis XIV it was fashionable to be a Hellenist; now we are all Orientalists. This is a step forward. Never have so many great minds at one and the same time explored the unfathomable depths of Asia. We now have scholars specializing in every Oriental tongue from China to Egypt. And so the Orient – whether image or thought – has become, for artist and intellectual alike, a sort of general preoccupation, and one to which the author of this book has perhaps himself unwittingly succumbed.[7]

The geographical region encompassed by this notion of the Orient was vague. For some like Hugo, it extended as far as India and China, but its core was generally regarded as the Middle East – that is, North Africa, the Ottoman Empire and Iran – a region which also became of very great political, strategic and economic importance to Europe in the nineteenth and twentieth centuries.

The phenomenon of Orientalism went through many

permutations and forms of expression, according to the culture and political outlook of its exponents. But one of the central features of this vision of the Orient, which is most evident in popular writings and visual imagery, but which also informed many works of scholarship, was the concept of a society where all aspects of life – culture, politics, economics and personal relationships – could be explained by reference to the religion of Islam. In this essentialist view, Islam offered an explanatory touchstone for the behaviour of people from otherwise diverse cultures, ethnic groups and social classes. It was frequently assumed that the dominant role of these supposedly rigid religious precepts created a timeless social order scarcely subject to the forces of social or economic change.

A further assumption, common to much European thought of the nineteenth century, was the inherent superiority of European culture. It was from this vantage point that the social practices and religious philosophies of other societies were judged. Islamic societies were regarded with special interest, and sometimes hostility, as a result of their history of particular political and religious rivalry with Europe.

2 Unidentified photograph in the collection of A. Hotz, Dutch consul in Beirut before World War I.

This extraordinary picture is probably the work of an amateur and must have been a private joke. The bizarre quality of the composition – a woman with two skeletons – is further enhanced by the Orientalia which surrounds them. The woman wears a headdress, waistcoat and cloak of vaguely Oriental style; on her left is the base of a *narghileh* and a *chinoiserie* vase, while to her right is a rose-water shaker and a small Oriental rug. The whole scene is set upon another Oriental rug. It is unlikely that these objects had any particular meaning for the participants, except to increase the exotic quality of the photograph.

As the monotheistic religion which, during the late Middle Ages and the Renaissance, had presented the greatest political and military challenges to Christian Europe, Islam had already attracted interpretations by Europeans based on hostility, ignorance and even fear, which a small body of more sympathetic literature was unable to counter. When in the nineteenth century the roles were reversed, and the major European nations were making economic, political and military inroads into the Middle East, they generally came armed not merely with the sense of confidence, technological and racial superiority characteristic of the age, but with a predetermined set of ideas and prejudices about Muslims and Islamic society. As Edward Said observes:

In the system of knowledge about the Orient, the Orient is less a place than a *topos*, a set of references, a congeries of characteristics, that seems to have its origin in a quotation, or a fragment of a text, or a citation from someone's work on the Orient, or some bit of previous imagining, or an amalgam of all these.[8]

In the world of visual images of the Orient, the same process of borrowing, from literature as well as from other visual sources, combined to create a kind of pseudo-culture with its own internal logic. The age of empiricism and colonial rule intensified but did not fundamentally alter these images.

Many of these visions and ideas incorporated the figure of 'Oriental woman', often taken to represent the Orient itself or its essential characteristics. In the multiplicity of visual and verbal images of women of the Middle East in painting, photography, fiction and travellers' tales, recurring themes can be discerned. Some of these themes emerged from intellectual or artistic movements in particular European countries, while others had more general application.

The Orient as the domain of the 'other', as Europe's cultural and spiritual opposite, was often conceived of as female. Jules Michelet saw the Orient (which for him included India) as the 'womb of the world' from which the 'cultured' male emerged. The French Saint-Simonians, seeking a source of redemption in nature for the ills of the Western world, also turned to the 'Oriental' female as the source of life. Some disciples of Saint-Simon went to Egypt on a visit which one of them pronounced to be 'no longer a voyage to the Orient, but a voyage towards Woman. The knights crusaded to free the tomb of Christ, we, the guild of Woman, are going to the Orient to seek not a tomb, but life.'[9]

Most Europeans did not share the reforming ideals of the Saint-Simonians, or the elevation of 'Woman' to the status of redeemer, but the image of the Orient as female – as mother or seductress – was a pervasive one. The idea of fertility and fruitfulness are embodied, for example, in the figure of the Egyptian peasant woman depicted in the pre-Raphaelite Holman Hunt's painting 'The Afterglow in Egypt'. Portrayed holding wheatsheafs and doves – later modified to a calf and a cage of birds – against the background of a harvested wheatfield, she is an emblem of fecundity and growth, a kind of earth goddess. But at the same time, Hunt also saw her as part of an evocation of the past. He wrote: 'I cannot believe that Art should let such beautiful things pass as are in this age passing for good in the East without exertion to chronicle them for the future.' Of 'Afterglow in Egypt', he said that it was intended 'to express nothing but that the light is not that of the sun, and that although the meridian glory of ancient Egypt has passed away, there is still a poetic reflection of this in the aspect of life there'.[10]

This search for the idealized past of the Orient was in constant tension with the romantic European's awareness that Western culture was rapidly impinging on this imagined world: hence the frequent ambivalence shown by such romantics towards colonization and domination of these regions by the Western powers. Discussing Orientalist painting, Linda Nochlin comments:

> The picturesque is pursued throughout the nineteenth century like a form of peculiarly elusive wildlife, requiring increasingly skilful tracking as the delicate prey – an endangered species – disappears further and further into the hinterlands . . . The very notion of the picturesque in its nineteenth-century manifestations is premised on the fact of destruction.[11]

This pursuit could take a physical form, or the form of fantasy. The physical pursuit of the picturesque increasingly meant travelling far from the cities into the desert. In Algeria, the French occupation rapidly took the sense of 'otherness' out of the coastal areas, so that by the 1840s and 1850s writers like Théophile Gautier and his friends were heading south into the desert to find it. In the Mashreq (the eastern part of the Arab world) British travellers such as C.M. Doughty, the Burtons and the Blunts were doing likewise.

Both literature and paintings portrayed the deserts as the domain of men. The romance of the 'wild, untrammelled' bedouin, especially popular in the French Orientalist school of painting, was a romance largely without women, an escape from the restrictions and taboos of Western society, the social conventions and smoke-filled cities. The fascination with 'empty places' attracted generations of

3 French soldiers in Algeria. Stereoscopic slide, second half of the nineteenth century.

This composition embodies, in a very simplistic way, a popular view of the encounter between the native inhabitants of Algeria and their colonial masters. The French soldiers pose in their bivouac against a backdrop of palm trees, while the local inhabitants appear decorative and complaisant in the foreground, the men sitting doing nothing while the woman parades before both groups of men with her water jar.

explorers, including a few women such as Gertrude Bell. In the accounts left by these travellers, male and female, the world they describe acknowledged women as little more than black shadows in the corner of the bedouin tent – relegated to a corner of their consciousness. These travellers lived in a world of men and admired the male values of nomadic societies.

Women's invisibility in this version of romantic escapism in the Orient is in strong contrast to their sexual exposure in the other version: the fantasy of the Orient as the site of sexual freedom and experiment. In this fantasy the Oriental woman was surrounded by the barriers created by the veil and seclusion. But behind these barriers, men reigned supreme, living in a sexual paradise in which four wives and unlimited concubines were permitted. The fantasy consisted of gaining access to this world – seen as the antithesis of Christian monogamy with its sexual taboos and emotional problems which the fantast wished to escape.

Of these sexual adventurers in the Orient, the best-known was probably the novelist Gustave Flaubert, who visited Egypt and Palestine with the photographer Maxime du Camp in 1848–49, seeking an escape from his own disturbed sexual and emotional life. As Edward Said points out, 'Woven through all of Flaubert's Oriental experiences, exciting or disappointing, is an almost uniform association between the Orient and sex.'[12]

For Flaubert, the physical embodiment of Oriental womanhood was the dancer Kuchuk Hanem (see also Chapter VI). He wrote to his mistress Louise Colet, advising her not to be jealous of his sexual adventures:

> As for Kuchuk Hanem, ah! Set your mind at rest, and at the same time correct your views about the Orient. Be convinced that she felt nothing at all: emotionally, I guarantee; and even physically, I strongly suspect . . . The Oriental woman is no more than a machine: she makes no distinction between one man and another man. Smoking, going to the baths, painting her eyelids and drinking coffee – such is the circle of occupation to which her existence is confined. As for physical pleasure, it must be very slight, since the seat of same is sliced off at an early age [a reference to female circumcision, practised in Sudan and Egypt, but infrequently in most other parts of the Middle East].[13]

Kuchuk Hanem was the silent, passive and apparently indifferent subject of Flaubert's experiments. Louise Colet, on the other hand, represented the emotional demands and ties which Flaubert frequently wished to escape. Despite his evident obsession with 'Oriental sexuality', however, he found it necessary to denigrate Kuchuk Hanem in order to placate his French lover.

The fantasies of the Oriental woman as the embodiment of sexual licence reach their visual heights in the work of the French Orientalist painters. The odalisque, symbol of sexuality, the exotic and sensual scenes of the harem and the naked beauties in the *hamam* (public bath) appear in paintings hung in galleries and museums for all to see – sexual danger and excitement at a safe distance. The themes of voluptuousness and abandon, of women waiting only to serve men are presented without the bedbugs which accompanied Flaubert's experiences. The vision of women imprisoned in the harem was haunted by another figure, the black eunuch who guarded the door of the harem – suggesting that patriarchal society in the Middle East would defend itself with violence against outsiders who tried to penetrate it.

But not all images of Oriental womanhood were as crude or direct as these. Some male visitors with rather more experience of the region than Flaubert purported to offer insiders' views of the lives and behaviour of Middle Eastern women. One of these was Gérard de Nerval. His travel narrative, *Voyage en Orient*, describes his three-month stay in Cairo and his subsequent travels in Palestine, Lebanon and Syria. His acquaintance with the life of Cairo was certainly more extensive than that of Flaubert but, like Flaubert, his basic preoccupation is with women.

His conclusions, however, are rather more ambiguous. Told by his neighbours in Cairo that it was improper for a man to live alone, he recounts his somewhat halfhearted attempts to find a marriage partner. Finally he settles for buying a female slave named Zeynab. But Zeynab does not turn out to be the pliant being he expects. A Muslim from Java, she quotes Islamic law on the treatment of slaves, demanding her rights and refusing to do any manual work. Nerval, the Western man, appears confused and often frustrated by Zeynab's behaviour. Yet he later retreats to a more familiar image of romance in the Orient. He falls in love with the beautiful and apparently docile daughter of a Druze nobleman in Lebanon, whom he vows to marry, though finally he does not do so and returns to Europe.

Writers like Nerval and Théophile Gautier assumed an air of superior knowledge in denigrating the popular myths of harem life but do not finally escape from many of the assumptions which lie behind these myths. Nerval expressed his romantic sentiments about the Orient and its complaisant women in the following flight of rhetoric:

> Yes, let us be young in Europe as long as we can, but go to spend our old age in the Orient, the country of men worthy of the name, the land of the patriarchs. In Europe, where our institutions have suppressed physical strength, woman has become too powerful. With all that power of seduction, of ruse, of perseverance and persuasion with which heaven has endowed her, the woman of our own countries has become socially the equal of man, and this

4 'Luncheon in the Temple of
Medinet Habu, Thebes, Egypt'.
Underwood & Underwood, 1987.
5 'Captain Furness Williams, Lt.
Langbein and Local Beauties'.
Aqaba (Jordan) during World
War I.

Two photographs suggesting the
unequal relationship between
Western males and young,
indigenous women. In the first,
the three young girls are posed to
suggest that they are serving the
Western tourist, as he eats his
picnic lunch in the shadow of one
of the great monuments of
Thebes. The second shows British
army officers having a drink on the
sands of the port of Aqaba, which
T.E. Lawrence helped to capture
in 1917, while they are entertained
by an encounter with local
children, referred to sarcastically
in the caption as 'local beauties'.

was more than was necessary to ensure that he should
inevitably and eternally become her victim . . . It is
essential that I shall unite myself with some innocent
young girl belonging to this sacred soil which is the original
fatherland of us all, and drench myself again in the
life-giving springs of humanity, from which flowed the
poetry and religions of our fathers.[14]

The novelist Pierre Loti took this theme of 'explaining'
invisible Oriental woman to the West a step further. In his
novel *Les Désenchantées*, published in 1906, he describes
harem life through the eyes of three young Turkish women.
Their characters were apparently based on three women
from a well-to-do family whom he had met in Europe.[15] He
portrays them as unhappy and discontented with 'aimless and
unprofitable' harem life which differed so much from the
expectations aroused by their education at the hands of
French governesses. In the novel, the three sisters cultivate
the friendship of André, a wandering European writer, and
pour out their frustration to him.

Although Loti avoids the usual exotic descriptions of
harem life, stressing rather its 'ordinariness' in European
terms, his treatment of the sisters' oppression, and of
André's secret meetings with them, when all he sees is their
glittering eyes behind their veils, relies on many of the
standard assumptions about Middle Eastern women.[16]

Loti's view of Eastern women as the prisoners of a cruel system of oppression was also taken up by those who regarded the status of women under Islam as a central part of their moral objection to the Islamic religion and social order as a whole. Budgett Meakin, a journalist and writer who recorded his experiences of seven years' residence in Morocco at the turn of the century, reflected this commonly held view: 'Of no country in the world can it be more truly said than of the Moorish Empire that the social condition of the people may be measured by that of its women. Holding its women in subjection, the Moorish nation is itself held in subjection, morally, politically, socially.'[17]

Among those who objected most vociferously to the treatment of women in the Middle East were missionaries who established themselves in the region in large numbers in the second half of the nineteenth century. S.H. Leeder, who saw his book *The Veiled Mysteries of Egypt* as an antidote to the 'severe and sombrous tone of much writing about the Middle East', observed that the writings of missionaries frequently seemed 'imbued with a strange dislike of everything Islamic'. He continued: 'Though the readers may be excited thereby at the degradation and darkness they are called upon to contribute to remove, they are certainly misled if they think they are gaining a fair view of the life and religion of the people described.'[18]

Raising the status of women was generally regarded as a crucial part of the missionary enterprise. This improvement would be achieved if women could be converted to Christianity, or rather, to the branch of it advocated by that particular missionary. This in its turn would raise the moral tone of the whole family. But like the romantics, some of the missionaries had difficulties with the question of whether their converts should emulate trends in contemporary Western society. The Reverend Henry Harris Jessup, an American Presbyterian who worked as a missionary in Syria for seventeen years, was of the opinion that contemporary

6 *'Miss Stuart's Farewell Meeting with the Women Converts'. Church Missionary Society, Isfahan, Iran, early twentieth century.*

The picture seems to suggest the centrality of the missionary's role as the figure on whom the converts rely for their new interpretation of the world.

DERVISHES OF CAIRO.

Mohammetan & Syrian Ladies of Damascus.

CIRCASSIAN GIRL

BRIDE AND BRIDEGROOM.

REV. W. B. BANTING AS PRIEST OF THE EASTERN CHURCH.

JEWS SHOP AT JERUSALEM.

BEDAWEEN OF THE DESERT.

MILL

VILLAGE LIFE.

WELL

An interesting representation of Eastern scenes was given at Kensington Townhall on Tuesday, Jan. 31, and the two following days, in aid of the Kensington Church School Board. The tableaux were under the direction of the Rev. W. B. Banting, Vicar of Little Brickhill, Bucks, who has travelled in Egypt and Syria, and collected the costumes and objects of interest that were exhibited on the platform. The Eastern troupe of forty-five local ladies and gentlemen and children were divided into groups of Jews, Eastern Christians, Mohammetans, and Bedaween. The platform was fitted up to represent a shop in the Bazaar, the divan and interior of the harem, Bedouin tents and a well which was surrounded by palm-trees, and some hundreds of Eastern curiosities connected with indoor and outdoor life were arranged all over the platform. When the performers in their various Oriental costumes occupied their places, the whole effect was thoroughly Eastern and most picturesque. The scenes represented included the bringing of the corn from the harvest-fields and being ground at the mill, bargaining in the Bazaar, the Mohammetan form of prayer, Dervishes howling and whirling, episodes in Eastern courtship, violent robbery by Bedaween, Eastern pilgrims received by the Patriarch at Jerusalem, a meal in the desert, snake charming, and an Oriental wedding.

7 *'Scenes from Eastern Life'*. Illustrated London News, *4 February 1893*.

Scenes representing a range of visual clichés associated with 'Eastern life'. Some were possibly engravings based on photographs. These tableaux were part of an exhibition staged in London in 1893.

society in the West was not a suitable example to follow. He wrote in 1873:

> May it ever be a work founded on the Word of God, aiming at the elevation of woman through the doctrines and the practice of a pure Christianity, striving to plant in Syria, not the flippant culture of modern fashionable society, but the God-fearing, Sabbath-loving and Bible-reading culture of our Anglo-Saxon ancestors![19]

The Development of Anthropology and Popular Ethnography

By the beginning of the twentieth century, there was a large body of travel literature, photography and other records of Europeans' encounters with the Middle East. Much of this focussed on the aesthetic and moral aspects of Western reactions to the cultures of the region and was coloured by the increasing power of leading European nations to influence them. At the same time, the development of new 'empirical sciences' such as ethnography and anthropology offered new ways of viewing the people of the Middle East.

This so-called scientific approach to the study of mankind, to the physical and cultural characteristics of races and peoples, operated on a number of levels. At the popular level it was manifested in the proliferation of exhibitions in museums and elsewhere which aimed to show the public the characteristics of races and cultures over which Europeans then held sway. This trend coincided with the rapid growth in photographic imagery to cover most areas of the globe.

The most gradiose of these displays were the succession of Great Exhibitions held in British, European and American cities from the 1850s to the 1950s. Here the evocation of empire and Western technological achievement, and the quaint customs of subject peoples, could be presented to the public on one site. These occasions generated an enormous quantity of visual imagery: postcards, stamps, posters and other memorabilia, as well as large numbers of articles in the illustrated press.

At these exhibitions, all the racial and social stereotypes of 'Oriental' and 'primitive' societies could flourish in replicas of Cairo streets, Dahomeyan villages and displays of native crafts put on for the entertainment of the Western public. As John Mackenzie writes:

> The 'native villages' were in fact among the most enduring features of all the exhibitions from the 1870s. They repay closer attention because here was the prime way in which people in the metropolis were brought into contact with the conquered peoples of the Empire. Here were the racial stereotypes illustrated, Social Darwinism established in the popular mind, and control of the world expressed in its

most obvious human form. Moreover, the numbers of programmes and postcards of these exhibits that can still be found seem to indicate that they caught the public imagination. Yesterday's enemies, the perpetrators of yesterday's 'barbarism' became today's exhibits, showing off quaint music, dancing, sports, living crafts and food, but now set on the path to civilization. In the exhibitions representatives of African and Oriental peoples were brought cheek by jowl with all the trappings of the worldwide economy. It was a concentrated and speeded-up version of what was happening in their own countries.[20]

This interest in displaying and ranking the world's cultures was accompanied by a growth in the popularity of ethnographic literature. As far as the Middle East was concerned, a large number of the so-called 'ethnographic studies' which appeared in the late nineteenth and early twentieth centuries in books, journals and magazines were little more than travellers' tales which placed often inaccurate ethnographic labels on the people they described. Few had the value of, for instance, E.W. Lane's *Account of the Manners and Customs of the Modern Egyptians*, first published in the 1840s. This work, whatever its preconceptions and methodological flaws, remained one of the most detailed and careful Western studies of a Middle Eastern society carried out in the nineteenth century.

While this wave of popular ethnography was accompanied by the development of the academic discipline of anthropology, the Middle East was by no means the most important field for early anthropologists. There were a few surveys by physical anthropologists: Ernest Chantre's work on Egypt and North Africa in the 1890s; and Henry Field's on Iran, Iraq and Egypt in the 1930s (see Chapter I). Early British social anthropologists paid relatively little attention to the Middle East, with the exception of Sudan, concentrating mainly on Africa, India and Polynesia. Until the 1940s and 1950s, there were relatively few social anthropologists of any nationality engaged in fieldwork in the Middle East outside North Africa. Besides the work in the nineteenth century of Sir Richard Burton, one of the founders of the Royal Anthropological Institute, some studies were made in the first half of the twentieth century of bedouin life. Apart from some French studies in Syria connected with the French Mandate authorities' efforts to settle the Syrian bedouin, there was also Alois Musil's study of the Rwalla bedouin in Syria and H.A.R. Dickson's work on the bedouin of Kuwait and Saudi Arabia, published in the 1950s. On urban and peasant societies, little work was done. Probably the most interesting studies of rural life in the Middle East before the 1950s (again with the exception of North Africa) was done by two women anthropologists – Hilma Granqvist and Winifred Blackman.

Hilma Granqvist, a Finnish anthropologist, spent a total of three years doing fieldwork in the Palestinian village of Artas in the period from 1925 to 1931. Her original project had been to pursue a study of 'The Women of the Old Testament' through observation of the lives of women in contemporary Palestine. But after she had spent a short time in the country, she came to the conclusion that in order to understand the life and position of women she needed to study one Palestinian community in detail. She settled upon the village of Artas south of Jerusalem, and soon abandoned her Old Testament preoccupations to concentrate on contemporary village society. Her method of work was unusual for that period in that all her books on Artas, published in the course of the next thirty years, examined village life through the narratives of women informants. In the 1940s, when she came into contact with the functionalist school of anthropology led by Malinowski and Radcliffe-Brown, she claimed that even in her earlier work on marriage in Artas, she had taken a 'functionalist' approach in relating the lives of individuals to their social roles in society.

Winifred Blackman's work on village society in Upper Egypt took a much more narrative and anecdotal approach and although she included many detailed observations on women's lives and work, her method of research did not provide the same insight into women's own perceptions of their lives as did Granqvist's approach. Blackman was a graduate of the Oxford University school of anthropology who first visited Egypt in the early 1920s, spending the winters of 1920–22 living in villages in Fayyum and Asyut provinces. She subsequently led two research expeditions to Egypt, including the Wellcome Expedition from 1927–31. Aside from numerous articles on her researches, she published her major work *The Fellahin of Upper Egypt* in 1927. Both Blackman and Granqvist took a large number of

9 *The anthropologist Hilma Granqvist, helping villagers with the harvest. Artas, Palestine, late 1920s.*

8 *Winifred Blackman with some of the women of al-Gherak, Upper Egypt, 1925.*

photographs in the villages where they worked.[21]

The situation in North Africa – particularly in Algeria and Morocco – was, however, quite different. Not only were there a number of British folklorists and ethnologists at work, but the region provided a major focus for French academic anthropology. Its practitioners also came to play a significant role in the formulation of French colonial policy, particularly in Algeria.

As Lucas and Vatin explain it in their book *Algérie des Anthropologues*, in the first period of the French colonial occupation of Algeria, from 1830 to 1871, the priority was to understand the working of Algerian society in order to conquer it. Since the strongest resistance came from the Berber regions, it was these which called for the most attention. The period from 1871 to the end of the century was one of intense efforts to import European colonists. During this time, Algerians largely ceased to be a subject of enquiry and became little more than an object of folkloric description, and a problem of colonial administration. Most anthropologists continued to concentrate on studying Berber society, rather than the majority Arabic-speaking community.[22]

These anthropologists sought to embody in their work a record of so-called 'traditional' society which was rapidly being eroded and changed under the economic and political pressures of colonial rule. Like anthropologists in other colonial situations, they strove to document what was disappearing, what they considered the 'pure' form of the society, rather than the 'hybrid' which colonialism was creating.

In these accounts of indigenous societies, women are often portrayed as the repository of traditional ways and values. M.W. Hilton Simpson, a folklorist who worked on Berber cultures in the Aurès mountains, remarked: 'Very many primitive customs, such as must be studied by anyone engaged in examining the daily life of a native race, are known only to the women.'[23] The view that women, particularly in Berber societies, were also a hidden source of power and influence was not uncommon among anthropologists working on Algeria and Morocco.

In some cases they went so far as to argue that there was a hidden element of matriarchy in these highly patriarchal societies. The notion that it was women who were really the guardians of traditional culture was also taken up by some French colonial officials seeking to subdue or remould Algerian society, Arab and Berber. In the 1930s, at the height of a French campaign to reform the status of Algerian women as part of the 'modernization' of indigenous society, a colonial governor, Maurice Viollette, wrote: 'Many people think that the indigenous woman counts for nothing. This notion is utterly false. The indigenous woman is extremely influential in Arab society.'[24]

In the eyes of male Algerian nationalists, however, this view suggested the need to 'guard' Algerian women against efforts to change their social roles. For nationalists too, women became a symbol of the integrity of indigenous culture which the French were trying to destroy. Frantz Fanon outlined how these nationalists perceived the colonial authorities' strategy:

> This [idea about the role of women] enabled the colonial administration to define a precise political doctrine: 'If we want to destroy the structure of Algerian society, its capacity for resistance, we must first of all conquer the women; we must go and find them behind the veil where they hide themselves and in the houses where men keep them out of sight.'[25]

Thus women also appeared as the prize, the disputed possession over which men, both colonialist and nationalist, were fighting.

Women on Women

The images of Middle Eastern women which emerged from the West were not, however, solely the creation of men. By the end of the nineteenth century, numbers of Western women had visited the Middle East, or lived there as the wives of the growing population of Western officials, doctors, engineers and businessmen. Women also made up a large proportion of the missionary workers who came from Europe and the United States as teachers and medical assistants. This was one of the few vocations open to women from modest backgrounds who wanted to work and to have some degree of independence. Finally there was a small group of independent women who spent time in the Middle East as travellers, anthropologists, doctors and even, in a few rare cases, as political advisers.

Women from all these groups contributed to the body of Western literature and imagery on the Middle East, but there is little evidence that gender alone distinguished their views from those of men, except in one respect: the fact that they had many more opportunities to observe the daily lives of Middle Eastern women, even those who lived in seclusion. However, what use they made of these opportunities varied very much from person to person. (For a more detailed account of Western women's visits to harems see pp. 77–9.)

Like their male counterparts, most women who left records of their impressions of the Middle East used their own culture as a yardstick by which to judge what they saw. However, their conclusions were frequently influenced by the way they perceived women's role in their own societies. Since the late nineteenth and early twentieth centuries were times of considerable debate about the image and status of women in Britain, Western Europe and the United States, the position they took on the issues of emancipation and women's sexual and social freedom was likely to affect their reactions to the problems of women in the Middle East.

Among independent women travellers, the desire to escape the constraints and limitations of life in their own societies was often a motive for launching out into unknown regions. Like men, they did not want to conform to the norms of their own society; however, their motives related more often to intellectual and social constraints than to a yearning for sexual freedom. For talented, energetic women, outlets at home were few and far between and if they had the money and initiative travel appeared as an escape from all these forms of frustration. Among the most outstanding examples of women travellers motivated by a desire to escape these shackles were Gertrude Bell and Isabelle Eberhardt.

Gertrude Bell, the daughter of a well-to-do and indulgent family, spent a good part of her adult life in the Middle East. Nevertheless she showed very little interest in the lives of women. In her books and photographs women appeared from time to time, but they remained peripheral to her main interest in politics and public affairs, which she considered the domain of men. As a Western traveller she seems to have been accepted in most circumstances as a kind of surrogate man. As a highly intelligent and independent woman who had made the most of her privileged background to enter into male domains in her own society as well as in the Middle East, she had scant patience with what she perceived as the narrower worlds of women and their problems. She even went so far as to campaign briefly against the suffragist movement in Britain.

Another legendary figure among women travellers was Isabelle Eberhardt who, like many other travellers, used the Middle East (in this case Algeria) as a place of escape from the tensions caused by the stifling conventions of bourgeois Europe. Eberhardt was able to play out a role which fitted her own apparently ambivalent sexuality, sometimes as a surrogate man moving in nomadic society, sometimes as the woman who was the lover of an Algerian soldier. She also did not appear to have had any great interest in indigenous women. Some of her writings suggested that she regarded Algerian women as sad and passive victims of men and of economic circumstances.[26]

Women such as Lady Isabel Burton and Lady Anne Blunt, who mostly travelled with their husbands, did not generally make very much of their encounters with women. In the nomadic societies which interested them most, the women of the community received relatively little space in their narratives. In Isabel Burton's case particularly even questions of marriage and personal relationships were narrated mainly from the male point of view. In Lady Anne Blunt's account, the exception is her vivid description of the personality of the first wife of Muhammad Ibn Rashid, whose harem she visited in Hail, northern Arabia.

The English writer and traveller Freya Stark, who made many journeys in the Middle East from the 1920s until the 1950s, has left a much more detailed record, in her writings and photographs, of her contacts with women. She was certainly much more willing to spend time in women's company and though her comments were sometimes tinged with condescension, she could also be perceptive and humorous. But Stark also shared the common nostalgia of travellers of this era for the 'old ways', which were gradually fading as Western influence grew. At the same time, like Gertrude Bell, she seems to have been basically in favour of Britain's imperial role, though she was critical of the practice of particular colonial administrations.[27]

It was frequently missionary women who painted the blackest picture of Middle Eastern women's lot, while they described the moral elevation of the convert, 'redeemed' from ignorance and oppression, in glowing terms. Although their zeal sometimes overrode concerns other than those of bringing women to Christ, many of these missionaries were also dedicated teachers and formed close, if unequal, relationships with women they taught or converted.

The personal position of missionary women in societies where women had little freedom of movement outside the home could also be ambivalent. Isabella Bird, speaking of women missionaries working in Iran, pointed out that their own freedom of action and movement were curtailed by the need to observe at least the external conventions of the society in which they were working. 'Women coming to the East as missionaries are by far the greatest sufferers, especially if they are young, for Eastern custom, which in their position cannot be defied with advantage, limits free action and abridges all the comforts of independence.'[28]

The belief in the moral superiority of Christian cultures, particularly as regards the treatment of women, was not confined to missionary women. It was a commonly expressed sentiment among women travellers who did not question the norms of their own society. Sophia Lane Poole, sister of E.W. Lane and author of *The English Woman in Egypt*, gave detailed accounts of her visits in the 1840s to upper-class Egyptian harems. She was a good deal less disapproving than many who came after her, but she stressed the otherness of the 'Eastern view of the world', as represented by harem life, and suggested that only by abandoning this view could women attain happiness:

The very framework of Eastern society is so opposed to the opinions of Europeans, that I will venture to prophesy it must be the work of several generations to root up prejudice before the mind of the Eastern [*sic*] can be prepared for the reception of our ideas of civilization. That

Christianity is the only medium through which happiness
may be attained by any people is most certain; therefore as
the Easterns are very far from being Christians, except in
the mere dogmas of their faith (inasmuch as they
acknowledge the Messiah though denying his divine nature
and atonement for sin), so they are very far from being
really happy.[29]

Most of the Western women who wrote about the lives and
status of Middle Eastern women did so with a consciousness
of how these lives compared with their own. Some even went
so far as to link explicitly their views on women in the Middle
East with those on the status of women in their own societies,
although the conclusions they reached varied considerably.
One such writer was Lucy Garnett, who spent some eight
years in the region, and whose two-volume account of the
lives of Muslim, Jewish, Kurdish and Armenian women in
Turkey was one of the most detailed written in the
nineteenth century. Garnett stressed the diversity of conditions under which Middle Eastern women lived, arguing that
segregation and seclusion in the various communities were a
matter of 'the special social and economic conditions under
which they live – some conditions necessitating a rigid
seclusion of women and others allowing an extraordinary
degree of independence. The subjection of women in the
East is, consequently, so far as it exists, the result of such
conditions, rather than of legal and religious enactments.'
   At this point, Garnett shifted her focus to the West where,
she argued, the subjection of women had been 'chiefly the
result of the substitution of the Law of the Christian Church
for the later Roman Law, under which women enjoyed
greater personal and proprietary privileges than are now
claimed by the most advanced champions of "Women's
Rights" '. Thus she argued that neither in the West nor in the
East was the subjection of women absolute; but that in the
West the constraints imposed on women were mainly legal
ones, while in the Middle East, they related mainly to custom
and socio-economic conditions. While today this may seem a
very simplistic argument, it differed from the conventional
wisdom of the time, which tended to posit a sharp dichotomy
between Western enlightenment and Eastern tyranny over
women. Yet Garnett ends her book (published in the 1890s)
on a surprising note, with a polemic against the Suffragist
movement and its demand for the political enfranchisement
of women in the West. This seems incongruous, but perhaps
indicates that such women observers were often unable to
disentangle their feelings about women's status in their own
societies from their assessments of women's condition
elsewhere.

   But I believe that I am at one with the vast majority of
Englishwomen in thinking that the assumptions of the

Women Suffragists – the 'brutality of men' and the 'antagonism of the interests of men and women' – are utterly false; hence, that no political slavery of women exists, and no political enfranchisement is, therefore, required; and hence that Womanhood Suffrage would, quite needlessly, introduce into politics an element altogether incalculable.[30]

By contrast, Hubertine Auclert, the French feminist and suffragist who visited Algeria at the turn of the century, argued that the disenfranchisement of women in France had a detrimental effect on France's colonial policy in Algeria, and therefore on its policies towards Algerian women. She appears to have assumed that if French women had had political rights they would have used them in support of other women – even those under French colonial rule. Referring to the need to end the practice of child-marriage in Algeria, she remarked:

If women in France enjoyed their share of [political] power, they would never permit the continued existence – in a territory under French control – of a law allowing the rape of children. Men tolerate this crime because they share a common outlook [on this question] with those who profit from it.

She added that since France did not permit polygamy on its own soil, it should not be allowed in territories under its control. Here, however, her arguments began to enter controversial ground. She admitted the brutality of French rule in Algeria, but argued not for its termination but for more assimilation of Algerians which, she considered, would improve the status of women. She also advocated the appointment of female French administrators in Algeria: 'The conquerors would be ill-advised if for lack of female administrators they neglected to put the views of Arab women in the balance to weight it in their favour – these women who had helped their husbands to defend their country against the French.' Auclert's feminism does not prevent her entertaining much the same set of notions about the nature of Algerian societies and of women in it as her male counterparts.[31]

There were a few Western women living in the region who directly supported the efforts of individuals and small groups of Middle Eastern women to change their situation. One of these was Eugènie le Brun, who married a prominent Egyptian, Rushdi Pasha, and converted to Islam. Despite her love for her husband, she found life in an upper-class harem difficult and was critical of many aspects of women's situation in Egypt. Thus, in the last years of the nineteenth century, she was quietly encouraging young women of her acquaintance who lived in seclusion to discuss their position and develop their own ideas. She started a salon for women, using both her social status as the wife of a prominent man and her position as a foreigner to do what most of her Egyptian women friends could not easily do. She also wrote two books, one on her impressions of life in an upper-class harem and the other based on research in the divorce courts, in which she was critical of the way the laws governing marriage and divorce affected women.[32]

From the 1920s onwards, when feminists from women's movements within the Middle East began to attend international conferences, Western feminists were made more aware of their needs and demands, which included rights to education and work, improved legal status within the family, and in some cases, women's enfranchisement. Some Western women who visited Turkey after World War I were very impressed by the reforms implemented by Kemal Atatürk, which were regarded at the time as something of a model for the rest of the region. But despite the contacts and personal friendships which developed through encounters between feminists from the different cultures, there was often a lack of understanding of Middle Eastern cultures on the part of Western feminists. Even Margery Corbett Ashby, President of the International Alliance of Women for Suffrage and Equal Citizenship in the 1920s and 1930s, who was considered a staunch friend, particularly by Egyptian feminists, took a somewhat condescending attitude towards Arab women in her private correspondence.[33]

Western feminists were not able to escape entirely from the Eurocentrism of their age, nor even from the imperial perspectives of their own nations. This resulted in a growing political divide between European and Middle Eastern feminists over nationalist resistance to Western imperialism in the region. In the period after World War II this rift was widened by the Arab–Israeli conflict – in which, with a few exceptions, the West has sided with Israel – and by the wave of anti-colonial struggles throughout the region, culminating in the Algerian war of independence.

The Impact of Political and Economic Change

The era from 1830 – when the French occupied Algeria – until 1950 was the heyday of European influence and control, direct or indirect, in the Middle East. The history of the region in the late nineteenth and early twentieth centuries was dominated by the changes these interventions brought about in economic and political life.

The literature and visual imagery of the West, however, tended to stress the static nature of Middle Eastern societies at the very time when Western intervention was causing rapid change. Where this change was acknowledged by Western observers, it was usually viewed in absolute terms as the 'destruction of traditional society'. Until comparatively recently, little attention was paid to the ways in which these societies adapted to new conditions, sometimes resisting, sometimes acquiescing in the domination of the West, but on both ideological and practical levels drawing on their own cultures to cope with change, as well as on new ideas and technologies from the West.

How wider economic and political changes affected social mores and family life is difficult to assess, especially where it concerns relationships between men and women. Indigenous sources which throw light on these relationships are only now being studied, and this is part of a hidden history which is at last beginning to be unearthed and explored. Photography is just one form of historical evidence which can be examined alongside other oral and written sources. On a broader social level, there are written sources such as censuses, court records, and reports on economic and social conditions by both colonial and indigenous authorities. Anthropologists have also used oral testimonies of women as well as oral traditions such as poetry and songs to explore women's lives.

Indigenous written records and memoirs are mostly by men, since few women were literate until the early twentieth century. There are, however, a few memoirs written by prominent women which are of considerable value: for instance, the autobiographies of Huda Shaarawi and Halide Edip, leaders respectively of the Egyptian and Turkish feminist movements, and the memoirs of Emine Foat Tugay, a granddaughter of Khedive Ismail. In the late nineteenth century, there was also a spate of biographical dictionaries in Arabic, some of which included biographies of notable women.[34]

But this kind of evidence raises a difficulty also encountered in the social history of other regions, particularly as it relates to women. What first-hand information there is focuses mostly on the lives of the literate elites, and while it represents an important and often exciting source on the history of women in the upper classes, it leaves the lives of the majority of women largely undocumented except by broader and more impersonal kinds of social data.

Even with this limited evidence, it is clear that social and economic changes in the Middle East at this time did not bear a simple or direct relationship to changes in gender or family relationships. The linear path from 'backwardness to modernity' so dear to Western journalists, photographers and – later – to some development theorists, certainly does not apply here.

How these changes affected particular aspects of women's lives will be explored further in the essays which follow but, broadly speaking, the impact of socio-economic change on women depended on a combination of factors: geography, class, religious and ethnic community. At the same time, their experience of change did not simply mirror that of the men in their own communities.

City dwellers tended to feel the impact of economic change

most rapidly and with most intensity. For example, Cairo and Istanbul saw considerable changes in both economic and social life between the 1880s and 1930s and experienced rapid population growth. The impact of French colonial rule on Algiers and the other cities of the Algerian coastal region was more immediate than it was in the hinterlands. Other cities, such as Damascus, suffered an overall decline in their influence and economic prosperity from the middle of the nineteenth century as the overland trade routes were eclipsed by the seaborne trade with Europe. Meanwhile, port cities such as Beirut, Haifa and Jaffa grew and flourished as a consequence of this trade. At the same time, other parts of the Middle East, notably the Gulf and the Arabian peninsula, were relatively unaffected by these economic currents until the 1940s and 1950s.

Away from the main cities, those who lived close to major trade routes or in the immediate hinterland of large towns and cities were drawn more quickly into a wider web of economic and commercial relations with the rest of the world than those in remoter areas. Peasants who, like those of the Egyptian Delta and the Lebanese mountain region, entered early into the cash-crop economy, became most exposed, for better or worse, to changes in world markets for the commodities which they produced.

Class, too, had an important bearing on the way people experienced change: there were often more similarities between the lives of, for instance, an Egyptian and an Iranian peasant, for all their differences in religion and social customs, than between those of an upper-class Egyptian living in Cairo and a peasant from Upper Egypt.

In the rural areas, where the great majority of the region's inhabitants lived, there were many alterations in the patterns of agriculture and land tenure. In Egypt, the changes were probably most dramatic. The world shortage of cotton during the United States Civil War in the 1860s allowed Egypt to gain an important share in the world market for cotton. Over the following thirty or forty years this radically altered the patterns of agricultural production to the point where most peasants in the Delta region who had previously concentrated their efforts on subsistence production became involved in growing cotton and other crops such as sugar for the international market. The profitability of cotton also led to the increased concentration of ownership of the fertile land in the Nile Valley in fewer hands, leaving a growing number of peasants without land of their own, or without sufficient land for family subsistence. A widening gap appeared between the landless poor and those peasants who prospered under the new system.

In Turkey and the Arab provinces of the Ottoman Empire, particularly in Syria, Lebanon and Palestine, the development of cash-crop economies was slower than in Egypt and less widespread, but in the longer term had many of the same effects. By the time the world recession began in 1929, few of the major agricultural regions were immune from its effects. The problem of landlessness and peasant indebtedness also became acute in many areas. In Algeria, this problem was exacerbated by the French policy of settling colonists on much of the best land, while in Palestine during the British Mandate period (1921–48), the buying up of land by the Jewish Agency for exclusive settlement by Zionist colonists added to an existing problem of landlessness among the peasantry.

These changes in crop patterns and access to land had effects on the way peasant families organized their work. It was not uncommon for women to be left with now-marginal subsistence cultivation or to be confined to household tasks while men controlled cash crops and irrigation systems. At the same time a number of factors led to a considerable movement of male labour out of the villages, which also had an impact on patterns of women's work.

In Egypt, the notorious *corvée* system of forced labour which was used on a vast scale by Muhammad Ali, and which continued until 1893, caused major disruptions in agriculture and often left women at home to manage as best they could while the men were away. In the rest of the Ottoman Empire the equivalents of the *corvée* were the periodic recruitment drives by the Ottoman army, which swept away the able-bodied male populations of whole districts, disrupting production and leaving women, children and old people to fend for themselves.

From the late nineteenth century increasingly large numbers of peasants, seeking an escape from land-hunger and poverty, migrated from their home area. Some moved within their own country: for example, from Upper Egypt to the Delta and from the interior of Syria and Palestine to the coastal towns in search of work. A sizeable number migrated abroad, as far afield as the United States, Latin America and Africa. These migrants frequently left their families behind, and women were expected, with the help of male relatives, to care for the family and whatever property they had. They were often, however, left in the invidious position of having responsibility for what was usually deemed to be 'men's' work without the power and authority which a man would have.

In the nineteenth century wealth and status in most regions of the Middle East rested on the ownership of landed property, and access to positions in the state bureaucracy and the army. In the Ottoman Empire officials frequently became landowners through the granting to favoured individuals of parcels of land, or of tax farms (*iltizam*). These tax farms frequently enabled their holders to acquire land by buying out peasants who fell into debt. In addition, landowners quite often played the role of agricultural merchants and moneylenders.

Ottoman attempts to impose a land code and land registration in 1858 led to the opposite of the intended effect: it strengthened the power of the large landholders at the expense of the peasantry. Fearing that registration of land might also lead to heavier taxation and conscription by the Ottoman authorities, peasants often allowed large landowners to register land in their names, and thus lost title to it. There were few further large-scale attempts at land reform, or other efforts to redistribute agrarian wealth in the Middle East until the 1950s.

The advent of Western economic influence and colonial rule had varying effects on this class. In some cases, landowners even under colonial rule continued to wield considerable political influence, and many prospered by associating with Western interests in the agricultural market and other business enterprises. Only in colonial states where settlers had an influence on politics – that is in Algeria and in Palestine – was there a direct challenge to the political and economic power of this class.

Women from these largely urban-based upper echelons of society generally shared in the economic fortunes of their families (see Chapter IV) but they also experienced marked changes in lifestyles during the century from 1850 to 1950. Until the early twentieth century they were on the whole strictly secluded, but from World War I onwards their fashions, social lives and personal freedoms probably changed more than those of any other class.

In the cities, the strata of craftspeople and merchants felt the effects of the rapid increase in the volume of manufactured goods coming into the region from Europe. Not all craft industries were decimated – some even found specialist markets and flourished – but in the longer term many of those men and women who depended on the production and sale of handicrafts experienced an economic decline.

Until World War I, the lives of the pastoral nomads who lived in the deserts of Syria, Iraq, Arabia, Egypt and North Africa had been less affected by Western economic and political incursions than the lives of other classes. But the political settlement imposed on the Middle East by the Great Powers after the war drew national boundaries which brought a gradual decline in the influence and independence of the major bedouin tribes of Syria and Iraq. Some individual tribal chiefs remained powerful by becoming settled landowners, but the livelihood of bedouin societies were seriously affected by the loss of freedom of movement imposed by these boundaries. In North Africa too, nomads were gradually pushed further and further into the desert or obliged by economic considerations to end their pastoral existence. Only in Arabia did the lives of nomads remain largely unchanged until the advent of oil exploration in the 1940s.

Many Western observers have laid more stress on religious

and ethnic divisions in the Middle East than on class-based differences. While there is no denying the importance of these forms of identity, they were by no means the only criteria for political action or social cohesion, nor has their role remained a constant one.

The polyglot Ottoman Empire, covering at its widest extent the area from the Balkans in the north to Yemen and the North African littoral in the south, and as far west as Algeria, rested on allowing a large degree of autonomy, both to particular regions and to religious and ethnic minorities. The latter were left to organize their own internal affairs under the so-called millet system. The degree to which particular communities were able to capitalize on this system depended on their economic status, geographical position and, by the nineteenth century, the ability of the much-weakened Ottoman central government to impose even the most minimal demands such as taxation. For example, in the Lebanese mountains, the Druze and Maronite communities were controlled by a hierarchy of Druze and Maronite families over which the Ottomans exercised only limited control. In their quarrels with each other and with the Ottomans, both these communities were, by the mid-nineteenth century, looking to outside protectors: the Maronites to the French and the Druze, on the whole, to the British.

Predominantly urban minorities such as the Jewish communities of the Middle East were not in a position to exercise comparable autonomy. Although they were in theory self-regulating communities, they were from time to time subject to arbitrary and sometimes oppressive interference from local or state authorities. Communal ties were also strained at times by class divisions within communities. For example, in the Lebanese mountain district of Kisrawan there was an uprising in 1859 which began as a revolt by Maronite peasants against Maronite landlords and middlemen.

In urban Jewish communities such as that of Istanbul, the more affluent families certainly participated in community affairs and charitable activities, but their lives were otherwise very different from those of its poorer members. The well-to-do and educated sections of the community mixed with the Ottoman establishment, while the rest led a much narrower, more segregated existence.

In cities throughout the Middle East, mutual prejudices, stereotypes and hatreds periodically flared into communal violence, but on a day-to-day level the various religious and ethnic communities generally coexisted, or led parallel lives which scarcely impinged on each other. In the countryside, divisions were usually less clear. In Palestine, for instance, Christian and Muslim peasants had much the same lifestyles, and while they did not customarily intermarry, sometimes lived in the same villages and even shared the same local saints. In Egypt too, there was little to distinguish the life of a

Muslim from a Coptic peasant except their beliefs, social rituals and the yearly round of festivals.

The growing importance of the European powers, however, contributed in some instances to an increase in communal tensions. Rival groups formed alliances with particular European powers, and these powers as colonial rulers often manipulated and further exacerbated communal rivalries. The French promoted the Alawites in Syria, the Maronites in Lebanon and the Berbers in Algeria and Morocco. British Mandate administrations in Palestine tended to favour indigenous Christians in their appointments to government posts, while in Iraq, the British imposed a Sunni ruler (King Faisal) on a predominantly Shia population.

As far as women were concerned, both class and communal divisions affected their lives. The purity and probity of women were highly valued in all communities and classes. Particularly where marriage was concerned, women were under enormous pressure to act in conformity with the norms of their class, tribe, ethnic or religious group. None the less in all but the most closed communities, women were rather more likely to have personal contacts with women of different ethnic or religious groups than they were with those of other social classes, except where there were relationships of patronage or employment across classes.

While the political manoeuvring of the Great Powers and of local political elites may have passed most people by, the results of their policies were less easily avoidable. The war-torn period from 1913–21, which marked the collapse of the Ottoman Empire, resulted, apart from battlefield casualties, in the deaths of hundreds of thousands of people from famine, especially in Lebanon. The Turks also ordered wholesale deportations of those suspected of Arab nationalist sympathies in Lebanon, Syria and Palestine. In Turkey itself, between one million and one and a half million Armenians were massacred, or perished after having been forced to flee their homes. Many more were driven into exile and were scattered throughout the Middle East and further afield. In the war between Greece and Turkey in 1920–22 there were also large displacements of population on both sides.

The inter-war period was punctuated with anti-colonial uprisings. Some were relatively brief and localized like the Iraqi rebellion against British rule in 1920 and the Druze revolt in Syria against the French in 1925–26. In Egypt there were mass protests against continued British direct rule from 1919–22 and prolonged unrest in the late 1940s protesting against the continued British occupation of the Suez Canal zone.

But the bitterest and most protracted struggle was in Palestine. Palestinian opposition centred on the Zionist Organization's policies of Jewish immigration to Palestine from Europe under the aegis of British Mandatory rule. This progressively created a new settler population greatly outnumbering the traditional Jewish Palestinian community. For the most part, these immigrants settled on land acquired for the Zionists' exclusive use in perpetuity. Moreover, the Zionist movement demanded that Arab workers should be excluded from all Jewish economic enterprises. This brought Palestinians into conflict with both the British and with the Jewish settlers themselves. By the 1930s, the conflict had escalated into a six-month general strike (in 1936) followed by a three-year rebellion with guerrilla groups fighting the British army in the rural areas, as well as in some towns, including Jerusalem. The final collapse of this rebellion, however, was a severe blow to the Palestinian nationalist movement and in the 1940s it was very much weakened.

After a truce during World War II, fighting again erupted between British forces, the Jewish military organizations – now striving to wrest control of Palestine from both the British and the indigenous inhabitants – and the Palestinians, by now on the defensive. When the British could neither impose a solution nor control the fighting, they withdrew, terminating the Mandate in 1948. Immediately, the State of Israel was declared, leading to the first of a long series of wars between Israel and the Palestinians and the surrounding Arab states. In the first of these wars (1948–49), some 800,000 Palestinians fled or were driven from their homes, becoming refugees in the surrounding countries. They were not permitted by the Israelis to return to their homes after the war and the Palestinians have remained without a state of their own to this day.

All these events have not only helped to shape people's political attitudes, but have also affected their personal lives and the wellbeing of their families. In the personal reminiscences of women as well as men, memories of these events are still strong, and have coloured their views of themselves and the world around them.

National Revival and the Role of Women

These complex changes also created intense debate in intellectual circles in the Middle East about the nature of society and the position of women within it. Just as in the West perceptions of the 'plight' of Middle Eastern women were taken as indicators of the backwardness or decadence of the society, so within these cultures the status of women was held by many intellectuals to be symbolic of the state of society as a whole. The written record of these debates is inevitably dominated by men, who had much higher levels of literacy and could more easily publish what they wrote. But the limited research carried out so far suggests that women were more involved in these debates – in private at least – than was previously supposed.

The common experience of foreign domination or of

10 Painting by Osman Hamdy Bey, Turkey, second half of the nineteenth century.

Hamdy Bey was one of a number of Turkish painters in this era to adopt European styles of painting, but he was the only one to adopt figurative painting. He went to Paris in 1857 and spent some twelve years working in the studio of Jean-Léon Gérome, leader of the Neo-Greek school of painting and a noted teacher at the Ecole des Beaux Arts. Gérome had also visited the Middle East and produced a number of Orientalist genre paintings. Hamdy Bey's work, when he returned to Turkey, reflected Gérome's influence. He combined a formal realism – he often used photographs as the basis of his work – with a romanticism reminiscent of European Orientalism. His paintings of women in the harem are obviously based on a more informed perspective than most of their European counterparts, but they often retain that air of languid mystery so common in Western paintings. This led to accusations that he viewed Turkey in his work as a foreign tourist would. (For his views on costume, see pp. 122–3.)

encroachment, whether by the Ottomans or by Europeans, created a sense of the need for national and cultural revival. In the late nineteenth century this expressed itself in various ways. In Egypt, under British rule from 1882, nationalists drew on the country's long history as an independent state, while in greater Syria there was a revival of Arab culture. In Turkey itself, two different strands of thought were evident: the first aimed to reform the empire, combining some ideas from the West with liberal Islamic thought; the second stressed Turkish nationalism, both pan-Turanism (the unity of all Turkic-speaking peoples), and, in the years leading up to the collapse of the Ottoman Empire, a narrower Turkish nationalism centred on the heartland of Anatolia. Meanwhile, in Iran nationalism focused on resistance to foreign interference in the nation's internal affairs, particularly by Britain and Russia. This national feeling often coincided with opposition to the Qajar dynasty, which was seen as capitulating to foreign pressure and incapable of reform. After World War I and the collapse of the Ottoman Empire came a new wave of nationalisms – Syrian, Lebanese, Palestinian and Iraqi – which developed mainly in reaction to French and British colonial rule.

Ideologies of national revival or revival of the *umma* (the community of the Islamic faithful) had various roots. Some argued for a reform of society through the rethinking of the tenets of Islam, while others took a more secularist approach, espousing various Western cultural and political ideologies. Islamic modernist thinkers in Egypt and Turkey argued that many of the more desirable features of Western culture, particularly its scientific advances, could be integrated into the Islamic tradition without changing its essence. Christian Syrian and Lebanese writers stressed the importance and continuity of the Arabic language and Arab culture while at the same time advocating social changes modelled mainly on Western ideas.[35]

Whatever the approach to this question of national revival, discussions of the role of the family as the bearer of moral and cultural values played an important part in the debate, and it was in this context that the question of women's status was usually raised. Women's role in the family could be viewed in two ways: as the educators of children, who could instil new, more enlightened principles, or as the symbols of conservatism and traditional values. In neither case, however, was their basic role within the patriarchal family questioned.

Many of the reformist intellectuals of the late nineteenth century, whether Islamic modernists or secularists, argued that if women were to be the educators of youth they too must be educated and be more able to think for themselves. The Turkish writer Namik Kemal said in 1867:

> The harm created by this situation [the lack of women's participation in public activities and their relegation to being simply a 'source of pleasure' and bearers of children] does not affect individuals only. The present idleness of women, who constitute more than half the human population, and their entire economic dependence disturb the balance of the general laws of co-operation and welfare of mankind. This is obviously as harmful as the paralysis that afflicts one side of the nation's existence . . . Women, both mentally and physically, are not inferior to men. In the old days women would participate in all men's work and even in war. In the country districts women still help their menfolk in agriculture and trade. The reason for women's idleness in our country is that they are considered completely ignorant and unaware of their rights and duties, and whether they are helpful or harmful to their communities. Innumerable evils emerge from this inferior position of women, especially in the upbringing of their children.[36]

The Egyptian reformer and advocate of women's rights, Qasim Amin, in his books *Tahrir al-Mar'a* (*The Emancipation of Women*) and *Al-Mar'a al-Jadida* (*The New Woman*) published at the turn of the century, caused a sensation by demanding that women should be allowed education and opportunities to work. He argued that Islam had been just to women (except in the matter of polygamy, which he opposed) and that women's inferior status in contemporary society was the result of the corrupting influence of 'customs and illusions' which had developed subsequently. Though he did not advocate political rights for women, he argued that: 'Where woman is free, the citizen is free; and the arguments used against freedom of women are exactly the same as those used against freedom of any kind.'[37]

Although these observations were considered radical in

their time, they were all being made not by women but on their behalf. Even the most liberal and progressive men still assumed that while women should be encouraged towards education and a greater role in society, they could not initiate such reforms themselves. But despite the restrictions placed upon them, women did not remain entirely passive. In a number of countries, notably Egypt, Turkey and Iran, small groups of women began to become involved in discussions of the need for change. By the early years of the twentieth century, some were prepared to take the risk of acting to secure these changes (see Chapter VIII).

Their role, significant though it was, was subject to two kinds of limitation. First, there were the boundaries set by continuing male hegemony in government, the economy and the family. Writing of Turkey under the Republican government which had initiated reforms redefining women's role in society, Deniz Kandiyoti comments: 'There is one persistent and underlying concern which unites nationalist and Islamic discourse: it is an eagerness to establish beyond doubt that the behaviour and position of women, however defined, is congruent with the "true" identity of the collectivity and constitutes no threat to it.'[38] In other parts of the Middle East, this congruence was not quite so explicit, but it still formed an underlying theme in debates about women's status in the family and society.

The second limitation relates to class. In general, the women who were most involved in, and benefited most from those reforms which were carried out – the spread of education and work opportunities for women, and reforms of their legal status – came from the urban middle and upper classes. These changes were much slower to filter down to the urban poor, the provincial towns and the rural areas.

While women from the poorer classes often experienced considerable changes in economic conditions, this did not necessarily change their position vis-à-vis men in any significant way. Judith Tucker, examining the way social and economic change affected Egyptian women in the nineteenth century, remarks:

> Although many women might manage to improve their situation through participation in family production or independent economic activities, social perceptions of them as dependent and subservient were undergirded not only by custom but by religious authority. The strength of such authority may well account for the fact that the disruptions of the nineteenth century, especially the undermining of family coherence based on shared production, did not lead to a radical transformation in family structure.[39]

Religious authority, then, could be used to bolster the status quo just as it could be deployed in arguments for changing women's status. This conservative view of women's status was also justified as a response to Western domination. If some thinkers argued that the nation or the *umma* needed to change to meet the challenges of an altered reality, others argued that the best defence was the preservation of 'traditional' values. Both these views could be discerned in the ideologies of most anti-colonial nationalist movements in the region from Iran to Algeria. In most cases these contradictions in attitudes to women's role in society remained unresolved when political independence from colonial rule was finally achieved.

The family, too, could act as a bulwark against social change, and in times of social or economic upheaval it was often the only form of security and continuity to which people could cling. This meant that while in some cases male members of families encouraged women to take new paths, on the whole, male control over women within the family tended to reinforce accepted norms of female behaviour. For example, ideas concerning the importance of family honour, embodied in control of women's sexuality, persisted despite economic and political upheavals, as they have done in different cultural and religious contexts in other Mediterranean societies. Despite the fact that by the 1950s many more women were receiving education and going out to work, both sexual control, and the demand that women submit to male authority within the family in return for protection, remained powerful.

Some women certainly chose to defy this authority by conscious acts of rebellion – by leaving their families and even by going to live abroad – which would have been virtually impossible half a century earlier. Yet women who had the strength and the resources to take this path often paid a considerable personal price for doing so.

Only within the last twenty years have these aspects of patriarchal control been challenged on an intellectual level, with feminists such as Nawal Saadawi and Fatima Mernissi questioning men's sexual double standards and the assumptions behind male control in the family. But even today criticism of this kind is not widely accepted. One of the factors which has inhibited these more comprehensive criticisms has been what Leila Ahmed has termed 'cultural loyalty', arising out of the Middle East's unequal relationship with the West. 'Feminism', she suggests:

> . . . is irreconcilably in conflict with all or nearly all currently entrenched ideologies. It is in conflict with the dominant ideologies in the West to more or less the same extent that it is with the Islamic. But Western women can be critical and radically critical of their cultures and prevalent ideologies – although these in the West as elsewhere also exert their pressures, perhaps more subtly than elsewhere, towards conformity and acceptance. For

the Islamic woman, however, there is a whole further dimension to the pressures that bear down on her urging her to silence her criticism, remain loyal, reconcile herself to, even find virtue in the central formulations of her culture that normally she would rebel against: the pressure that comes into being as a result of the relationship in which Islamic society now stands with the West. The Islamic civilization has a very special, even unique, relation with the West so that the issue of cultural loyalty and betrayal, perhaps at issue in any culture in this new age of the simultaneity and accessibility of a range of cultures, is experienced with unique force and intensity in that civilization.[40]

The roots of this ambiguous relationship, and the images and self-images of women which resulted from it, are to be found in the history of the years from 1850 to 1950. This book explores how photographs of women during that century both reflected and helped to shape these images.

Chapter I
The Development of Photography in the Middle East

Through Western Eyes: European Photographers

Photography came to the Middle East only a few years after its invention in 1839. Egypt and Palestine were among the earliest testing-grounds for this new medium, as photographers joined artists on the grand tour of the Orient. During the first two decades of photography, the Middle East often appears to be a world uncannily empty of people, and full of stark historical monuments. Yet from time to time a few human figures appear, seemingly transfixed by the camera, because of the long exposure times – up to two minutes – needed to take a picture.

Perhaps the best known of these early photographic tours was undertaken by Maxime du Camp, who visited Egypt and Palestine in 1848 and 1849 with the novelist Gustave Flaubert. A large number of du Camp's photographs published after this trip include such human figures, posed on the skyline of Egypt's ancient monuments. Du Camp described how he used Hajji Ismail, one of the sailors on the Nile steamer in which the party travelled, to pose for him, usually wearing only a loincloth. 'In this way,' he remarks, 'I was able to include a uniform scale of proportions on every one of my plates.' To persuade the man to remain still for the required length of time, he turned the camera into a threatening object: 'I told him that the brass tube of the lens jutting out from the camera was a cannon, which would vomit a hail of shot if he had the misfortune to move – a story which immobilized him completely.'[1]

Hajji Ismail was one of the first in a long line of people whom European photographers would persuade, cajole or intimidate into posing for photographs, transforming a situation of unequal power into a visual image. The pursuit of unwilling subjects often added to the excitement of the photographic enterprise. This is not, of course, to say that everyone who appeared in European photographs of the Middle East did so against his or her will, but simply that the relationship between photographer and subject was rarely one of equality or spontaneous co-operation. The subject was chosen by the photographer and had little or no control over the resulting photograph.

In the period up to World War I a large proportion of the photographs taken in the Middle East were the product of commercial studios or of photographers seeking to profit by their work from publication in magazines or books. This

1 'Laveuse Egyptienne' – Egyptian Washerwoman. Pierre Trémaux, salted paper print, 1847–54.

Trémaux's published album of photographs of Egypt, Sudan and Ethiopia was among the earliest showing human figures in the Middle East. This picture must have been taken at roughly the same time as Du Camp photographed Hajji Ismail. The long exposure time required probably accounts for the woman's strange, stiff pose: most of Trémaux's subjects were photographed propped against walls. Yet the overall effect is uncanny, almost ghostlike. Trémaux gives a description of how he took this photograph. '[This woman] is a washerwoman who, on my invitation, got up from her work without letting go of either her washing or her soap. She stayed still in front of the photographic apparatus until I gave the signal. Then all she did was to reach out her hand saying the word *bakhshish* (give me something) and went back to her work without concerning herself with the outcome of my activities, and without saying another word, so sparing of words are these poor creatures, especially with Europeans.'
This photograph contrasts with the impression Trémaux gives in his narrative – that all women in Egypt were strictly veiled. But in his commentary on other photographs, he points out that poor women, like the one in this picture, did not always cover their faces, even in front of strange men.[1]

commercialism, combined with the photographers' monopoly in the choice of subject, goes some way to explain the rapid development of a range of photographic clichés about the people of the region. These clichés picked up and echoed for a wider audience some of the Orientalist themes in literature, painting and anthropology, but they also developed a life of their own.

By the 1860s photography had become big business in Britain, Europe and the United States, and by the 1870s, the major cities of the Middle East had been drawn into this commercial network. At first, demand was not generated locally but by the growing influx of tourists and the growth of Western interests in the region. In 1830, France occupied Algeria which, by the 1840s, was already being promoted as a place for more venturesome Europeans to visit. The first organized tours of Palestine began in the 1850s and in 1868 the first Cook's tour party arrived in Egypt. After the opening of the Suez Canal a year later, a constant stream of Europeans passed through Egypt en route to India and the Far East.

For these reasons the photographic trade spread rapidly, probably more so than in any other region outside Europe and the United States, with the possible exception of India. Commercial photographic studios produced pictures for purchase in a variety of forms: postcards, stereoscopic slides mounted on card, lantern slides, and loose prints to be mounted in albums. In Europe by the 1870s postcards were legalized as a new and attractive form of postal communication. They also became popular as collectors' items.

Stereoscopic slides, which gave the illusion of a three-dimensional picture when seen through a stereoscope, by the juxtaposition of two photographs taken at slightly different angles, became all the rage in Europe in the 1860s and 1870s. The stereoscope had a particular appeal for viewing salacious or pornographic photographs, in private or in peep shows. Charles Baudelaire, who held photography in profound contempt because of its commercialization, commented in 1859 during the early years of the stereoscopic boom:

A little later a thousand hungry eyes were bending over
the peepholes of the stereoscope as though they were the
attic windows of the infinite. The love of pornography,
which is no less deeply rooted in the natural heart of man
than love of himself, was not to let slip so fine an
opportunity of self-satisfaction. And do not imagine that it
was only children on their way back from school who took
pleasure in these follies; the world was infatuated with
them.[2]

The Development of the Commercial Photography Market

The major Western photographic companies also rapidly came to see the appeal of postcards and stereoscopic slides as souvenirs of travel, adventure and exoticism, of which the Middle East provided a seemingly inexhaustible store. Some Europeans also established studios in the cities of the Middle East: for example, Sébah and Joaillier in Istanbul, the Bonfils family in Beirut, Lehnert and Landrock in Cairo, and ND Photos in Algiers. These studios produced thousands of photographs in a variety of forms, often buying up or poaching each other's negatives to achieve wider sales. By 1876 the Bonfils studio had its own mail-order catalogue, and other studios followed suit.

Many of the photographs destined for this audience of tourists and Westerners who had never visited the region were taken in studios. This was partly because of the problems of gaining access to subjects, especially women. While it was usually easy enough to photograph street scenes, or views of the countryside, it was often difficult to obtain close-up shots of people. There were also very real difficulties of using cameras in the field, until the latter part of the nineteenth century when they became lighter, smaller and easier to handle. Until this time most of the more popular photographic printing techniques such as the albumen process also required instant processing in the field. Most of the major operators did have mobile studios in horse-drawn vans, and occasionally hauled their equipment around on animal-back. But a substantial proportion of nineteenth-century photographs were taken in indoor or outdoor studio sets even though they purported to be 'real-life' scenes.

In Europe, photographic studios were used to make portraits of clients on demand as well as for the creation of such 'scenes'. But in most European commercial studios in the Middle East, particularly those which served the tourist market, there was much less portrait work for clients and a good deal of scene-making. The studio was used as a kind of theatrical set in which to present images of unnamed people whose only identity appears in the (often erroneous) captions which categorize them by racial type, religion, tribe or, occasionally, class.

In this genre of photography, the images of Middle Easterners, particularly women, did not differ dramatically from similar types of photographic image created by Westerners of people in other parts of the world. The figure of the woman as an erotic and exotic object of the European's gaze can be seen in the reclining, almost naked African woman posed against a studio backdrop representing 'the jungle'; in the Japanese 'geisha' girl with her robe slipped from her shoulder; in the bare-breasted Samoan women posed as if playing cards; in the 'odalisque' with her semi-nudity, her jewels and her water pipe. All these studio photographs use pose and juxtaposition of objects to suggest sensuality, sexual availability or primitiveness. In the same way, studio portraits of 'native types', whether of Peruvian Indians, Polynesians, Algerian Kabyles or Zulus, all tended towards the same quality of archetypal anonymity.

Yet in the Middle East there were certain distinguishing features in the way this type of photography developed. Many of the images which hardened into clichés, especially in the photography of women, were drawn from a pre-existing repertoire of themes already established by the genre of Orientalist painting which had developed, particularly in France and Germany, from the first half of the nineteenth century. Roland Barthes rejects the idea that 'it was the painters who invented Photography (by bequeathing it their framing, the Albertian perspective, and the optic of the camera obscura)'. He argues that it was the chemists who were responsible for its creation.[3] Yet in subject matter and construction, if not in aesthetic intention, it might be argued that Orientalist painting had a very considerable influence on nineteenth-century studio photography of the Middle East.

Though most of these photographs may seem banal and flat when compared, for instance, with the paintings of Ingres or Delacroix, the subject matter, perspective and manner of presentation were often very similar. Common subjects in these paintings – the harem, the odalisque, the white mistress with her black slaves – were all replicated in studio photographs. And just as in the painters' studio, one can be virtually certain that nothing appearing in these photographs is accidental or unintended – except occasionally the model's expression. Especially in the early decades of photography, people were draped, posed and clamped at the photographer's pleasure.

The difference between paintings and photographs, however, lies in the way they appear to the viewer. As Barthes suggests, this product of chemistry has a claim to 'represent a reality' in a way no artist would claim for a painting. The process of photography, therefore, could transform these imaginative arrangements in the studio into 'proof' of the way people in the Middle East and elsewhere looked and behaved.

At the same time, there was a good deal of blurring of the distinctions between the two genres in the late nineteenth century. It became quite common for painters to work from photographs rather than from life. For instance, a volume of photographs of Syria produced by Charles Lallemande in the 1860s as part of a grandiose and unfinished project entitled *Galerie Universelle des Peuples*, contained some 600 photographs illustrating 'native costumes and people'. Although it was also used to produced a series of stereoscopic slides, it was intended primarily as a source for artists wishing to paint these subjects.[4]

Studio Fantasies

Although these three studio photographs show women from different cultures, the way they are constructed, and the assumptions which lie behind them, are in many ways similar. In each case, the subject is isolated in the studio with 'props' to represent supposedly typical aspects of her culture, which is thereby visually reduced to a collection of objects, impervious to time and to change. The women's poses, and their physical exposure to the camera, also suggest the photographers' common intention to present them as objects of sexual scrutiny and desire. Thus the African woman is stretched virtually naked in an inviting pose before a 'jungle' of pot plants and *papier mâché* which the photographer – and probably many of the viewers would regard as an 'appropriate environment.' The two Algerian women recline against 'Moorish' rugs with a tentlike backdrop. Here, the image of sexual availability is compounded by the hint of a liaison between the two women, a theme quite common in Orientalist writings and visual imagery. The Japanese woman's pose is more restrained, in keeping with the Western belief in the greater sophistication of Japanese culture. Yet the cultural object in the picture, the *sanisen* (a musical instrument), is little more than an adjunct to the projection of the woman's sexuality.

2 *'Girl Playing Sanisen'. Studio portrait, Japan, c.1880.*

3 *African woman. Studio portrait, late nineteenth century.*

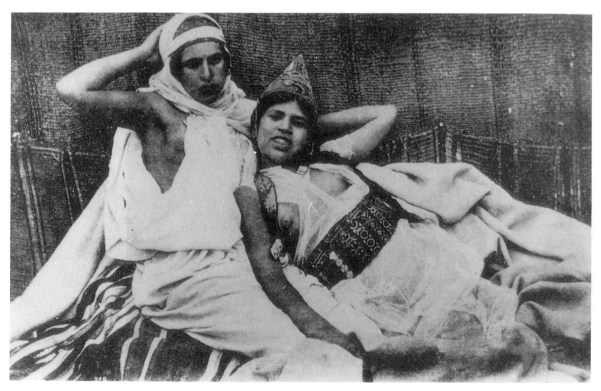

4 *'Jeune Mauresque et Femme Kabyle' – Young Moorish Woman and Kabyle Woman. ND Phot. Postcard, probably Algiers, late nineteenth century. The woman on the right was a model who frequently featured in photographs from this studio.*

5 'Group of Bedouin from East of the Jordan'. Bonfils, late nineteenth century.

The photographer has posed these women with elaborate care, down to the positioning of their hands, to create a composition in many ways closer to an imaginative painting than to photographic naturalism in its use of line and perspective. The desert scene is set by the use of a painted backdrop and artificial rocks. Whether or not the women were bedouin, and whether or not they came from the region suggested in the caption, is impossible to tell.

6 An Egyptian woman. Zangaki. Studio portrait. Port Said, Egypt, probably 1870s.

Zangaki was a photographer thought to be of Greek origin who established a studio in Port Said in the late 1860s, undoubtedly to cash in on the increased tourist trade after the opening of the Suez Canal in 1869.
This composition contains a variety of incongruous motifs: the Pyramids and Sphinx (shown on the painted backdrop) symbolizing ancient Egypt frame the veiled woman of 'Islamic' Egypt. Her black *burqu* (face veil) and bare feet suggest that she is not well-off, and contrast oddly with the floral carpet, mother-of-pearl inlaid table and vase, which form the studio furniture. The Western design of the carpet and vase are also out of keeping with the rest of the decor, though they do suggest the increasing presence of Western consumer goods in Egypt in the second half of the nineteenth century.

7 Jewess of Tunis. Late nineteenth century.

Most commercial photographers took series of pictures of 'native types', divided according to ethnic or religious group. Among women in particular, distinctive costumes, often richly decorated, made them attractive subjects. Yet in this photograph, the cultural distinctiveness of the Jewish woman's dress in Tunis is belied by the studio backdrop which shows a fanciful European-style landscape.

8 'An Egyptian Peasant Woman and Her Child'. Painting by Joseph-Florentin-Léon Bonnat, 1870.
9 'Arab Woman with Her Child'. Egypt, c.1900.

This method of carrying children was very common in Egypt and was used to a lesser extent in Syria and Palestine. It became the motif of numerous photographs and several paintings of the Orientalist genre. It was used to express both the picturesque and melancholy aspects of the Orientalist view of women.

In the Bonnat painting, sensuality mingles with an air of pathos. It was apparently based on a sketch of a peasant woman which he may have made during the ceremonies marking the opening of the Suez Canal in 1869, but he is also thought to have used photographs of this subject as an aid to composition. Two years earlier, Bonnat painted an 'Ascension of the Virgin' which bears a resemblance to the composition of this painting: the iconography of madonna and child was seldom far from the minds of artists and photographers portraying women and children in the Middle East.[2]

The photograph, taken at a later date, stresses the mystery of the veiled woman, contrasted with the sensual nakedness of the child. This, too, is a self-consciously 'artistic' composition, with the carefully posed limbs and concern for the effects of light and shadow. The woman's pose is, however, also reminiscent of another common motif in painting and photography of the Middle East – the woman carrying a water-jug on her shoulder or her head.

This overlap between 'art' and 'documentation' was further complicated by the fact that until the 1900s, the growing numbers of illustrated magazines published all over Europe did not have the technology to print photographs directly on their pages and normally used engravings or drawings, which in their turn were frequently made from photographs. Paintings were often rendered in the same way, so that the distinction between the two media virtually disappeared.

Whether presented as engravings in magazines or photographs in books, the genre of studio photographs proved very versatile. Despite their often evident artificiality, they appeared as illustrations to books of travels and even to what purported to be ethnographic descriptions of life in the Middle East. Some travel books used such studio shots interspersed without comment with the author's own photographs taken in the field. Even a classic of European description of Middle Eastern life, E.W. Lane's *An Account of the Manners and Customs of the Modern Egyptians*, included in the 1895 edition posed studio shots of women to 'illustrate' the text.

In photography as in painting, images which drew on Orientalist perceptions of the character and role of Middle Eastern women were among the most saleable items in the commercial market. At the crudest end of this market, there were photographs of women in varying stages of undress, sold to soldiers, sailors and tourists. Two Algerian writers describe the way images of women were presented to fulfil and reinforce the European's stereotypes of the Middle East and its women:

> An entire industry was there to serve him: coloured pictures showing some of the regional characteristics of the *mouquère* [Arab woman] – the young girl from the desert (Nailia) or the Aurès, the young Kabyle woman or the city woman from Algiers, Oran or Constantine, ludicrously attired, or in a state of 'Oriental' undress; postcards for tourists and soldiers; cheap novelties; bizarre or salacious tales peddled on street corners; songs . . .[5]

12 The most explicit versions of this sub-eroticism were produced mostly in the cities of North Africa and Egypt; they were more rarely seen in Turkey, Lebanon, Iran and Iraq, and seldom in Syria or Palestine.

It seems, however, that Ottoman officials had, by the end of the century, become unhappy about the way their society was being portrayed in visual images. In November 1900 an imperial decree forbade the introduction into or sale in the Ottoman Empire of images bearing the names of God or Muhammad; pictures of the Kaaba or any other images relating to the holy city of Mecca; Muslim buildings and ceremonies; and portraits of Muslim women.[6] Although

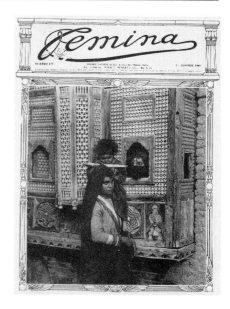

10 *'Captive dans son palais'* – Captive in Her Palace. Cover photograph from Femina magazine, Paris, 1 January 1906.

This picture is supposed to depict a woman locked up by her father, a notable religious figure of Cairo, after he had ended her marriage to someone of whom he disapproved. In fact it is a 'staged' photograph taken years earlier, probably by Zangaki. It is one of a number of photographs using the same *mashribiyya* (latticed) window, set close to the ground, as the background for a variety of posed scenes, for example Zangaki's 'L'Amour egyptienne' – Egyptian Love (11, opposite). Close examination of the woodwork and masonry shows it to be exactly the same as that in the *Femina* picture. All these scenes are highly improbable, since the point of *mashribiyya* windows was to allow women to see out without being seen from the street. The same photograph had also appeared in *Lady's Pictorial* of 7 July 1900, illustrating an article whose main themes were the 'Mohammedan's indifference to suffering' and the foibles of Cairene servants – especially their failure to comprehend the notion of dusting.

These photographs were not only fabricated clichés about the lives of women in the Middle East, masquerading as 'real' scenes, but were often reproduced in the context of writings which further elaborated these Orientalist fictions.

these regulations, like many others made by the Ottoman authorities at this time, seem to have gone largely unheeded, they do suggest a token effort at self-defence against the deluge of culturally unacceptable images being made and sold.

But photographers, amateur and professional, continued to pursue these popular images of women. Studio portraits vied with the interest aroused by the veiled figures of women to be seen in the streets of Middle Eastern cities. Some photographers were fascinated by the physical beauty they saw in some rural dwellers, especially women who were not veiled. Lucie Duff Gordon, writing in 1863 from Cairo, echoed the sentiments of other travellers and artists: 'If you have any power over artists, send them to paint here. No words can describe either the picturesque beauty of Cairo or the splendid forms of the people in upper Egypt, and above all in Nubia. I was in raptures at seeing how superb an animal man (and woman) really is.'[7]

13   Western views of the historical significance of the Middle East also affected how its inhabitants were perceived. The region attracted great interest as the site of the great monuments of Pharaonic, classical and biblical antiquity. This interest in the glories of the past has continued as a theme of both commercial and amateur photography to the present day. It often has the effect of making the indigenous inhabitants who appeared, like Hajji Ismail, in the foreground of many such pictures seem like picturesque visual markers, dwarfed by history.

But it was the biblical significance of Middle Eastern life which held the greatest attraction for many Westerners. Both the growth of tourism and pilgrimage to the Holy Places of Palestine and the intensification of missionary activity in the whole region produced a deluge of books, slides, postcards and other memorabilia of 'biblical' Palestine and its inhabitants. The images which resulted combined Western religious imagery with a penchant for the picturesque and an ambivalence about the effects of 'progress', an ambivalence which both fed and mirrored the views of many Orientalists.

The photographer Adrien Bonfils, son of Félix Bonfils who founded the leading commercial studio in Beirut in the 1870s, created many of these images. Unusually for a photographer, he committed his view of what he was doing to paper:

> Twenty centuries have passed without changing the decor or physiognomy of this land [Palestine] unique among all; but let us hasten if we wish to enjoy the sight. Progress, the great trifler, will have swiftly brought about the destruction of what time itself has respected . . . before progress has completely done its destructive job, before this present which is still the past has forever disappeared, we have tried to fix and immobilize it in a series of views.[8]

Biblical image-making became an industry. Some photographers took whole series of photographs in Palestine to illustrate editions of the Bible, biblical histories and travel books. The earliest of these was Alexander Keith's *Evidence of the Truth of the Christian Religion*, published in Edinburgh in 1844 and containing engravings based on daguerrotypes (one of the earliest photographic processes) made by his son George. In time, the people of Palestine and the surrounding region were enlisted by photographers to become part of this biblical past. Some photographers like Adrien Bonfils, whose photographs of Jerusalem and the Holy Land were very successful, especially in the United States, took to using models. To create material for an illustrated Bible, he is said to have proceeded as follows: 'After choosing scenes he wished to re-create from the Old and New Testaments, he went to the sites, grouped together peasants, shepherds, and bedouins and tried in this way to reconstruct biblical events.'[9] Apparently it was usual to pay a nominal sum to these 'models'. Sometimes, it seems, they did not appreciate the fee he offered for their services. One group of lepers Bonfils had photographed threatened to touch him if he did not pay them better.

For the most part, however, photographers did not create scenes with models but simply took pictures of daily life in Palestine and attached a caption with a biblical reference or quotation. Thus contemporary Palestinians – women fetching water, a man ploughing a field, a shepherd with some goats – could exchange their present existence for a biblical image, becoming for the viewer Mary, David or a figure in one of Christ's parables. Eric Matson, who worked from the 1890s until 1948 as a photographer with the American Colony, a small religious community in Jerusalem, took many such pictures for the tourist and pilgrim market. In one hand-coloured series some of the captions were: 'The 23rd Psalm, portrayed in the land of its inception'; 'Ruth the Moabitess'; 'Bethlehem Juda: scenes of the first Christmas'.

Many people brought up in Europe or the United States, particularly if they were from a Protestant community, were steeped in the imagery of the Bible and would probably 'see' a biblical significance in these scenes even without the help of such captions. In fact travellers were able to find these scenes even in countries other than Palestine. Lucie Duff Gordon describes seeing a tall bedouin woman in Egypt 'walking away towards the desert in the setting sun like Hagar. All is so Scriptural in the country here.'[10] Apart from the romantic nostalgia of these visions, the wide circulation of biblical stereotypes of Palestinians suggests a picturesque backwardness which has coloured Western views of them to this day.

Apart from serving the needs of pilgrims and tourists there were other ways in which Western preoccupations with Christianity affected images of the Middle East. One of the effects of Darwinism on Christian, and especially Protestant,

12 'Femme mauresque' – Moorish Woman. ND Phot. Postcard, North Africa, late nineteenth or early twentieth century.

Studios such as ND Phot. produced hundreds of postcards of this kind. This particular example was sent by Michel Coste, from the Fez region of Morocco to his wife Anna in Coursan, in the Aude region of France, in September 1914. He may have been a soldier, or simply a tourist. The message reads: 'Dear wife, Am still in good health. Hugs to the children, a thousand kisses, your husband, Michel. Letter follows.'
It is hard to imagine that this innocent message would have accompanied such a photograph if the woman portrayed had been a European. Her suggestive pose might have been thought highly improper and inappropriate by the recipient. But the fact that this woman was an Arab means that the suggestion of sexual allure could safely be regarded as part of the local colour a postcard was expected to provide.

46

13 'Type de femmes fellahs à Karnak' – Type of Peasant Woman at Karnak. J.P[ascale] Sébah. Egypt, late nineteenth century.

Sébah, thought to be Turkish in origin, worked mainly in Istanbul with a French photographer named Joaillier in the second half of the nineteenth century, but he also had a studio for a time in Cairo. Scenes such as this were common subjects for photographs. In Egypt particularly, the inhabitants could be juxtaposed against the backdrop of the great monuments of antiquity. In this photograph, the women have an air of uneasiness – probably because their poses have been arranged by the photographer – which contrasts with the clean assured lines of the reliefs above them.

thought was to highlight the need to 'prove' scientifically the authenticity of the stories told in the Bible. In 1868 the Palestine Exploration Fund began a full-scale survey of Palestine west of the Jordan, using the Royal Engineers (including the young Kitchener) as surveyors. Apart from the military and intelligence value of the maps and topographical information which emerged, its stated aim was to establish the historical authenticity of biblical sites and to document life in the Holy Land. In the course of their work the team took numerous photographs to document and authenticate their findings, and these photographs also found their way into books, magazines and lantern slide shows.

Furthermore, in the growing numbers of Sunday schools all over Britain, children were increasingly shown photographs and lantern slides of the Holy Land as a way to make the biblical stories more 'real'. Thus generations of children grew up with images of the Middle East associated almost exclusively with the Bible.

Missionaries of all denominations also used photographs and slide shows as an aid to fundraising, showing the record of their work among the 'heathen'. As photographs became easier to take they showed their own pictures of converts, smiling mothers and clean children whose newfound well-being was the result of missionary labours: the triumph of Christianity, order and hygiene over dirt and ignorance. Many of these pictures were designed particularly to appeal to the women in their congregations at home, to encourage them to make donations or even to enlist in the ranks of the missionaries.

Photography, Anthropology and Ethnography

Among the scientific theories which made their mark on Western thinking in the late nineteenth century was one which divided the world into a hierarchy of races and ethnic groups. This notion informed much of the popular imagery

14 'Puits de Rebecca à Harran (Charres). Lieu biblique illustré par Abraham, Eliezer, Jacob, Rebecca, Rachel (Mesopotamie)' – The Spring of Rebecca at Harran. Biblical Site Illustrated by Abraham, Eliezer, Jacob, Rebecca, Rachel. Capucin Fathers. Postcard, Iraq, early twentieth century.

Harran is a site in northern Iraq near the Euphrates mentioned in Genesis XI.31 as being on the route taken by Abraham and his tribe on their journey from Ur in Iraq to Palestine. The Capucins evidently took some of the local inhabitants, perhaps bedouin from this region, to play the role of these biblical figures. The fathers produced a series of postcards, some documenting daily life, but others, like this one, stressing the continuity and changeless quality of life through the centuries since biblical times.

of the non-European world, including the Middle East, and in photography was embodied in the enormous numbers of images of 'native types'. These images to some extent took their cue from the new disciplines of anthropology and ethnology.

In physical anthropology, photography rapidly came to play a crucial part in documenting and classifying people according to the 'evolution' of their physical features, head shape and size and cranial capacity. A specific style of photography was evolved to suit this kind of investigation. As early as 1862, the *British Journal of Photography* carried an article describing the methods used at the Academy of St Petersburg:

> Each figure is produced in profile and in a front view with the head uncovered, and the hair shaved off so that the measurements of the three principal dimensions of the cranium can be taken without difficulty. As it is much easier to take photographic portraits of a large number of living individuals than to collect the same number of authentic crania, it follows that photography will furnish an excellent method of determining the mean proportions of the skulls of the different races of men.[11]

This kind of research was rather less common in the Middle East than in Africa, India and other parts of Asia, but there were some examples – for instance, the work of Ernest Chantre on North Africa and Egypt. In *Recherches Anthropologiques dans l'Afrique orientale: Egypte*, published in Lyon in 1904, Chantre used field studies done in 1898 and 1899 to examine the cranial capacity and facial features of various categories of Egyptians (a total of 694 men and 164 women), which he compares with those of ancient Egyptians using measurements made from mummies.

Chantre remarked that he could not have obtained the photographs of women without the assistance of his wife: 'The women could not have been examined without the

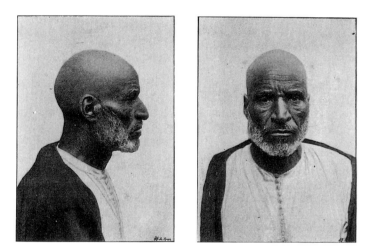

15 'Fellahin de Gizeh'. Ernest Chantre, Egypt, 1898–99.

These are anthropometric photographs from Chantre's study on Egypt.[3] The peasant woman from Giza wears a head-covering, which defeats the aim of the anthropometric photograph – to show the size and shape of the cranium. She also departs from the standard pose by resting her face in her hand. Her male counterpart conforms more exactly to the norms of this kind of photography.

intervention of Madame Chantre who took part in all my anthropometric work.'[12]

Another, later, practitioner was Henry Field who was in charge of the Chicago Museum of Natural History's anthropological expedition to the Near East which began its field work in 1934. But in anthropometric surveys which they conducted in Iran and Iraq, they were not able to take photographs of the women they examined.

Alan Sekula points out that this type of photography represents part of the positivist fascination with the human form and physiognomy. In Europe it manifested itself mainly in the adaptation of these standardized portraits for the purposes of social control: the categorization of 'criminal types' – the police mug-shot – and the examination of the inhabitants of mental asylums. In these forms the technique was not much used in the Middle East until the 1950s with the gradual introduction of photographs for identity cards.

This positivist outlook on anthropology and ethnography was not confined to cranial studies. The craze for popular ethnographies put together by travellers and writers in the

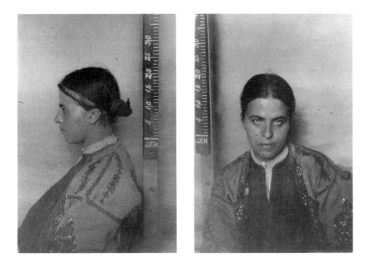

16 A young married woman from Bethlehem. J.E. Hannauer, c.1902.

J.E. Hannauer was a clergyman at St George's Cathedral in Jerusalem who was also an amateur enthnologist and antiquary. In 1902 he was sent a camera and tried his hand at some anthropometric photography. But, as he wrote from Jerusalem to J.D. Grace: 'Attempts to obtain photographs of types of individuals – I find this more difficult than I anticipated as many people with characteristic features strongly object to being photographed with their heads bare, and yet this is essential.' In this case, he must have persuaded, or intimidated this woman to pose, uncharacteristically, with her head uncovered.

late nineteenth century drew heavily on these ideas. Such works usually marshalled a ragbag of commercial and personal photographs to illustrate them, labelled according to racial and ethnic categories. This approach remained characteristic of much comparative anthropology even after new techniques of photography allowed a more naturalistic and flexible approach to camerawork. It provided a way of collecting comparative details of dress, artefacts and supposedly typical physical traits of different races, tribes and religious groups.

Early in the twentieth century, Albert Kahn, a wealthy French banker who was part of a humanist intellectual circle which included figures such as the philosopher Henri Bergson, brought a different perspective to this tradition of 'collecting the world' through photographs. Kahn established a grandiose humanist project which he called 'les Archives de la Planète'. He marshalled a team of photographers and sent them round the world to collect both stills and film footage of 'social life and customs'. Several of these roving cameramen visited various parts of the Middle East in the first two decades of the twentieth century. His intention seems to have been to establish the value and variety of cultures in the world rather than to arrange them in a racial hierarchy, yet his view of the project also reveals a romantic notion of pristine cultures which need to be preserved on film before they disappear in the face of Western 'progress'. His aim, he said, was to 'record once and for all those aspects and patterns of human activity whose inevitable disappearance is only a matter of time'.[13]

The availability of hand-held Kodak cameras in the West by the end of the nineteenth century gave many more people access to photography. Travellers could supplement their postcard collections with their own albums of snapshots. Many produced images remarkably similar to those found in commercial photography, seeking out the same sights and monuments, often influenced in what they considered

18 'Femme d'el-Salt' – Woman from el-Salt (Jordan). Paul Castelnau, Jerusalem, 3 August 1918.

An unusual study of an old woman. Although the lined faces of old men often attracted the interest of the photographers, women of that age appear less often. Paul Castelnau was one of several photographers whom Albert Kahn sent to the Middle East to contribute to his 'Archives de la planète'. Castelnau worked for Kahn for three years, from 1917 until 1919, visiting Egypt, Arabia, Palestine and Cyprus in 1918, a period of great dislocation, as the Ottoman armies retreated through Palestine and Syria before the advancing British and allied forces. On the whole, Castelnau's photographs do not record this turmoil, seeking rather to document 'types' and social customs rather than contemporary events.

17 Women of the family of Audeh abu Tayyi, a chief of the Howeitat tribe, with, probably, Muhammad al-Ma'rawi, Gertrude Bell's guide. Gertrude Bell, southern Syrian desert, 29 January 1914.

This is an unusual photograph for Gertrude Bell. She was a keen and competent photographer, but took few pictures of women. At this time, she was on the outward leg of a long journey from Damascus to Hail in Arabia. The fact that she photographed these women at all was largely an accident. She had wanted to visit Audeh abu Tayyi, who was a very well-known figure among the bedouin tribes of this region, and went to his encampment to meet him, only to find that he was away. In his absence, she passed some time socializing and taking pictures of the women in the camp. If Audeh had been there, the chances are that she would have paid them scant attention. She wrote in the version of her diary which was later published: '29 January . . . we came presently to Audeh's big tent. He is away, raiding the Shammar [tribe], according to his wont: but I stopped for half an hour, drank coffee and photographed his tent and his womenkind – more particularly his very handsome sister, Aliyah.'[4]

The women standing in this photograph is very probably Aliyah and the woman sitting in the background one of Audeh's wives. An unsolved puzzle is why Aliyah is holding the hand of Bell's guide, Muhammad al-Ma'rawi. The most likely explanation is that they were relatives. In a further (unpublished) diary entry for that day, written on 30 January, Bell also mentions the identities of Audeh's wives, but in a way which reflects her interest in tribal alliances, rather than in the women themselves.

19 (left) & 20 (above) 'Mendiante persane' – Persian Beggar Woman. Engraving (19) by Pranishnikoff after a photograph (20) by Jane Dieulafoy, Tehran, 1880s.

worthy of a photograph by pre-existing images and stereotypes.

There were, of course, exceptions. Among those who travelled extensively in the Middle East were some people who took photographs which to varying degrees belied the standard images. On the whole, the male travellers of the early twentieth century – for instance, H. St J. Philby, Wilfred Thesiger, Bertram Thomas – left a photographic record which stresses politics and exploration, and the individual men – politicians or tribal leaders – whom they met. Only a few, like Alois Musil, who made a study of the Rwalla bedouin in Syria, actually took pictures which give any sense of the life their subjects lived.

Some of the women travellers who were able to enter the lives of women as well as men give a rather broader photographic picture. Of these, the British traveller Freya Stark provided perhaps the widest range of photographs from her extensive travels. Another important woman traveller of the first decades of the century, Gertrude Bell, was also an enthusiastic photographer, but her main focus, like that of her male compatriots, was largely on exploration, archaeology, architecture and political life. She spent too little time with women to provide more than a fragmentary photographic record.

Jane Dieulafoy was a Frenchwoman who travelled extensively in Iran with her husband in the 1880s. In contrast to the studio photographs shown earlier, this powerful portrait is accompanied by a detailed explanation of the circumstances under which it was taken, transforming a portrait of a 'Persian type' into that of an individual in a tragic predicament. Dieulafoy wrote that she took this photograph in Tehran while visiting a clinic run by the Catholic order of the Sisters of St Vincent de Paul. Among the people waiting in the courtyard: 'I saw a young Muslim woman whose face bore witness to her deep suffering. This poor beggar woman had just left her son, close to death with diphtheria, in the care of the sisters. Crouched in a corner of the courtyard, she was still as a stone. Powerless to save her son's life, she had given him, without hope, into more experienced hands than her own. Silent, her swollen eyes dry of tears, and wrapped up in her own pain, she

Those who studied or lived in particular communities obviously produced photographs which set less distance between photographer and subject because they are well known to each other. Ernest Hoeltzer, an official of the Iranian telegraph service who married an Armenian woman in Isfahan and lived there in the late nineteenth century, provides a closer view of that community, men and women, than could be given by an outsider.[14]

Women anthropologists working in the Middle East in the 1920s and 1930s, such as Winifred Blackman who surveyed a number of villages in Upper Egypt, Matthéa Gaudry who studied the women of the Aurès and Hilma Granqvist who lived in the Palestinian village of Artas, all took photographs which, to varying degrees, gave a less stereotyped picture of the lives of people they knew and who knew them. Though many of these pictures were of poor technical quality, some at least offer a more nuanced view of the life of women and of their community.

Yet almost all of these Western observers viewed Middle Eastern societies as existing in a sort of time warp. They were acutely aware of the changes which increasing Western influence was bringing to the region, and some actively supported or furthered this influence. But the focus of their photography was often influenced by a desire to seek communities untainted by these changes – most preferred the bedouin tribes of the desert, and the Kurds, the Berbers and the Druze in their mountain strongholds. The photographs Westerners took of these societies often embodied a romantic nostalgia, and sometimes an explicit wish to capture a vision of these 'pristine' societies before they disappeared for ever.

At the same time, the spread of colonial rule was creating new images to be superimposed on the old stereotypes: 'backward' people were shown to be reaping the benefits of Western rule in the form of schools and hospitals, while those who resisted were portrayed as gangs of criminals and wreckers. These images can be seen in the private albums of colonial officials, and much more emphatically in the rapidly expanding international media. The era from World War I until the 1950s saw European power in the Middle East reach its greatest extent, and this coincided with the heyday of the illustrated magazine in Europe and the United States, and the blossoming of the skills of photojournalism. As Tom Hopkinson has pointed out, it was the introduction of the small, compact Leica camera which allowed press photographers the possibility of taking pictures in a relatively spontaneous way instead of the cumbersome posed arrangements of the kind known to journalists as 'firing-squad pictures'.[15]

In the resulting photographic coverage of the Middle East, nineteenth-century stereotypes and visual clichés of wild bedouin on camels, harems, biblical characters and Oriental

was unaware of anything going on around her.'[5]
The original photograph is a powerful evocation, almost shocking in its exposure of private grief. The engraving, which appeared in Dieulafoy's book and in at least one magazine article, substantially modifies her expression to one closer to resignation.

decay became intertwined with power politics and the news values of the mass media.

Photography could sharpen the dichotomies often posed between new and old, modern and backward, Western and Eastern. Change was frequently represented by the juxtaposition of images: of the bedouin against the motorcar; the veiled woman against the woman in chic Western clothes; the 'biblical' Palestinian peasant against the 'modern' Zionist settler. None of these images offered any explanation for what was happening within those societies.

The Development of Indigenous Photography

Photography, like many other Western technologies of the nineteenth century, was spread round the world by European colonialism, trade and exploration. In some regions it remained almost exclusively in the hands of Europeans until well into the twentieth century. But in certain areas, including the Middle East, India, Japan and parts of Latin America, groups of indigenous photographers emerged

21 'Femmes fellahs' – (Egyptian) Peasant Women. Abdullah Frères. Probably a studio portrait, Cairo, 1886–95.

Abdullah Frères' studio in Cairo, which operated from 1886–95, did much of the same type of commercial work as Lekegian, Zangaki, Arnoux, and Lehnert & Landrock. Yet on the whole their studio portraiture had a more direct quality and was less inclined to elaborate artifice. But, undoubtedly, like all other photographers, they would have paid, or otherwise induced, subjects like these to sit for them.

within a few decades of photography's invention in 1839.

In the Middle East there were two kinds of incentives to take up photography: first, its obvious commercial potential in cities such as Istanbul, Jerusalem, Beirut and Cairo which had both resident European communities and a growing tourist or pilgrim trade. In Iran, Turkey and, to a lesser extent, Egypt, there was also the attraction of imperial patronage.

By the end of the nineteenth century there were numerous local photographers operating commercial studios in the major cities. Many belonged to minority ethnic or religious communities, most notably the Armenians. There is no certainty about the precise reasons for the Armenians' early predominance in the photographic business. One reason may have been that Armenians had long played an important role in crafts such as metal working, engraving and miniature painting in a number of Middle Eastern cities. All these crafts provided skills of relevance to the early techniques of photography. On the whole, the Armenian communities in these cities also had closer than average relations with Europeans, which gave them opportunities to learn the new skills of photography and to find a clientele.

Certainly these factors played a part in the success of one of the earliest Armenian commercial studios – that of 'Abdullah Frères' – which began operating in Istanbul in 1858. Two years earlier, Vichen Abdullahian had taken a job as a retouch artist in the photographic studio of a German chemist named Rabach. Vichen's two brothers, Kevork and Hovsep, had also trained in fine arts, Kevork having studied in Venice, and in 1858 they bought Rabach's business and quickly established their reputation. In the 1860s, they began to work for the Ottoman court and in 1874 were given exclusive copyright on all photographic portraits of the Ottoman imperial family. They were given this position by Sultan Abdul Aziz and retained it under Sultan Abdul Hamid II until the 1890s.

In Jerusalem, another of the important figures of early Middle Eastern photography, Yessayi Garabedian, began in 1855 to experiment with a camera. Born in Tlas in Anatolia, he went to Jerusalem in 1844 to study for the priesthood at the Armenian Patriarchate. He returned to Istanbul in 1859 to study photography with Abdullah Frères, and visited Europe in search of information about the rapidly evolving techniques of photography, subsequently writing several manuals on photography, the first to be produced in the region. He became Armenian Patriarch of Jerusalem in 1865, apparently rather reluctantly, but established a photographic workshop in the grounds of the Patriarchate which trained the first generations of Jerusalem-based photographers, the best-known of whom was Garabed Krikorian.

A network of Armenian photographers developed during the second half of the nineteenth century in Turkey,

22 'Nazimeh Sultan bint Abdul Aziz Khan' – Nazimeh Sultan, Daughter of Sultan Abdul Aziz. Kargoupolo Photo, Istanbul, 1870s–80s.

From the later years of the reign of Sultan Abdul Aziz, portraits of members of the Ottoman court and harem, commissioned by the Sultan and others in his entourage, became increasingly common and set the fashion for the Ottoman elites to have photographs taken of themselves and their families.

Lebanon, Palestine and Egypt, and further afield. They also became involved in importing photographic materials. One of the earliest of these importers was Onnig Diradour, who later became Kodak's agent in the Middle East, and by the end of the century was selling these materials as far afield as Mosul in Iraq.[16]

If we compare the output of commercial photographs for the tourist market by these local photographers – Abdullah Frères in Istanbul, and later in Cairo, Lekegian in Cairo, Krikorian in Jerusalem, to name only a few of the largest businesses – with that of the European-owned studios such as Bonfils, or Lehnert and Landrock, we find that there is surprisingly little difference in themes or techniques. For the most part these photographers supplied the tourist market with much the same clichés and stereotypes as their Western colleagues, although in their portrayal of women some, like Abdullah Frères, generally avoided the more suggestive poses frequently shown in this type of photography.

But taking these photographers' output as a whole, there were a number of factors which distinguished their work from that of most European commercial photographers working in the Middle East. If the tourist market constituted one of their clienteles, they had others as well. Imperial patronage was important both in Istanbul and Tehran. In Turkey both Sultan Abdul Aziz and his successor Sultan Abdul Hamid became patrons of photography. Abdul Hamid also started a photographic workshop in the military engineers' school.

In the 1860s and 1870s, the era of the *Tanzimat* reforms, the Ottoman Empire was under considerable pressure from the European powers to institute political reforms and modernize its economy. Photography was viewed as an embodiment of modern technology, in itself a symbol of progress, which also offered a convenient means of documenting other kinds of 'progress' and reform. Abdul Hamid made full use of this opportunity. During the 1880s he employed a number of photographers, principally Abdullah Frères, to take photographs of some of the empire's new achievements.

These were compiled into some fifty-eight albums, gold-tooled and bound in red morocco, which were sent in 1893 as gifts to the heads of state of France, Great Britain, the United States and Germany. The albums were put together with an overtly propagandist purpose: to show the modernization of the Ottoman Empire. The result is an entirely different image of the region from the one which appears in the repertoire of Western commercial photography, though this image too contains a considerable element of distortion. Instead of harems, picturesque scenes and 'native types', there are photographs of dockyards, mines, factories, army cadets, naval officers, divers and firefighters, and posed groups of pupils from recently established schools. This is a

23 'Elèves de l'école des filles à Kutchuk Moustapha Pasha' – Pupils of the Girls' School at Kutchuk Moustapha Pasha. Abdullah Frères, Turkey, before 1893.

This photograph was one of a series taken by Abdullah Frères of groups of schoolgirls in Turkey, in an album which was part of the collection Sultan Abdul Hamid II sent as a gift to Western heads of state in 1893.

24 Portrait of his fiancée. Ali Sami, Istanbul, c.1880.

Ali Sami was a Turkish photographer who had trained and worked in the Ottoman army school (*Mühendishane-i Berri-i Humayun*). But for this photograph he evidently rigged up a 'studio' in a garden, to take advantage of the natural light. The 'set' consists of a cloth attached to the garden wall, in front of which his fiancée is posed in a drawing-room scene, to rather incongruous effect. Ali Sami's fiancée was a painter, hence the small paintbrush she holds in her right hand.

largely male world – only in the school photographs are young girls to be seen, demonstrating that the government was paying attention to female education – but elsewhere, virtually no women are visible.

In Iran too, royal patronage played an important part in the development of photography. As early as 1860, Nasir ed-Din Shah established a school of photography in Tehran Polytechnic (Dar ol-Funun) and made one of his favourite courtiers, Aga Reza, court photographer. Nasir ed-Din became a keen photographer and even took snapshots of himself and of members of his harem.

By the end of the century a new clientele was emerging for portrait photographs among the upper and middle classes in several parts of the Middle East. But the demand for this type of photography spread unevenly, both in terms of region and community. In centres of tourism and pilgrimage, where local photographers were already well-established, commissioning of portraits first became fashionable. In Jerusalem, for example, the Armenian Patriarchate's photographic workshop did a thriving business taking photographs of Armenian pilgrims visiting the city, and later, of prominent members of other communities. By World War I, Garabed Krikorian and his son John, and the Lebanese-born Khalil Raad were profiting both from the tourist business and from local clients in Jerusalem.

In Lebanon it became very fashionable among well-to-do Christian families to have cabinet portraits or photographic *cartes de visite* made, and a number of photographers, both Armenian and non-Armenian, had established themselves in this line of work by the end of the nineteenth century. By this time photographers had also begun to set up businesses in the small towns of the Lebanese mountains, broadening the social range of people who appear in photographs. In Egypt and Turkey too, not only was photography well established and accepted in the large cities by 1900, but photographic studios were beginning to appear in provincial towns. This certainly widened the range of people who might appear in portrait photographs, though it still did not mean that the poorest sections of society were likely to have their photographs taken.

Photography seems quite rapidly to have acquired connotations of fame and social status. The Egyptian singer Umm Kulthoum recalled in her memoir that while she was still a girl, just becoming known as a singer in the Delta province where she lived (around the time of World War I), her father, who was a poor village shaikh, took her to have her photograph taken.

> Our fame was spreading and our fee went up. The six of us, my father, myself, Khalid and the three other shaikhs now received 100 piastres per concert. Soon it went up to 150 piastres. By the standards of the little village of Tammay, we were rich! So my father decided we should try to behave like rich people. Rich people had photographs taken of their children, so why shouldn't he, Shaikh Ibrahim, have a picture taken of his children?
>
> We went to a photographer in Zaqaziq, which seemed a big city to us. We were supposed to be quiet and serious, but when Khalid and I saw the man standing behind the camera with the big black cloth over his head, we were convulsed with laughter. The photographer was annoyed and spoke sharply to my father. Did he not know that children in a picture were supposed to be solemn, serious and above all motionless as statues? After many attempts, we finally calmed down and the exasperated photographer was able to take what he called 'a proper picture'.[17]

In Syria and Iraq, less affected by the influx of Westerners, photography developed at a slower pace, though by the end of the nineteenth century there were already several local photographers working in Damascus – for instance, Sulaiman Hakim and Bishara al-Samna – and several Armenian studios in Aleppo. In Iraq well before World War I there were several commercial photographers in Baghdad and Basra, and in Mosul, photography was pioneered by Naom Sayegh, a member of the Chaldaean community, who learnt his skills from European missionaries who were working there. The British occupation during World War I brought a new spate of photography. Not only did the British army bring its own photographers but it also stimulated a market for tourist souvenirs.

In the hundred years after its invention, photography developed many roles not foreseen by its pioneers, and the record it has left of the Middle East is in many ways a strange and ambivalent one. By far the largest volume of images were created by Westerners with strong ideas of what people and places should look like. Yet photography gradually developed various roles and functions within Middle Eastern communities: as a vehicle of propaganda; as an expression of status or family cohesion; and, once hand-held cameras were available, as a form of amusement and recreation. At the same time, styles of photography remained largely derivative, taking the norms of composition and styles of portraiture almost entirely from European models.

As a record of life in the Middle East in this era, the corpus of photography which has come down to us in archives and private collections contains a number of gaps and distortions. These derive in part from the cultural and other presuppositions imposed by photographers, both local and foreign, but are also the result of the uneven distribution of photographic attention over different regions and classes. Photographers, both local and foreign, were mostly concentrated in cities and even those who travelled around usually kept to the easily accessible regions where there were popular tourist or religious sites. Thus, for instance, there were large parts of rural Turkey and Iran which were scarcely ever photographed. Even in Syria and Palestine, photographers tended to concentrate on areas of particular historical interest and ignore others.

There were also whole regions where photography did not develop locally until much later, and where relatively few travellers with cameras went. Until the 1940s and 1950s, this applied to the whole of the Arabian peninsula. There were a few outstanding exceptions: for instance, the Dutch Orientalist Snouk Hurgronje's photographs of Mecca taken in the 1880s; some other scattered instances of photographs taken by pilgrims to Mecca and Medina; and photographs of the Hejaz taken by T.E. Lawrence and his associates during World War I. Gertrude Bell took a small number of photographs of her visit to Hail in northern Arabia in 1913–14, and after the war H. St J. Philby took many photographs of his travels in Arabia, but relatively few which showed people rather than deserts. By the 1930s a few photographers, most notably Freya Stark, had discovered how photogenic Yemen was. In the Gulf a few travellers and political agents took pictures and there are some local family collections. But compared with the volume of photographs which were taken in Turkey, Lebanon, Palestine, Egypt, North Africa and even Iran up to the 1940s, the quantity of photographs coming from the Arabian peninsula was minuscule.

But the photographic record was also skewed by differences in the photographic treatment of various classes and communities. This is particularly evident where the portrayal of women is concerned. Western photographers could rarely, if ever, take pictures of upper- and middle-class women who lived mostly in seclusion. Such photographs as exist of this class were taken by local photographers for the private albums of families, or were snapshots taken by the families themselves.

On the other hand, the less well-off, and those who lived in rural areas, rarely had such access to photography. They were almost always photographed by outsiders, mostly by Westerners, or at least by commercial photographers working for the tourist market. While in Europe, the US and Japan, a tradition of socially concerned documentary photography developed in the late nineteenth and early twentieth centuries, there was no comparable trend in the Middle East. Thus there was no alternative view of these sections of society to that of the tourist, the traveller and the anthropologist. Hence there is a division in the photographic record between those classes and communities which generated photographic images on their own terms, and others – the urban poor and petty bourgeoisie, peasants and bedouin – whose images remained largely outside their control.

Power and Patriarchy: Women as Subjects of Photography

John Thomson wrote, of his photographic experiences in China in the 1860s:

> I frequently enjoyed the reputation of being a dangerous
> necromancer, and my camera was held to be a dark,
> mysterious instrument which, combined with my naturally,
> or supernaturally intensified eyesight gave me power to
> see through rocks and mountains, to pierce the very souls
> of the people and to produce miraculous pictures by some
> black art.[18]

In the Middle East too, photography often seems to have been regarded by both those behind the camera and those in front of it as an exercise in power. Those in front of it frequently felt threatened by its power to 'freeze' them into an image. Muhammad Ali, the ruler of Egypt, was quoted once as saying that photography was 'the work of the devil'. An Ethiopian notable, speaking of the photographer Edoardo Ximenes, saw photography as an act of possession: 'This man has too much in his camera and I think it is enough. Does this man want to take away the whole country?'[19]

There was also another way in which the camera might be seen as a threat. In cultures where the regulation of women's visibility was an important aspect of patriarchal control, photography might suggest not only an assertion of the photographer's power over the subject, but a loss of male control over women. Western photographers frequently scoffed at native ignorance and fear of this new technology, as in this anecdote about Afghanistan, which appeared in January 1890 in the *Photographic News*.

> Some traveller in the country of the Pathans [Afghanistan] beyond Quetta, who had a camera with him, gave the natives their first knowledge of photography, and this appears to have been received with much disfavour, for, on the Surveyor of the Madras Government Department proceeding thither on a professional mission, he met with a hostile reception [he had a theodolite with him which people mistoook for a camera]. The dislike to [*sic*] the camera, it appears, springs from the fact that it takes pictures upside down. But in addition, the Pathans imagine, when the surveyor is using his theodolite, that he can see through the walls of houses, with the appalling result that the ladies of the house are photographed standing on their heads by the infidel! It was a mistake for the first photographer in the Pathan country to allow the natives to look at the ground glass screen of the camera. He forgot that a little learning is a dangerous thing.[20]

This story offers several clues to common Western views both about photography and colonial power and its relation to culture. The Pathans must be kept at the lense-end of the camera as subjects: access to its viewfinder, to the position of the photographer, makes them dangerous, because they cannot expect to grasp the technology which is anyway the property of the West. The possession of that knowledge and the desire to retain exclusive possession of it is part of a broader relationship involving inequality of power. But the other theme which emerges is that of the camera as something which reveals what should not be revealed: the women of the Pathans' household.

This aspect of patriarchal control often conflicted with the wishes of the photographer, and sometimes, as photography became more widespread and popular, with the wishes of women themselves. This was also a consideration influencing which women appeared in photographs, and how they were presented. It is often suggested that because Muslim tradition does not sanction the portrayal of the human figure, photography would not be easily acceptable in the Muslim Middle East. But in fact there was no simple, hard and fast norm. In Iran, and in the Mogul Empire, the prohibition had never been strictly observed and there was a long tradition of figurative court painting, and in elite milieux there seemed to be little objection to photography on those grounds. In both Iran and Turkey the fact that photography received the patronage of the Shah and the Sultan respectively must have lent it greater legitimacy.

Although it is true that photography became popular among Christian communities at an earlier stage than in other parts of society, and that the majority of the first generation of photographers came from these communities, by the early twentieth century it was by no means uncommon to find photographs of prominent Muslim as well as Christian and Jewish families. Clearly, however, this did not apply to more conservative circles or to much of the urban middle class, and a reluctance to allow women to be photographed remained far more common than objections to photography as such. Among Jewish communities, attitudes to photography seem to have varied. The liberal elites generally regarded photographs of both men and women as quite acceptable, but in more orthodox communities it was frowned upon.

The practice of photography by Middle Easterners seems to have remained largely a male preserve in the period up to the 1950s. Only a handful of women appear to have worked in photographers' studios, usually employed in retouching, colouring or printing, as part of a family enterprise. As hand-held cameras became accessible to the wealthy by the 1920s and 1930s, there were obviously women who took amateur pictures at home, but women professionals seem to have been very few and far between and virtually no details are known about them. There is one documented instance of a professional woman photographer in Nazareth whose name – Miss Karimeh Aboud – appears on postcard views of the city dating from before World War I. A portrait also exists of a woman professional photographer named Sadiye Yalmiz in Ankara, probably in the 1930s or 1940s, but nothing is known of the background of either woman. It also appears from scattered references that there may have been a few female photographers in some countries who went to people's homes to take pictures, so that women would not have to go out to a studio.

On the whole, however, men took photographs of women and men frequently dictated if, or on what terms, women appeared in photographs. Where women appear in family photographs, this was sanctioned because these pictures were intended to be seen only within the family circle. But where women posed for commercial photographers, the question of choice and control was rather different. The question of how women came to appear in commercial photographs, whether taken by local or by Western photographers, is difficult to answer with any certainty, since photographers left few records of how they acquired models.

Certainly some of the women who appeared in posed studio scenes would have been paid or offered some other inducement to do so. It is often said that most of these women came, in the nineteenth century at least, from non-Muslim communities. This may be so, especially in cities such as Istanbul and Beirut, but the fact that they would pose probably also meant that they were not from the well-to-do sections of these communities. In the Bonfils studio in Beirut, the large numbers of photographs of women taken in the studio from the 1870s onwards may be explained by the fact that Félix's wife Lydie apparently took most of them.[21]

Once in the studio, the woman could be posed and dressed, or undressed to fit a chosen part, and one of the few certainties about these photographs is that the women were seldom in real life what they appeared to be in the photograph.

In city streets or in the countryside matters were rather

25 'Arab Women of Algiers'. Lehnert & Landrock. Published in National Geographic Magazine, *January 1914, illustrating 'Here and There in North Africa' by Frank Edward Johnson.*

This photograph of veiled women at the entrance to a cemetery in Algiers evokes the same sense of mystery as that which excited W.H. Barbrook. The caption describes the women's weekly visit to the cemetery as an occasion when, secluded from the eyes of men 'the ladies, laying aside their veils, indulge in impromptu picnics, with much laughter and gossip'. The idea that women had secret lives hidden from men gave these shrouded figures, so often photographed by Westerners, a particular kind of allure.

different, since the photographer could not always induce a desired subject to pose. If the women themselves did not object, then their husbands, fathers or brothers might do so. But for some, these obstacles were part of the excitement of the chase, and indeed photography rapidly accumulated a vocabulary reminiscent of hunting. In *Camera* magazine in 1886, W.H. Barbrook expressed this sentiment when taking photographs in Algiers. He notes 'the inveterate dislike of the true Mohammedan to be photographed', but continues,

> We were in one of the cemeteries and spied a group of veiled women seeking consolation from an itinerant marabout. I succeeded in getting the subject before I was discovered, when my Arab boy rushed up to the women and, dancing wildly round them, told them what had been done. There was a spice of excitement in photographing under such circumstances.[22]

Where the subjects of photographs were not known to the photographer, it is difficult to know, except from internal evidence – the demeanour and expression of the subject – whether any coercion or inducement had been used to make them pose, and these signs within the photograph are not always easy to interpret. The following group of photographs, of a variety of types, offer some idea of the range of relationships in which female subjects might stand to male photographers.

Power and Persuasion: Photographers and Their Female Subjects

The following group of photographs (26 to 34) shows women as isolated and largely passive subjects. They differ from many of the photographs in subsequent chapters of this book which, accidentally or by design, show women as social beings, engaged in work or part of a social group.

Although these photographs may make the subjects seem passive, there is a marked diversity in the relationships of power with the photographers who took the pictures. In the majority of instances, these photographers are male, and most are Westerners. The differences in these relationships are reflected to some extent in the expressions and gestures of the sitters, though their exact meaning is often difficult to read with any certainty. The following interpretations do not pretend to be definitive.

In the first two photographs (26 and 27), the women are the involuntary objects of Western photographers' interest. Yet in the second picture, one of the two women takes the initiative in demanding money in exchange for allowing them to be photographed (see also Caption 1).

In the next photograph (28), the photographer is also the employer of the subjects of his photograph, male and female, leaving them little alternative but to pose for him. Mac-Alister not only used this power to induce these obviously reluctant subjects to pose, but he also tried, rather unsuccessfully, to make them adopt positions suitable for anthropometric studies.

In 29 and 30 the subjects are almost certainly models, who would be posing for money or some other inducement, though it is rarely possible to document these transactions. It is often assumed that women who posed for commercial photographers were dancers or prostitutes. Both Westerners and Middle Easterners tend to assume that since respectable women were, generally speaking, publicly invisible, those made visible in this way were automatically disreputable. The very fact that a woman might take money for posing would also, in the eyes of many, put her beyond the pale of respectability. But the reality was probably less simple. The norms of respectability, particularly as regards photography, varied from place to place, and what was acceptable in one city, in one ethnic or religious community or in a particular class, would be abhorrent to another. Whatever the woman's status, as a studio model she would have little control over the resulting photographic image. Only facial expressions give any indication of their feelings, frequently vacant and alienated, as in these two photographs, or sad and ill-at-ease.[23]

In the two following portraits, however, the relationships of power between sitters and photographers are quite different. In 31 a husband is photographing his wife. This may have been a relationship of unequal power, but of a different order than that between photographer and model. In 32 the sitter is a client who by virtue of her class and the importance of her family is in a position to command the photographer, who is evidently, from her point of view, performing a service.

Photograph 33 is the only one in this group known to have been taken by a woman and portrays two women from different cultures as equals with the photographer, as well as suggesting the relationship between the two subjects. In 34 the young girl gazes directly into the camera, seeming to express her confidence in the person behind it.

As the subjects of photographs, then, Middle Eastern women were subject to a variety of constraints. Sometimes they would be prevented by male disapproval from being photographed at all. Those who objected to the attentions of Western photographers in the street or countryside could only express resistance by gestures of defiance or by covering their faces. Women photographed as models by commercial photographers frequently drew disapproval upon themselves and were also subject to the stereotypical views considered saleable by the photographers. Even photographs of women destined only for family viewing usually reflected in dress and gesture what was considered 'suitable' to their class and status, norms often internalized by women themselves.

26 'Egyptian Woman and European Tourist'. Beginning of the twentieth century.

The European woman in the picture is also carrying a camera, as her companion photographs this scene. The Egyptian woman is thus subjected to a double scrutiny, from one side by the camera, and from the other by the woman who might decide to take a photograph of this 'picturesque' Egyptian filling her water jar.

27 'Nazareth, femmes allant à la fontaine' – Women Going to the Fountain. F.A. Salles, 1891.

Salles commented that the older of the two women, who is holding out her hand, demanded *bakhshish*. In one sense this confirms the common tourists' stereotype of indigent and demanding 'natives', but at the same time the expressions on the women's faces suggest that they may well have been having a joke at the expense of this particular tourist.

28 Workers on the site of the Tel Gezer archaeological excavations, south east of Jaffa, Palestine. Robert Alexander Stuart MacAlister, 1902–09.

Local workers, both men and women, were often hired from surrounding villages on many of the major digs in Palestine in this period. They did manual work, mostly carting rubble away from the excavations. MacAlister, the director at Tel Gezer, said to have been a very arrogant man, took a series of photographs of these workers, attempting to arrange them according to anthropometric principles – standing in line, first full face and then side face. In most cases he met with some resistance, particularly on the part of the women, who were clearly uneasy at being photographed, but they were presumably not in a position to object, since they were in the employ of the photographer.

28

29 'Mohammedan Types of Baghdad'. Boesinger & Co. Postcard, Baghdad, early twentieth century.

A studio photograph playing on the contrast between veiled and unveiled, visible and invisible. The heavily veiled model on the right is, none the less, wearing very fancy high-heeled shoes. It is said that it was Boesinger's practice to employ prostitutes as models for his pictures. Although this is by no means certain, it may be that a Western photographer in Baghdad at this time, before World War I, would have had difficulty finding any other women to pose in the studio.

30 Persian women in indoor dress. Late nineteenth century.

The first director of Rotterdam's Museum of Ethnography (where the photograph is held), Werumeiis Buningh, speculated that these women were likely to be dancers, 'although their dress does not show it'. Certainly, their pose and general demeanour does not suggest that they belonged to the elite, as their dress would indicate. (Compare this photograph with the one of women wearing the dress of the aristocracy in Chapter IV, Caption 10.)

29

30

31 Portrait of Adla Sakkal, by her husband, Bishara al-Samna. Damascus, 1912.

Samna was one of the early professional photographers in Damascus. Despite the formal pose and decor, there is an unusual sense of intimacy in this photograph which belies the impersonal setting. Her direct gaze at the camera contrasts with the blank stares frequently adopted by studio models.

32 Nazira Jumblatt. Ajjaj Abu Shakra, studio portrait, Baaklin, Shouf, Lebanon, 1930s.

Nazira Jumblatt (the mother of Kamal Jumblatt) was a member of one of the most powerful Druze families in Lebanon. An awareness of her status is evident in her self-confident demeanour. Here the photographer is servant rather than master. He also chose a low camera angle, which makes his subject appear more imposing.

33 Sitt Louisa and Nafise Isna'in. Hilma Granqvist, Artas, Palestine, 27 July 1930.

Sitt Louisa was Louisa Baldensperger, so named because she had lived in Artas for many years and was considered virtually a member of the community. It was she who made it possible for Hilma Granqvist to do her anthropological field studies in the village and introduced her into the society of women there. Nafise Isna'in was the maternal grandmother of Safiya, who became one of Granqvist's main informants on the lives of Artas women. This picture gives the sense of a relaxed familiarity between the two women and the photographer.

31

3

33

*34 Portrait of a young girl.
Turkey, probably early 1930s.*

This photograph, taken for the
family, emphasizes the young
girl's eager, lively face. Her
brother wears his Republican sea
cadets' uniform with aplomb, but
it is she, gazing directly at the
photographer, who dominates the
photograph.

34

Chapter II
The Seen, the Unseen and the Imagined:
Private and Public Lives

1 'Femmes d'Alger dans leur appartement' – Women of Algiers in Their Apartment. Painting by Eugène Delacroix, 1834.

According to one French source, Delacroix had the 'rare privilege' of entering a harem such as he portrays here. But from Delacroix's own notebooks, it seems more likely that his models for this picture were members of the Moroccan or Algerian Jewish community with whom he had friendly contacts during his visit to North Africa. He mentions on a number of occasions painting some of the Jewish women he met. Delacroix visited North Africa in 1832, accompanying le Comte de Morney on a mission to the Sultan of Morocco, two years after the French began their occupation of Algeria. 'Women of Algiers' was one of about ten major paintings in the Orientalist genre which resulted from this visit. They evoke a sharp contrast between a violent and turbulent male world of the streets and deserts and a closed, largely passive female world contained in the harem.

Grace Ellison, an Englishwoman who visited Istanbul at the turn of the century as the guest of a well-to-do Turkish family, gave some lectures on her experiences when she returned to London.

> When I said I had actually stayed in a harem, I could see the male portion of my audience, as it were, passing round the wink. 'You may not put the word "harem" on the title of your lecture,' said the secretary of a certain society. 'Many who might come to hear you would stay away for fear of hearing improper revelations, and others would come hoping to hear those revelations and go away disappointed.'[1]

Fantasies about harem life pervaded the Orientalist imagination and did much to cloud understanding of the social, domestic and sexual lives of women in the Middle East. The power of the harem image lay in the notion of a forbidden world of women, of sexuality caged and inaccessible, at least to Western men, except by a leap of imagination. It was this leap of imagination which shaped the literature, paintings, engravings and photographs which purported to reveal the life of women behind the walls and barred windows of the harem. Women appeared first and foremost as possessions: as the playthings of men in the harem, or as objects of commerce in the slave markets which figure in numerous Orientalist paintings.

As Grace Ellison's remarks imply, reactions to these images were of two kinds. The first was to indulge in the excitement of an exotic sexual fantasy beyond the reach of the constraints and taboos of European culture. The harem, pictured in this way, was identified with complete male

2 'Le Pacha et son harem' – The Pasha and His Harem. H. Arnoux, Egypt, 1870s–80s.

Arnoux, thought to be French, worked in Egypt as a photographer from the 1860s onwards. This photograph is typical of studio fantasies of the harem: the elderly patriarch is surrounded by his wives or concubines, in an elaborate studio decor reminiscent of a baroque painting, with all the objects associated with harem life prominently displayed: the *narghileh* (water pipe), the black slave offering coffee, the rich clothes and slippers in the Turkish style. Ironically, the setting of this photograph is probably less accurately portrayed than that in the Delacroix painting, though many of the details are similar.

domination over women's lives and the apparently untrammelled sexual pleasures of four wives and unlimited numbers of concubines. The strict control of women's appearance and behaviour in public was assumed to be the corollary of unbridled licence within the harem.

The other reaction to this vision of promiscuity and indulgence was one of disapproval or disgust, and the denigration of a culture which could permit women to live in conditions apparently akin to those of a brothel. The Middle Eastern scholar Nabia Abbott, writing in the 1950s after living for many years in the United States, observed that in the West, 'the term "harem" has come to connote everything vicious and to exclude everything wholesome in the relationships of the sexes'.[2]

Seclusion and Segregation

The word *harim* in Arabic means a sacred, inviolable place, and it also means the female members of the family. From the same root comes also the word *haram*, which bears a double meaning: forbidden, or sacred and protected. But *haram*, or *hurma* was also used in upper- and middle-class Arab society as a respectful form of address to a married woman. In Turkey and Iran the equivalent term was *hanum* or *khanum*. But the most common use of the word *harim* (*haremlik* in Turkish) was to denote the space in the family home reserved for women (commonly spelt harem). Among the urban elites of the Arab region, Turkey and Iran, this separation of space was accompanied by the seclusion of the women of the family from the sight of all men except husbands and close relatives.[3]

Segregation of space and control over the visibility of women were forms of patriarchal control which emphasized the need to channel and contain women's sexual power. Some commentators argue that this concept of women's sexual power differs from that which developed in European cultures. The Moroccan sociologist Fatima Mernissi, for example, contends that restrictions placed on women in the Islamic cultures of the Middle East are not based on a view of women's biological inferiority: 'On the contrary, the whole system is based on the assumption that women are powerful and dangerous beings. All sexual institutions (polygamy, repudiation, sexual segregation, etc) can be perceived as a strategy for containing their power.'[4]

This view of women as possessing powerful, even uncontrollable sexual passions has taken many forms, including popular sayings, myths and stories. In Morocco, for example, there is a saying that women are *hbel al-shitan* (Satan's leash) implying that they are capable of dragging men away from virtue and also of tying them up (in Arabic this word is also a euphemism for impotence). Thus women who are not kept under strict control appear, in this imagery, as objects of both fear and blame. Their sexuality needs to be channelled into marriage and their visibility controlled to prevent other men from succumbing to their powerful sexual urges. In this view, men's sexuality is less problematic and they are offered numerous socially acceptable ways of indulging their sexual desires.

Although the idea that women's sexuality is dangerous is evident in many aspects of Christian European culture – as is the desire on the part of men to control it – a variety of strategies, practical as well as ideological, were developed to suppress or sublimate this sexuality. The figure of the nun, the celibate woman who dedicates her life to God, is complemented on the ideological level by the image of the Virgin Mary, the mother figure untouched by human sexuality.[5] In Islam, no equivalent roles have been created for women which similarly defuse the notion of sexual danger.

In practical terms, the desire to control women was often expressed in terms of safeguarding family honour and was manifested primarily in the physical segregation of women's space from that of men. Rules controlling the visibility of women in public were not, of course, confined to the Middle East. They could be found in other Mediterranean societies and, until the late nineteenth century, in 'genteel' society in many parts of Europe. But generally speaking, in the Middle

East these rules resulted in a much clearer physical demarcation between male and female society than existed in most European cultures. The boundaries of women's worlds were not, however, set in quite the simple ways suggested by popular Western visions of the harem. Although a high degree of sexual segregation was quite common, strict seclusion of women was practised only by the relatively small proportion of well-to-do urban families in which women did not play an active economic role and could therefore be confined to the home and to the role of childbearers.

In the cities, poorer women would generally veil when they went out in the street and did most of their work at home, but they could not be completely secluded, first because they often had to work to support the family and, second, because their homes were too small to allow for strict seclusion. Eugènie le Brun described the ways different social classes in Cairo practised segregation and seclusion as follows:

In palaces [the woman] is isolated from the rest of the household by high walls and massive doors; in bourgeois families the demarcation line is simply based on an

3 'Damas. Intérieur de la maison juive Stambouli' – Damascus. Interior of the Home of the Jewish Stambouli Family. Bonfils (Catalogue No. 431), before 1901.

While women from this wealthy Jewish family would probably have lived largely secluded from public view – like the upper classes of other communities – unlike the same class of Damascene Muslim they would not have been strictly segregated from men. Hence it was possible for a Westerner like Bonfils to enter such a Jewish household and take pictures of women, something which would not have been permitted in a Muslim home.

unwritten law – which does not imply that it is any the less respected. As to the common people, their dwellings are too small to allow any such division, so the men invariably receive [their male guests] in the cafe.[6]

Among the non-Muslim communities of the Middle East, practices relating to the regulation of women's space varied too much to allow any generalization, and depended very much on class and social status. Women in minority urban communities, however, were sometimes subject to an additional constraint on movement – that they were expected to remain within the boundaries of their own neighbourhoods. This was especially the case if the community in question feared hostility or aggression on the part of other groups. It was also common to insist that women marry only members of their own community.

But for the majority of people who lived outside the towns and cities, whether as settled peasants or nomads, the need for women to participate in the family labour force made strict seclusion impossible. Patterns of sexual segregation varied greatly from one community and region to another, but seclusion could be practised only among richer families where women did not need to work.

Hidden Away from the World?

In the popular Western imagery of seclusion, women were locked away from society and, apart from intrigues and jealousies, had no significant relationships except with their male sexual partners and/or oppressors. Paintings, photographs and literature usually stressed passivity and stillness – not the stillness of inner content, but the stillness of women waiting for the man who was the sole reason for their existence. The only form of power available to them was the power of sexual attraction.

The role of photography in creating and reinforcing this mythology was a singular one, and very influential in shaping popular conceptions. Since seclusion and male control of women's visibility for the most part denied Western photographers access to women in their homes, most 'harem scenes' were studio reconstructions composed by the photographer. In this respect, the photograph, like the painting or engraving, was a figment of imagination, which assumed the privileged position of the voyeur entering this closed and private space, and allowing the viewer to do likewise. But while painting is explicitly an act of imagination, photography is more readily assumed to show 'real' scenes.

For those who travelled in the Middle East, the invisibility of women in urban areas did much to reinforce the idea that their existence was rigidly confined to a hidden private realm from which they could not escape and into which no outsider could enter. In their narratives, Western male travellers frequently treated women's seclusion as a challenge: even

4 'Jeune mauresque' – Young Moorish Woman. Postcard, Algeria, late nineteenth century.

Malek Alloula, commenting on this picture in his book *The Colonial Harem*, notes the way in which the photographer, by placing the camera inside the bars of the harem, claims possess on of the woman photographed, already half-naked and sexually available.[1] From this 'privileged' position, the viewer can see both the frustration of the Algerian man who is excluded by the bars of the harem, and enjoy the sense of being inside a forbidden space.

the sober E.W. Lane engaged in a little of this voyeurism: 'A man may also occasionally enjoy opportunities of seeing the face of an Egyptian lady when she really thinks herself unobserved; sometimes at an open lattice, and sometimes on a housetop.'[7] In a late edition of his *Account of the Manners and Customs of the Modern Egyptians* published in 1895, a studio photograph was inserted on the page opposite this statement to emphasize the point. It shows a woman wearing a *burqu* (face veil) at an open lattice window. This was a popular photographic theme which appears in large numbers of late-nineteenth-century studio photographs, and many studios had 'sets' which included a latticework or *mashrabiyya* window (see p. 44).

For the photographer, male or female, seeking to capture glimpses of the domestic life of women in the cities of the Middle East, there were certainly many difficulties. Homes in most long-established cities in the region generally turned blank walls to the street, or had lattice windows (such as the *mashrabiyya* windows to be seen in Egypt and the cities of Arabia) from which the inhabitants could look out on to the street without being seen. For the traveller, these walls and screens appeared as the definitive boundary between the

5 'Moorish Women of Algiers'. Gervais Courtellement et Cie, Algiers, before 1895.

An unusual photograph, in that most pictures of veiled women in North African cities present them as silent figures. Even when they walk in groups, they usually seem isolated from each other and from the world around them. These women would probably have come from the poorer classes, since well-to-do women would be less likely to sit in the street chatting. The man in the background, however, directs a suspicious stare at the photographer.

6 'Porte centrale de la cour de Suleymaniye' – Central Gate of the Courtyard of the Suleymaniye (Mosque). Sébah & Joaillier, Istanbul, late nineteenth century.

In this photograph, the camera records the presence of this group of women walking in the street outside the mosque, yet it does not 'see' them as the focus of the picture. Although they dominate the foreground, the composition of the photograph relegates them to being a picturesque detail added to the architectural beauties of the Suleymaniye mosque. The caption further focuses the viewer's attention away from the women's presence in the photograph.

8 Cairo street scene: Tancrède Dumas, probably 1870s.

Dumas was a French photographer based in Beirut who also worked in Egypt. Since the technology of photography at this time did not allow for swift snapshots, this photograph was probably more posed than is immediately apparent. The unveiled woman in the foreground, gazing directly at the camera, is contrasted with the two veiled women in the background. She might have been a peasant or bedouin woman (who would not normally be veiled), though among the urban poor, too, veiling was less strictly enforced. However, she draws her head-veil slightly across her face in the presence of the man behind the camera.

7 A street scene, Kuwait. Freya Stark, 1937.

Strict seclusion and veiling of women remained the norm for much longer in the towns and cities of the Gulf region and the Arabian peninsula than in other urban areas of the Middle East. Here, the veiled silhouette, surrounded by high walls and shadowed doorways, stresses the public 'invisibility' of women in a way which is unusual in Stark's photography.

9 'Mussulman Ladies at Home'. Signed by P. Naumann, published in The Ladies' Realm, July 1898, accompanying an article by Laura B. Starr, 'Ladies of the Harem'.

The decor in this photograph bears a striking resemblance to that of the Arnoux picture in Caption 2. It may be one of Arnoux's prints reused by another photographer – quite a common practice. Despite the rich decor of the illustration, Laura Starr, claiming more familiarity with harem life 'than the ordinary tourist', disabuses her readers of the idea that harems at that time were all 'Oriental magnificence'. She claims that, despite 'curious old customs still in force', the women she encountered were often strongly imbued with Western ideas. None the less, she stresses the notion that women in harems were preoccupied with 'visitors, flirtations and intrigues', despite the restrictions imposed by seclusion. The photograph, though entirely unconnected with the writer's experiences, to some extent echoes this idea, with the models posed to convey an air of waiting and expectation.

public and private spheres, and reinforced the notion that this boundary marked off, in an absolute way, the domain of women.

The sense of frustration this provoked in some Westerners can be seen in the following account, by Jane Dieulafoy, a Frenchwoman travelling in Iran in the 1880s with her husband, of her efforts to use her camera to break through this boundary. Her description of how she and her husband managed to snatch a picture of some women in the courtyard of a house makes the taking of a photograph seem an act of intrusion:

> In the centre of a courtyard the head of the household was chatting with two young women, doubtless his relatives. Unaware that they were being observed, they had left their faces uncovered . . . [I hid] behind part of the wall, asked my husband to pass me the cameras, and set them up as quickly as possible, delighted to have captured such a charming interior and one so jealously guarded in Persian circles.[8]

Somewhat more detailed and less speculative accounts of harem life began to emerge in the late nineteenth century as it became fashionable for Western women travelling or resident in the Middle East to visit a harem, though they hardly ever took photographs. Some of the most enterprising women travellers had already visited harems: Sophia Lane Poole and Harriet Martineau in the 1840s in Egypt, and later, Isabel Burton in Syria, Isabella Bird and Ella Sykes in Iran, and Lady Anne Blunt in Arabia.[9]

The picture painted by these women varies considerably according to their own ideas and the particular society in question, but as such visits became part of the tourist ritual, the voyeuristic element in these encounters frequently came to the fore. With neither common language nor comprehension of each other's cultures, these encounters could be almost comic in their air of mutual incomprehension. Written accounts of harem visits by the less informed tended to dwell on appearances, especially clothing and decor, and usually confirmed the stereotypes of luxury and indolence.

More knowledgeable and careful observers offered much more diverse opinions, but even women such as Sophia Lane Poole were fascinated by physical appearances and dwelt on them in long descriptive passages. The fact that most of Lane Poole's visits were to the homes of the very rich, including relatives of the Egyptian ruler Muhammad Ali, meant that her descriptions often conform to the Western ideas of the harem as a 'gilded cage'.

In other respects, however, her views did not reflect the usual clichés. While she made clear her disapproval of the system of seclusion, she none the less remarked on the gentleness, good humour, intelligence and invariable graciousness of manner which she found among the women whom she met in the upper-class harems of Cairo. She also remarked on the sense of discipline which prevailed:

> The ideas entertained by many in Europe of the immorality of the harem are, I believe, erroneous. True it is, that the chief ladies have much power which they might abuse; but the slaves of these ladies are subject to the strictest surveillance; and the discipline which is exercised over the young women in the Eastern harem can only be compared with that which is established in the convent.[10]

A very different view was taken by Harriet Martineau, whose brief visit in the 1840s to two harems, one in Cairo and one in Damascus, filled her with horror. She describes the women she saw there as 'the most injured human beings I have ever seen, the most studiously depressed and corrupted women whose condition I have ever witnessed'.[11] A highly intelligent woman who had contributed to the political and social debates of her day, Martineau none the less rushed to this judgement on the basis of very scant experience. In the case of the harem she visited in Cairo, she was without even an interpreter and so could not communicate with the women she saw. The home in Damascus she found less oppressive but though the women of the harem laughed and appeared to be enjoying themselves, she emphasized the jealousies between them. It is hardly surprising that the tiny minority of active, independent European women should find harem life repugnant in its restrictive narrowness, but it is perhaps indicative of their attitudes to other cultures that they should be willing to make such sweeping judgements on the condition of women on the basis of such limited experience.

There was a handful of European women, however, who went so far as to suggest that the harem system had its

10 'Woman [named Turkiyyeh] Seated in House, Hail [northern Arabia]'. Gertrude Bell, March 1914.

Gertrude Bell, in her account of her long and arduous journey to Hail (capital of the Rashid dynasty) in 1913–14, leaves a less bleak picture of a woman living in seclusion, though her own sense of claustrophobia at being so confined is evident. Upon her arrival in Hail she was kept, in the politest way, a virtual prisoner on the orders of Muhammad ibn Rashid. She was lodged in one of his summerhouses and received by an old lady caretaker. Turkiyyeh was a Circassian woman who belonged to ibn Rashid's harem and who 'was sent down from the Qasr [palace] to amuse me'. Bell describes her as a 'merry lady'. Bell usually spent little time with women on her travels except, as in this case, when she was obliged to do so. Her sense of alienation in this environment is evident in her comment afterwards: 'I felt as if I had lived through a chapter of the *Arabian Nights* during this week.'[2]

virtues. One of this number was Lucy Garnett, whose two-volume survey of the lives of Turkish women published in 1890–91 is one of the most detailed Western accounts. In a book which provided a briefer overview she remarked: 'From the foregoing description of the homes of Osmanlis [Muslim Turks] of all classes, it should, I think, be apparent that the harem, far from being, as is so often supposed, a "detestable prison" is the most cheerful and commodious division of an Osmanli's house.'[12]

Descriptions of harems by those who experienced life in seclusion were few and far between, and were mostly written by women who were remarkable for their self-awareness and interest in the question of women's status: for example Huda Shaarawi, Halide Edip and Eugènie le Brun. They reflected exclusively the life of the upper-class harem, but their accounts none the less differ from those of outside observers in several crucial respects.

While they generally stress, like Sophia Lane Poole, the strict hierarchies which governed harem life – of old over young, mistress over slave and servant, and the crucial role of the mother of the male head of household – they also talk of the web of personal relationships within the harem. They

11 'Mauresque et mulatresse' – Moorish Woman and Black Woman. Probably Algiers, before 1895.

The image of the veiled Arab woman, with her unveiled black slave, appears in numerous Orientalist paintings and in commercial photographs, particularly in North Africa. This photograph suggests both the unequal relationship of class and power between them, but also a certain interdependence. Although some women slaves, particularly black slaves brought from Sudan, Ethiopia and other parts of Africa, were harshly treated and often suffered sexual abuse at the hands of their masters, many also became very much part of the families in which they lived. In well-to-do families, their close contact with the secluded women of the house meant that they often acted as intermediaries for these women with the world outside the harem (see also pp. 153–4).

include, inevitably, accounts of bitter rivalries and jealousies, but also of great affection and friendship, particularly between children and older women; and the relationships of dependants which grew up between mistresses and slaves. These relationships were not necessarily confined to members of the household, since for many families paying visits to relatives was a major form of entertainment and social contact. Among the well-to-do, it was also quite common to have female relatives coming to stay for long periods of time. Women whose marriages had broken down might return, sometimes with their young children, to the family home, and some families took in indigent relatives, friends and even former slaves.

Thus women were not entirely cut off from society; even those without wide networks of relatives received information and gossip from the women who came to the homes of the rich as tradespeople, dressmakers, marriage brokers and others who provided services required by wealthy women living in seclusion. Neither do the accounts of these 'insiders' give the impression that women were entirely passive or helpless. Rather they suggest that the limits of women's power and influence depended mainly on their age and status in the household.

By the end of the nineteenth century, the most simplistic Western images of the changeless, passive life of the harem, portrayed in the popular literature and photography of the time as bypassed by history, were less relevant than ever. Even the exotic decor was changing. Grace Ellison related that, in the years just before World War I, she sent a photograph of the women's drawing-room in the harem of an affluent Turkish family to a British newspaper. It showed a rather cluttered room with little to distinguish it from a European drawing-room of the same period. Ellison's caption to the photograph as later published in her own book reads: 'This photograph was taken expressly for a London paper. It was returned with this comment: "The British public would not accept this as a picture of a Turkish harem." As a matter of fact, in the smartest Turkish houses European furniture is much in evidence.'[13]

The newspaper editor could not accept the picture because it did not conform to the stereotypical photograph taken in a studio, and therefore did not appear 'real'. For his audience, the imaginary notion of the harem was the only acceptable one. The alien quality of this imagery did not allow Europeans to entertain the idea that Middle Eastern harems could even physically resemble their own homes.

What is also striking in this otherwise unremarkable photograph is that, decorating the walls and side tables, are a number of portrait photographs. By this time, in cities such as Istanbul and Cairo it was becoming quite common for members of richer families, women as well as men, to have their photographs taken.

12 Ethiopian girl and Egyptian boy. Portrait, Egypt, 1898.

An Ethiopian girl with the son of a well-to-do Egyptian family who had brought her up. She was later given some land and a marriage was arranged for her. It was not uncommon for orphans, or the children of relatives and even of slaves, to be brought up in wealthy households. The appearance of the girl in the portrait with one of the sons indicates acceptance of her as part of the family.[3]

At first there were objections to the photographic portrayal of women who still appeared veiled in public. But
gradually the objections became less generalized and women
themselves found ways round the prohibition. Dorina
Neave, an Englishwoman who lived in Istanbul in the latter
part of the nineteenth century, described how women she
knew used a small subterfuge to get their pictures taken:

> As they were allowed to take a child to the photographer,
> they would pretend that they were obliged to hold the
> child during the process of having his [sic] photograph
> taken, and if by chance the lady appeared in the picture,
> no exception could be taken, as they had not been to the
> photographer for that purpose.[14]

It seems that not only did women find ways of having their
pictures taken in the studio, but photographers also visited
upper-class and royal harems with the express intention of
taking photographs of women. In Egypt, according to
feminist historian Margot Badran, male photographers were
admitted to such harems from the reign of Khedive Ismail in
the 1870s. The women who appeared in these photographs
wore indoor clothing – in other words, they were unveiled –
and mostly wore Western-style clothes. Certainly by the
early twentieth century photographs of secluded women in
their homes were quite commonly included in family albums.
Clearly they were intended for the eyes of the family alone,
but as Badran points out, 'it is an irony that women who
remained their whole lives veiled and living strictly segregated lives were posthumously unveiled when, many decades
later after their deaths their photographs circulated in
public'.[15]

The alterations in fashions and behaviour suggested by

*14 Portrait of his sister. Ali Sami,
albumen print, Istanbul, 1880–90.*

This portrait, by a Turkish
photographer trained in the
Ottoman army school
(Mühendishane-i Berri-i
Humayun), gives a view of a
woman in a domestic setting which
might have surprised those who
believed in the exoticism of
women's home lives in Turkey.
Note the framed photographs on
the dresser and on the wall.

*13 'The Family of Izzet Bey'.
Studio portrait, Istanbul, late
nineteenth century.*

This is an example of the kind of
studio portraits being
commissioned by well-to-do
families in cities such as Istanbul
by the late nineteenth century.
They were still intended to be seen
only in the home, within the circle
of family and friends. Note the
variety of the women's dress.
While the older women wear the
yashmak (face veil) and *charchaf*
(cloak), the young girls wear
Western-style clothes. The girl,
seated in the plaid skirt, also holds
a book, an indication of the
growing prestige attached to
education, even for girls.

15 *Huda Shaarawi at home as a young girl. Cairo, c.1890.*

Huda reclines, in a pose almost mockingly reminiscent of many Orientalist images, yet her expression holds none of the passivity or lethargy associated with those poses. Despite her submission, under pressure, to an early marriage, her tenacity and intelligence allowed her to continue her education and gradually broaden the horizons of her life.[4]

photographs of this kind, however, only hint at the wider changes which were affecting the lives of upper-class women, particularly those who lived in large cities such as Cairo and Istanbul. Badran also notes that in Egypt by the 1890s rich families were moving to new European-style villas in the suburbs. The same trend was also evident in Istanbul.

Even for women living in seclusion, certain kinds of travel: to visit relatives, or to perform the pilgrimage, had always been permitted, but by the end of the nineteenth century improvements in transport, both within the Middle East and between the Middle East and Europe, greatly extended the possibilities of travel. Women from wealthy families visiting Paris or London experienced a different lifestyle which, though it sometimes evoked doubts and criticisms, certainly widened their horizons. These changes, combined with the trend towards allowing more upper-class women access to education (see Chapter VII), encouraged the younger generation of women to question the boundaries, both physical and mental, which were imposed on their lives.

The collapse of the regime of Sultan Abdul Hamid in Turkey in 1908 and the social and political turmoil of the World War I period marked the end of the era of total seclusion for upper-class women in Turkish cities. In Egypt, too, by the 1920s the harem system had effectively broken down. In other parts of the region – North Africa, Syria, Palestine, Iraq and Iran – the same pattern of change was occurring but considerably more slowly.[16] Among the middle classes, and in provincial towns, the physical boundaries of women's lives altered less dramatically, but education and the gradual changes in social norms brought adjustments in the way patriarchal control was exercised. Ann-Marie Goichon, writing of changes in the lives of women in the conservative bourgeoisie of the Moroccan town of Fez, described the gradual relaxation of physical control over women's activities in the 1920s:

16 *'Veiled Ladies Waiting at a Wayside Station between Baghdad and Basra'. Marjorie Armstrong, 1932.*

This snapshot by a British woman travelling in Iraq indicates how the spread of railways, which occurred in the late nineteenth and early twentieth centuries throughout the region, contributed to women's greater mobility. Usually there would have been separate compartments reserved for women.

17 'Veiled Ladies in a Carriage'.
On the shores of the Bosporus,
Turkey, late nineteenth century.

For the photographer, this was an
attractive and picturesque scene
which would undoubtedly appeal
to Westerners; for the women,
who from their dress belonged to
the upper classes, and therefore
probably lived in seclusion,
excursions of this kind were
among the most popular forms of
entertainment. Some years later,
in 1905, when Huda Shaarawi
visited Istanbul from Cairo, she
remarked on the relative freedom
of movement permitted to Turkish
women of her class: 'They go to
coffee houses, take boats and
drive in carriages with a little black
veil on their faces and sometimes
go unveiled.'[5] By this time, both
the style of dress and attitudes to
women appearing in public had
also undergone some changes
since the late nineteenth century.

The women would undoubtedly be delighted to enjoy
greater freedom. Nevertheless, over the last three or four
years there has been quite a noticeable change in this
respect – and it is the men who have contributed to it. Four
years ago the people of Fez maintained that, 'Even if the
idea of going out occurred to them [the women] they
would never dare to admit it.' Here we are not speaking of
those excursions for which some ingenious pretext has
always been found, but rather of outings which do not
need to be concealed. These are now much more frequent,
and travel is seen as both desirable and respectable.[17]

Although it is clear that changes in men's attitudes were
crucial to the relaxation of women's seclusion, women
themselves played a part in pressing men to allow these
changes. Long before there were organized women's movements, some women were trying to alter their positions
within their own families. Evidence of women's attitudes
towards seclusion in the late nineteenth and early twentieth
centuries is only fragmentary and tends to come from those
who were the most articulate critics of the harem system.[18]

But it has to be borne in mind that whatever the
unwelcome aspects of this form of male control, for many
women seclusion also represented the achievement, or the
maintenance of social status, a sign that husband or father
was able to maintain the family in respectability. In Europe
at this time, a comparable indicator of social status might
have been that no well-to-do family could countenance its
women taking paid employment outside the home.

One of the arguments of those who campaigned against
the harem system was that the boundaries imposed on
women by seclusion were not just physical, but mental and
spiritual. Mrs Badr ol-Moluk Bamdad, one of the early
campaigners for women's education in Iran, argued that
historically, seclusion had made women ' . . . unaware of

18 'Members of the Harem of Sultan Abdul Hamid with two Eunuchs Setting off to Exhibit Themselves in Vienna after the Sultan had been Deposed'. Probably Istanbul, 1909.

The unnamed photographer added the following commentary which indicates the ambiguities of both the women's and the photographer's attitude to their intention to 'exhibit themselves'.

The imperial harem had been composed mainly of Circassians, many of them brought to Turkey originally as slaves (see p. 154). Some of these women were reclaimed by their families after the Sultan's establishment was broken up but some, like these women it seems, were left to fend for themselves.

'They had arrived in Vienna on 29 September to perform their harem dances. Among them was the Sultan's favourite, Princess Sobrah, the last to enter the harem. When they were turned out of the harem, they had to find some means of livelihood. It was dance that attracted them.'

The photographer continues, asserting that, 'This is a unique event in the history of Turkish women,' and claims that they were the first women ever to put themselves on show, since, even in foreign countries, this is forbidden by the Quran. 'Moreover,' he adds, 'they will appear unveiled. After Vienna, they will tour all the countries of Europe. They have promised themselves that outside their performances they will adhere strictly to the rules of the Quran. The photographer found it extremely difficult to persuade them to pose in front of the camera, and without their veils.'

Thus women who had seemed exotic to Westerners because of their seclusion, now became exotic in their public exposure, while apparently in their own minds trying to maintain their own norms of culturally acceptable behaviour.

their own capabilities and spiritual worth. They saw themselves as feeble herbs in society's garden, only able to survive when shaded from the sunshine by robust trees, or when dependent like parasites on strong healthy plants from which they drew sustenance.'[19]

Among the generation of well-to-do women who became adults in the 1920s, a more forceful approach to the subject could be discerned. The following speech, delivered in 1928 to a largely male audience by Doraya Shafiq (see p. 232), a young Egyptian woman in her twenties, directly challenged men's efforts, and by implications their right to impose these physical controls over women's space. She concluded that if men persisted in trying to do so, they would be defied. Yet at the same time she suggested that the observance of religious principles is a better guide to behaviour than seclusion behind high walls:

> You build walls around your daughters and surround them
> with ever more doors and guards. Have you forgotten,
> then, that walls can never be high enough to counter
> feminine guile? Your daughters will always have some
> servant or old woman to help them communicate with the
> outside world. You show them the world through the
> framework of their imagination, so that all they see of it is
> illusion and, at the first opportunity, they fall into the
> abyss. The more you restrict them, the stronger will be
> their reaction. Why do you not draw support from
> religion? Give your daughters a clear conscience and let
> them out into the world: their sense of duty will stand them
> in good stead when the sturdiest of walls would crumble.[20]

The Camera and Women's Horizons

Looking at the mass of early Western photographic images of women in the Middle East, it may be tempting to equate their visibility to the public eye, and therefore to the photographer, with the division of their lives into 'public' and 'private' spheres. This formulation, however, would be just as simplistic as to assume that it was possible to distinguish neatly between a 'public' world of men and a 'private' world of women.

As will become apparent, there were many variations in women's social and economic roles, according to their age and class and to the particular circumstances of their own families and communities. The public/private dichotomy often employed in descriptions of these roles may not prove to be the most illuminating way of seeing them. As anthropologist Roxan Dusen suggests, it may be more useful to examine what she calls the 'social horizons' of particular groups of women. These horizons were set by a variety of factors, most importantly by economic circumstances and by social constraints imposed according to male notions of what constituted proper behaviour for women in that community.

Sexual segregation and seclusion did not mean simply the creation of a boundary between public and private space but the control of women's movements and visibility whether they were at home, at work in the fields or walking in the street. Control of the physical space in which women moved took many forms: the segregation of the home into men's and women's quarters; the designation of separate spaces for women in public places and on public transport. An extreme case was the rule enforced in parts of Iran that women had to walk on a designated side of the road. Even in villages, where women's visibility was much greater, it was quite common for there to be unwritten rules about where women could go and how they should conduct themselves in public.[21]

These forms of control over women's use of space, public or private, are very difficult to discern in photographic record, which of its nature lays stress on more tangible factors of visibility and physical appearances. Only in the occasional crowd scene is it possible to see whether that particular society or community imposed spatial segregation on women. Furthermore, not all Western photographers were even aware of the ground rules which governed women's behaviour. The fact that photographic studios produced images which took no account of these rules further confuses the issue.

The camera could record changes which took place in the visibility of well-to-do women who had previously lived in seclusion, showing them unveiled in public places and performing new social and economic roles. But these photographs could also be misleading as to the extent and nature of these changes. Photographs disseminated in the Western media often projected an image of the 'modern woman' in Egypt, Turkey or Iran, suggesting a generalized transformation of women's lives to fit the model of European middle-class women. This did little more to explain the experiences of Middle Eastern women than the older stereotypes of the 'Oriental woman' of the harem.

One of the results of sexual segregation in all classes of society was the creation of largely separate women's worlds, not necessarily confined to the four walls of the home, with their own culture – songs, stories, religious practices – overlapping at times with that of men, but seen by both sexes as different and distinct.

Whether secluded or not, women would at times support each other against their menfolk's demands, or negotiate through older women respected in the family or community. Joy, at a birth or a wedding, and grief at death were usually expressed collectively. Even in peasant societies where women worked with men, in agriculture or crafts, their social lives tended to be more or less separate. Many daily chores – fetching water or firewood, going to market, making food,

19 'Egyptian Women Visiting the Mahmal at Abbassieh'. S.H. Leeder, Egypt, published in his book The Veiled Mysteries of Egypt, *1912.*

For both men and women it was the height of piety for a Muslim to perform the pilgrimage to Mecca, just as it would be for many Christians and Jews to visit Jerusalem. Women of all classes, whether secluded or not, had gone on the pilgrimage from the earliest days of Islam, and like men, on their return, received the respectful title *hajje*. In this picture, Leeder shows a group of women who could not go to Mecca, but did the next best thing by going to Abbassieh to see the *Mahmal*, the holy carpet carried ceremoniously to Mecca on each year's pilgrimage.

doing embroidery or weaving – were done by groups of women, both family and neighbours. In urban societies, women went in groups to the public baths, to the cemetery on Fridays or feastdays, or to picnic with their children. Both urban and rural women attended religious festivals and went on pilgrimages. The more private aspects of women's culture were rarely evident in the photographic record but photographs of women's activities which took place in public do exist.

20 *'Femmes allant au bain' – Women Going to the* hamam *(Public Baths). H. Béchard, Cairo, late nineteenth century.*

In Orientalist paintings, the theme of the *hamam* was used to portray naked female bodies, the outstanding example being Ingres' *Le Bain Turc*. The camera, however, had to leave these fantasies to the viewers' imagination and here presents the exterior view – the veiled women outside the doors of the *hamam*. But the *hamam* had an important social function as a legitimate meeting-place for urban women of all communities and most classes. Before the twentieth century, only the very rich had baths in their own homes. Consequently the women who ran the women's sections of the *hamam*s were often influential figures, closely involved in the affairs of the neighbourhood and privy to its secrets.

21 Women in a courtyard. Beirut, c.1905.

An amateur photographer's glimpse of women gathered around a well in a courtyard. In both town and countryside, fetching water was a regular daily chore and women often used it as an opportunity to socialize with neighbours and relatives.

22 Women and children in a park. Tehran, Iran, 1860s–90s.

The exact location of this scene is unknown, but from its layout, this would seem to be a typical upper-class Persian garden with avenues of pine trees intersecting at its centre, and probably fruit trees in the background. This would probably have been a private garden and the women would have been there at the invitation of the owner or the garden-keeper. Judging from their dress, they were evidently quite well-to-do. The light foliage on the trees in the background suggests that it was springtime, and the most likely occasion for this kind of social gathering would have been the *sizdah-be-dar*, thirteen days after New Year. This day was considered ill-omened and people would not stay in their homes. Women and men, in separate groups, would go out and spend the day in a pleasant place such as this. They would have lunch and chat and were sometimes entertained by strolling musicians. The children, boys and girls, could run around and play. This was entirely a social and family occasion, not a religious festival.[6]

23 Women mourning at the graveside. Hilma Granqvist, Artas, Palestine, late 1920s.

Granqvist, who was doing anthropological fieldwork in Artas, caught this moment of private grief apparently without the women being aware of, or concerned by, the presence of the camera. It is in marked contrast to the more distanced photographs of cemetery scenes taken by those who, like Hildburgh, had no involvement with the community. Granqvist wrote that men in the village often expressed disapproval of what they considered women's 'excessive' public displays of grief over a bereavement, yet this can also be

21

22

viewed as a cathartic release of feelings, usually expressed in the company of other women.[7] In this photograph, however, these women seem to be sharing a quiet moment by the graveside.

24 'Mohameddan Cemetery on [the Feast of] Bairam, Damascus'. W.L. Hildburgh, c.1902.

It was a widely practised custom for families, and particularly women, to honour the dead by visiting the cemetery on feastdays or on Fridays (the Muslim holiday). This was as much a social as a religious occasion and was not simply an act of mourning. In this photograph, Hildburgh, a folklorist who travelled widely in the Middle and Far East, remained at some distance from the groups of people gathered round the graves. From the angle of the photograph, it is possible that he took the photograph over a wall overlooking the cemetery.

25 'At the Sheikh's Stone,
Fayyoum Province, Egypt'.
Winifred Blackman, 1923.

The shrines of local saints (male
and female) and *shaikhs* (religious
teachers) attracted the sick and
those in need of help, in the hope
of cure or solace. Here a sick
woman is being consoled by
another woman. Blackman has
chosen to make the two women,
seated on the ground, the focus of
the photograph. The men,
standing, thus appear peripheral
observers of the women, who are
absorbed in their own concerns.

26 'Day for Women to Visit the
Commercial, Industrial and
Agricultural Exhibition at Cairo'.
18 March, 1931.

This snapshot appears in the
album of a Dutch couple returning
to Holland from Indonesia by way
of Egypt. Although by the 1930s
some women of the elite would
attend mixed social gatherings,
many middle-class women were
not free to do so, and some efforts
were made to encourage women
to attend public events by having
separate times at which women
could go, rather than spatial
segregation. These women's dress
also indicates the gradual change
in styles which was occurring –
only two of the women in the
foreground are still wearing small
face veils, though all have their
heads covered.

25

26

Mohammedan throngs during "Sacrificial Week," outside the eastern Wall of Jerusalem, Palestine. Copyright 1900 by Underwood & Underwood.

Underwood & Underwood, Publishers. New York, London, Toronto-Canada, Ottawa-Kansas.

Works and Studies ~ Washington, D.C. ~ Arlington, H. Littleton, H.H.

27

28

27 'Mohammedan Throngs During "Sacrificial Week" [i.e. the Eid] Outside the Eastern Wall of Jerusalem'. Underwood & Underwood, stereoscopic slide, published 1900.

Commercial photographs such as this one, showing crowd scenes, can sometimes give some insight into the relationship of men and women in public space in a particular culture. In this picture, it is evident that there are no rigid divisions imposed between men and women, who mingle in the crowd, although in the small knots of people within the mass, men and women seem mostly to congregate separately.

28 'Baluchi Pilgrims [from Iran] Disembarking on the Shatt al-Arab for Nejf'. Freya Stark, Iraq, 1937.

Nejf and Kerbala in Iraq are the two major shrines of Shia Islam, after Mecca and Medina. Women like this Baluchi, who might otherwise seldom have left their home town or village, might travel long distances in order to make the pilgrimage.

Chapter III
Family Portraits

1 The Acar family. Derounian Brothers, Aleppo, Syria, c.1906.

This photograph, probably taken in the family's home, shows an Ottoman official with his wife and daughter. The daughter Nihal was, unusually, an only child. She later attended a French convent, Notre Dame de Sion, in Istanbul (which she greatly disliked) and subsequently married Afif Gediz, an entomologist who had studied in Germany.

To anyone accustomed to the exotic dress and indolent poses of the people shown in many commercial photographs of the Middle East, the portrait of the Acar family may seem startling, not least because in its style and presentation of the 'family group' it so closely resembles Western family portraiture of the same era. However, the relationship between the images projected by these family photographs and the social and personal lives of their subjects is not a simple one.

In the West, the use of photography for family portraiture began soon after its commercialization in the 1840s, and by the end of the nineteenth century these studio portraits could be taken quickly and quite cheaply. In the 1890s the invention of the simple, hand-held Kodak camera also allowed families to take their own pictures without recourse to the studio. In the Middle East, the evolution of portrait photography followed a similar pattern, but it occurred much more slowly. Until the 1940s and 1950s, the clientele for studio photographs was mostly drawn from the more affluent strata of society and only the wealthy were likely to own cameras.

Among the well-to-do, however, by the end of the nineteenth century photographic portraits had become fashionable in cities where the photographic trade was well developed. Many such families still possess substantial collections of portraits from the late nineteenth and early twentieth centuries. Older members of these families often remember having group photographs taken on special occasions, and recall, as children, trouping off to the photographic studio to be cajoled or bullied into suitable poses.

Taken with the handful of personal memoirs from this period, family portraits offer some internal evidence of how middle- and upper-class families in different parts of the Middle East wanted to be portrayed. They also serve as a counterweight to the generally stereotyped Western views of Middle Eastern family relationships and of women's role in the family. Yet the question arises – why do these portraits commissioned by Middle Eastern families appear so similar to those taken in Europe at around the same time?

One explanation lies in the way this genre of photography was developed and disseminated from Europe. The techniques and styles of photographic portraiture were largely imported into the Middle East from Europe. These styles, it has been argued, had their roots in a European tradition of portraiture stretching back to the Renaissance. In her book on family portraiture in the West, Julia Hirsch argues that these antecedents influenced not only the aesthetics of portrait photography but also continued the aristocratic tradition of presenting the family as 'strong, gracious and cohesive'. At the same time the imperatives of commercial photography led to the production of standardized images which gave the majority of these portraits a 'homogenized air of propriety'.[1]

The European fashion for the *carte de visite* and the 'cabinet portrait' was taken up by photographers in the Middle East who served local clienteles. These standardized genres stressed uniformity: people appeared in isolation from their cultural and social environments, decorously posed in the studio with heavy drapes and overstuffed chairs. They were usually posed full face to the camera, staring directly out at the viewer, as if from a stage. Both the format of the photograph and the poses create this apparent homogeneity, not only across classes but across cultures.

Thus studio photographs of families from Bombay, Cairo, or the American Midwest all bear the same hallmarks.

Admittedly, in the formal portraits commissioned by the families themselves, the power relationship between the subjects and the commercial photographer was very different from that between the photographer and a model, paid or unpaid. In the former case the sitters were clients paying for a service. Yet it seems likely that in most cases the photographer retained a good deal of initiative in deciding how the family should be presented and might endeavour to impose that view.

The other explanation for the popularity of this genre of photography lies in the changing self-image of the upper classes who were its patrons. At least until the period of World War I, family portraiture in the Middle East represented a narrower class segment of society than it did in Europe and was also concentrated in particular regions and communities. It is, for example, more common to find family albums dating back to the pre-World War I period among families in Egypt and Turkey, where the upper classes were strongly influenced by European lifestyles and fashions, than it was in Algeria, Iraq or Iran. In Syria, Lebanon and Palestine, family portraiture became fashionable earlier in Christian than in Muslim communities. The Armenians, who

2 The Kapamadjian family. M. Arslan, Istanbul, late nineteenth/early twentieth century.

This was a prosperous Armenian family active in business and cultural life in Istanbul. The very formality of the portrait, as well as the style of dress, projects a sense of affluence and self-confidence. The grandmother (seated) forms the centre of the family group. The youngest member of the family (the little boy with the hoop) lays his hand on his grandmother's, stressing the relationship of the various generations. Whether these poses were decided by members of the family or the photographer can only be a matter of speculation. This photograph is in the archives of the Armenian Patriarchate in Jerusalem and was probably sent by the family, as was customary, as a gesture of thanks to the Patriarchate after they had returned from a pilgrimage to Jerusalem.

3 'The Family of Daoud Candela'. Naom Sayegh, Mosul, early twentieth century.

The bridal couple in the centre form a focus for the entire extended family, which came from the Chaldaean (Christian) community in Mosul. Naom Sayegh, himself a Chaldaean, was one of the earliest local photographers active in Mosul and took numerous photographs of Chaldaean families, many of which celebrate as much a sense of community as of family.

had played such an important role in the development of photography in the region, were particularly strongly represented. Since Armenian photographers were working in Turkish provincial towns from the 1880s onwards, the photographic record of this community encompassed a more socially and geographically diverse sample.

By the 1920s, however, photography had become respectable among all but the most conservative of urban elites and was an accepted means of celebrating family cohesion, prestige and success. In this sense, the motives for commissioning family portraits were probably little different from those of European families. But many of these portraits give the impression that the family's self-image and aspirations were being fitted into a European frame: not only in composition and decor, but in dress and general demeanour, these photographs suggest a lifestyle which imitates that of Europe. They seem to imply – in contrast to the Western fantasies presented in tourist postcards – that behind these seemingly familiar expressions of family prestige lie personal and social roles similar to those of a well-to-do European family.

Memoirs and family histories from Middle Eastern societies suggest, however, that the meanings of these images were more complex. The urban upper classes, particularly in societies such as Egypt which came under direct Western control, were most likely to be affected by Western cultural ideas and to absorb these norms into their own estimation of prestige and status. But it would certainly be rash to assume that the families in these portraits automatically fitted into the mould of the Western bourgeois family.

The era in which these photographs were taken – from the 1880s to the 1940s – was one of considerable social change, and it is unsafe to generalize about the coincidence between the image of the family in a portrait and the social and personal relationships and expectations which lay behind it.

Take, for example, the fact that in significant numbers of these portraits men and women appear together in the photograph. This might be interpreted as an indication that the family in question had thrown over the rules of seclusion and sexual segregation commonly observed in the upper classes. By the 1920s this was certainly a trend in some regions among the liberal elites, but in many cases this apparent breaking down of sexual barriers could also be explained by the fact that the photograph was intended only for the family's eyes.

Images of Marriage and Family Life

Nowhere is the ambiguity of these family images more evident than in wedding photographs. Pierre Bourdieu, examining the introduction of photography into a rural French community, notes that its first role was to represent those occasions which were of most importance to family and community – marriages, birth and death.[2] Among the elites of the Middle East, marriage photographs gained in popularity from the end of the nineteenth century and gradually became part of the ritual of marriage festivities.

For wealthy families, weddings had always been an opportunity for lavish display, with entertainments often lasting many days. But until the late nineteenth century, the bride and groom would appear together only briefly during the festivities. Male and female guests and relatives rarely mingled, with separate celebrations taking place in the harem.[3]

By the end of the century, when photographs of wedding couples first became fashionable, in cities where Western influence was strong there had already been some changes in the way weddings were conducted. As early photographs make clear, there had also been alterations in the fashions for bridal dresses, with Western-style bridal gowns much more in evidence than the distinctive wedding attire which had been peculiar to particular cities or regions (see Chapter IV).

Photographs can offer unequivocal evidence of these changes in fashion, but what of the relationships between the couples who appear in these portraits? It is obviously impossible to generalize across all the different regions and communities of the Middle East, but the iconographic meaning of the wedding photograph for a Western viewer can be set against its possible range of meanings for people in the Middle East.

In the West, the image of the man and wife, posed together in isolation, had a significance which went beyond a statement of family prestige or family alliances. By the end of the nineteenth century, in the rising middle-class cultures of Western Europe and the United States, the wedding couple was increasingly represented as the core of a nuclear family, living separately from the rest of their family in a union

4 'Meccan Woman in Bridal Costume'. Snouk Hurgronje or assistant, Mecca, published 1885.

The bride's dress was bejewelled and extremely hot and heavy. She was expected to sit for some hours receiving female wedding guests before she was joined on this 'throne' by the bridegroom. The city of Mecca is closed to non-Muslims, and the Dutch Orientalist Snouk Hurgronje has left one of the few detailed accounts of social life in the city for this period. Thus his uncorroborated interpretations have to be treated with some caution, particularly as he may have come into contact only with certain sections of Meccan society, which may not have been entirely representative.
He suggests that because many pilgrims remained in the city for several years, there were large numbers of short-term marriages. According to Hurgronje, the Meccan women who contracted these marriages were by no means always victims of fly-by-night husbands, and frequently chose these temporary partners on terms favourable to themselves, regarding the marriage as a business deal. He adds, however, that for such marriages of convenience, the couple would usually dispense with the elaborate and costly ceremonies and costumes shown in this photograph.[1]

5 *Shaikh Munther and his bride.
Metn region, Lebanon, 1895.*

This photograph was probably
taken by a local photographer,
either in their home or in a studio.
Shaikh Munther came from a large
and prosperous Greek Orthodox
family in the Metn region. At the
time this picture was taken he was
nineteen and his bride sixteen.
In the first half of the twentieth
century, the men in the family
were mostly businessmen,
intellectuals or politicians.
According to a member of the
present generation of the family,
the women of that era are 'like
shadow figures' in the family
memory. Even her great-aunt,
born in 1898 and regarded as the
repository of family history,
always talks about what the men in
the family did, and says little
about the women. It seems that
because they stayed at home and
reared children they were
perceived as having no history. In
the eyes of women as well as men,
family history was seen as rooted
in the achievements of men.
In this community there was no
physical segregation of the sexes,
but 'the men made all the
decisions, including who women
should marry. Only in the last two
generations has there been any
change in this.' None the less,
from the 1890s onwards, it became
customary for women in the family
to receive an education, mostly at
Catholic schools. As the family
businesses – agriculture and trade
in silk, rubber and sugar –
prospered, some branches of the
family moved to Beirut, further
improving the women's access to
education. Some sections of the
family also migrated, to Palestine
and Egypt, and even further afield
to Latin America.[2]

which depended primarily on the sexual and personal
relationship between husband and wife. While this ideal may
seldom have fitted the realities of family life, the wedding
photograph embodied this aspiration, with its overtones of
romantic love and the choice of a partner for life.

In apparently similar photographs taken of couples in the
Middle East at this time, this Western bourgeois vision rarely
reflected either reality or even expectations. Most marriages
were still arranged by the couple's families, and in upper-
and middle-class society, it was quite common for couples
not to have met before their betrothal. Hence the wedding
photograph, with its ritual proprietary or affectionate gestures, had little bearing upon the couple's relationship, or
lack of it. Yet for the photographers, these poses and
gestures were simply part of the required imagery for a
wedding photograph. In particular cases, the picture of the
bridal couple posed together, apart from their families, may
also have reflected a new attitude towards marriage as more
of a partnership between individuals, but such photographs
were certainly not confined to those who viewed marriage in
this way.

The Kamil Family

6 Hafiza (centre), *great-grandmother of Saad Kamil, with her two daughters. On the left is his grandmother Zakiya. Egypt, early twentieth century.*

Hafiza and her sister Sophia came to Egypt as children in the 1860s after their family had fled the turmoil in their native Caucasus. According to the family, the sisters left the Caucasus on horseback with their mother, father and uncle. The uncle subsequently turned back, and the rest of the family made its way to Istanbul. Their father died during or after this journey and the mother and children went on to Egypt to seek the protection of a Circassian relative who lived in Sharqiyya province. He looked after them and married the sisters into well-to-do families, Sophia to a *pasha* (a rich landowner). Despite the fact that she spent her whole adult life in Egypt, Hafiza never learnt to speak Arabic properly, though her children did.[3]

7 Fathi and Aziza Radwan, children of Hafiza's daughter Zakiya, Egypt, around the time of World War I.

Fathi, here trying to look tall and proprietorial, claimed to have been much influenced by his three sisters. He later became a politician, and in his memoirs, *Al-Khalij al-Asha'iq*, he wrote a sympathetic account of his relationship with them, saying that their influence and support had been important in his career. It was not unusual for brothers and sisters to maintain close relationships into adult life, though brothers tended to play a protective, and sometimes a constraining role.

6

98

All three of Zakiya's daughters –
Munira, Aziza and Amina –
married men of the professional or
upper class. Note the changes in
style of wedding-dress and
presentation of the bridal couple
in these studio portraits.

*8 Marriage of Munira to Kamil
Ahmad al-Birri, Cairo, c.1920.*

He was a schoolteacher and later a
director of schools. The couple
travelled extensively in Egypt
because of his work.

9 Marriage of Aziza, Cairo 1924.

Her husband was a lawyer whom
she did not know before the
betrothal: the marriage was
arranged by the family. They had
no children and he died in 1948.
Aziza adopted one of the sons of
Amina (below) who died of
cancer. Aziza is described by the
family as a strong personality who,
as a schoolgirl, took part in the
anti-British demonstrations of
1919 (see Chapter VII Caption 2).
As an adult she did not become
directly involved in politics or in
the women's movement until the
end of the 1940s, after her
husband's death, when she was
encouraged to do so by her
brother, Fathi.

10 Marriage of Amina, 1930s.

Amina, the youngest sister,
married within the extended
family. Her husband, a landowner
and specialist in apiculture, was
the grandson of Sophia. Amina
died young, of cancer, but is
remembered by the family for her
great interest in history and in
Egyptian nationalism, which she
imparted to all the children in the
family.

Although there were always women who through sheer tenacity or obstinacy managed to fend off unwelcome marriage partners whom their families wished to impose, for the most part there was little choice and limited bargaining power. This was especially the case when the bride-to-be was very young. The pressures which parents or guardians could bring to bear on a young girl are vividly illustrated in Huda Shaarawi's account of her marriage at the age of thirteen (in the late 1890s) to her cousin Ali Shaarawi, a man in his forties.

Huda's father, a wealthy Egyptian landowner, had died when she was very young. Her mother, threatened with the loss of their landed property to her dead husband's family, decided to marry Huda, her eldest child, to Ali Shaarawi, who had been for many years the family's *wakil* (agent) who oversaw its property and financial interests. The decision was announced to Huda without prior explanation and she was asked, as a minor, whom she wished to act for her in signing the marriage contract. When she wept and refused to reply, Sayyid Agha, one of the family's eunuchs, whispered to her, 'Do you wish to disgrace the name of your father and destroy your poor mother who is weeping in her sickbed and might not survive the shock of your refusal?'

The marriage went ahead but, much to Huda's joy, after fifteen months it became evident that Ali had broken the terms her mother had written into the marriage contract, in which he had promised to free his slave/concubine and to remain monogamous. When it came to light that he was seeing his concubine again, Huda's mother insisted on a separation which lasted until Huda was twenty.[4]

Huda had known Ali Shaarawi as a relative and family friend since she had been a small child, but had obviously regarded him as a father- or elder-brother figure, certainly not as a potential husband. By the 1920s and 1930s, it had become less common among the urban elites for couples to be complete strangers to each other, but in earlier generations, this had been the norm. Even among Christians in Lebanon, where social divisions between the sexes were generally less strict, Asad Kayat, who later became an advocate of women's rights, was considered very daring when in the 1830s he demanded to see his bride before the wedding ceremony.[5]

Although marriage alliances were ultimately sanctioned and negotiated by male members of the family, it was usually the potential bridegroom's mother who, with the help of other female relatives and perhaps a marriage broker, would initiate the search for a bride for her son. This was an older woman's most powerful role in the family in most classes and communities. In urban societies where elite women were secluded, photography came to play a rather one-sided role in these negotiations by giving young men a chance to scrutinize potential fiancées without actually meeting them.

11 Family wedding-group.
Turkey, 1952.

At first glance, a conventionally
posed wedding-picture, similar in
appearance to many taken in
Europe at the same period. Yet
the formality is broken by the look
of affection the bride is
exchanging with her mother, in
the row behind her, probably
caught by the photographer purely
by accident. Her daughter
particularly likes this photograph
because she says, for her, it
expresses the close bond which
existed between her mother and
her grandmother.

According to Eugènie le Brun (who had married into an
upper-class Egyptian family out of choice) the production of
a photograph provided an opportunity for the man's mother
and female relatives to promote their favoured candidate:
'What does the young man do on this occasion? Would you
believe it – nothing at all; he listens [while] his mother, sisters
and aunts, with the help of a skilful photographer, paint a
ravishing portrait of his fiancée for him . . .'[6]

A Syrian researcher, Kazem Daghestani, wrote in the
1930s that in the more conservative milieu of the Damascene
upper classes, it was common to use fashion magazines to
pick out likenesses of potential brides: 'We witnessed a
similar sort of scene on numerous occasions: the female
relatives would show the future bridegroom fashion plates in
magazines in an effort to conjure up an image of the young
girl (or girls) under consideration.'[7] The irony here is that, in
the search for ideal types of womanhood, the future bride
was being stereotyped into the mould of a fashion model, in
all probability chosen from a Western magazine.

This substitution of photographs or other visual images for
the presence of the woman who is a potential marriage
partner has continued in some areas and classes to this day. It
undoubtedly enhanced the mother's power to persuade her
son to accept the bride of her choice. It also helped to
reinforce visual stereotypes among particular classes as to
what constituted beauty and attractiveness in a young
woman. It also symbolized the passivity expected of a young
woman in regard to her marriage: she was scrutinized
without having the opportunity to scrutinize in return.
Potential brides were rarely offered the chance to see their
suitors, or even photographs of them. Only the most
strong-minded women would attempt to insist on this.

12 Aziza Galal. Egypt, probably
early 1920s.

Aziza was an orphan and her
marriage was arranged by her
brother-in-law who, when a friend
of his expressed a desire to marry,
suggested that he should choose
Aziza. According to Aziza, he
showed his friend this photograph
of her. She, being by her own
account a strong-minded young
woman, refused to consider the
proposition without first seeing
her prospective husband. Finally
her brother-in-law relented and
allowed her to walk into the room
when her future husband was
present, with strict instructions not
to talk to him except for a greeting
and to behave modestly. She
found him 'short and not good-
looking' but agreed to marry him.[4]

If the antecedents of marriage were somewhat different from those in the West, so were expectations for the couple's future. The image of the married couple in the West suggests a monogamous relationship 'until death us do part'. In Christian communities in the Middle East, this was an accurate reflection of the young couple's prospects, since in most rites divorce was not permitted. For Muslims, however, whether Sunni or Shia, neither monogamy nor lifelong marriage was necessarily assumed at the time of the wedding.

Polygamy was certainly not the universal norm suggested by popular Western imagery. Its prevalence varied from society to society and from class to class and the expense of maintaining more than one wife was a considerable deterrent in less well-off families. Among peasants and bedouin the main motive of polygamous marriages was to secure more labour power than a monogamous household could provide (see Chapter IV). Among the rich and in court circles the most common reasons seem to have been to secure a male heir if the first wife bore no sons; to secure an advantageous alliance with another family; or because men unilaterally asserted their right to sexual satisfaction and a variety of partners.

In the period when most of these wedding photographs were taken – between the 1880s and the 1940s – polygamy remained legal everywhere except in Turkey where it was abolished under the civil code of 1926. In urban society, however, it was generally on the wane by the 1920s. According to the observations of Eugènie le Brun, among the Egyptian elite circles in which she moved, polygamy was becoming less common by the early years of the twentieth century. Using the yardstick of the Western family unit, she wrote that by this time, the 'ordinary' (monogamous) family had become the norm. Daghestani's study of the family in Syria in the 1930s concluded that in Damascus and Aleppo, still comparatively conservative in their social mores, not even the ten richest men in each city had more than one wife apiece. Among younger members of the educated upper class in these cities, he added, polygamy was also rare.

Not a great deal is known about women's views of polygamy, though these probably varied very much according to the status and expectations of the women concerned. There were popular sayings in a number of societies, urban and rural, which suggested that men as well as women were aware of the potential for strife in polygamous relationships, describing them, for example, as the 'bitter life'. The few biographies of upper-class women suggest that polygamy often made life difficult and painful for the wives concerned.

The Turkish feminist Halide Edip stressed the emotionally destructive effects polygamy could have on the whole family. Her father married two wives, and according to her memoirs, both he and the two women were deeply unhappy. 'On my childhood, polygamy and its results produced a very ugly and

13 'Wealth and Beauty for the Price [mahr – dowry or brideprice] of Twenty-five Fils!' An advertisement for a lottery for office space published in several versions in the magazine Radio Misriyya *during June and July 1938.*

The visual pun of the building and the bride is elaborated in the text of the advertisement. It reflects and plays on the equation commonly made between wives and property. The price of the lottery ticket is presented as the *mahr* or dowry, because like the *mahr* it purchases 'entrance' to the building/bride. Paying this small sum opens up the 'delights of beauty and property'. In the drawing, the men, though not the women, are seen leering at this double image of possession.

14 Family group. Cairo, 1936.

Portrait of a well-to-do family taken by a friend who was an amateur photographer. It became a ritual to have such photographs taken when the family gathered for major feasts such as the *Eid*. The family is grouped under a portrait of the grandmother who had died a few years before, and her husband sits directly below her picture.

15 Women in a divorce court in the Izbekiyya district of Cairo. Photograph published in Al-Dunya magazine, 1938.

The accompanying article offers some anecdotes on why people get divorced, including arbitrary reasons such as: 'My wife brought me bad luck.' The journalist also interviewed a judge who stressed that children were the main victims of divorce.
Women in Egypt had always had some access to the courts on matters of personal status, but the law was heavily stacked against them, and for poor, uneducated women, or those who were not articulate in putting their case, the likelihood of success was further diminished.[5]
The photograph shows women from a variety of social backgrounds. Note that by this time most of those who are wearing veils have them made of almost transparent material.

distressing impression. The constant tension in our home made every simple family ceremony seem like a physical pain, and the consciousness of it hardly ever left me.'[8]

In some upper-class circles, and certainly in royal courts, where polygamy was probably most common, there were, however, very different expectations of marriage and relations with men. Eugènie le Brun records some conversations she had with women from upper-class harems in Egypt which suggest that some of these women regarded status, rather than emotional attachment, as the key to their relationship with their husbands, though it is unclear how representative the views of her interlocutors were.

Le Brun seized on one account given her of a woman's

unhappiness and jealousy when her husband decided to take another wife to say that she thought polygamy victimized women. But another woman in the group argued that this instance was something of an exception: 'Do not be too hasty in your judgement, my child,' she said. 'Not everyone is of the same disposition. Many women of similarly high birth have accepted an identical situation with equanimity. [This woman] was an exception, believe me.' Another young woman observed that wives were more concerned with the external manifestations of affection than with affection itself. She added: 'I always heard my mothers congratulate themselves on my father's utter impartiality towards them. It was of small importance whether he loved them equally, just as long as he treated them equally.'[9]

Probably an equal source of pain and hardship for women was the ease of divorce, a prerogative which could be exercised quite arbitrarily by men. Women, on the contrary, could only with difficulty initiate divorce proceedings, except in cases of desertion, or if the right of divorce was written into the marriage contract. If the marriage bond was severed women were obliged to return to their own families. Although it was generally the custom for a woman to live in her husband's home, she would frequently retain close ties with her own family, and the family home remained a place of retreat in the case of divorce or of quarrels with her husband's family.

By the early twentieth century, it became more common for families to have photographs taken of large gatherings, either at home or in the studio, often encompassing several generations of the family. These probably reflected more accurately than wedding photographs the continuing importance of ties between different generations and between siblings, as well as the networks of relationships beyond the nuclear-family unit. These pictures in many cases reflect the importance which family members themselves attributed to these ties. Sometimes, even in the formal and ritualized poses, it is possible to discern relationships of power and authority: the family hierarchies of young and old, men and women.

Western Views of Middle Eastern Families

While family albums provide a record, however equivocal, of the lives, fashions and aspirations of the urban elites, most photographs of families from other classes in the era from the late nineteenth century until the 1940s were taken by Westerners. For the majority of people outside these elites, photographs were rarely either affordable or necessarily considered desirable until well into the twentieth century.

Apart from the imaginative evocations of the upper-class harem already discussed, there were many other photographic 'reconstructions' of what purported to be Middle

16 Two young cousins. Amateur photograph, Cairo, 1930s.

Photographs taken with hand-held cameras began to make their appearance in family albums from about the time of World War I. This photograph was taken by a man who was apparently in love with one of the two girls in the picture. Although this is a snapshot, the photographer, and perhaps the subjects, chose to adopt a formal pose more characteristic of a studio picture.

17 'A Judaean home, suggestive of "The Wise Men Seeking the Christ Child" '. Eric Matson, Palestine, probably before World War I.

Matson transforms a group of Palestinians, who may or may not be related, into an image of the Holy Family. For a Western viewer, such a picture needs no caption, and no date, because the arrangement of the figures tells its own story. The origins and personal histories of the people in the picture are irrelevant; what they represent to the Western viewer is 'The Nativity', the iconography of which had been shaped by centuries of art, and which has also created an idealized image of the nuclear family.

Eastern families, both inside and outside the studio. Some of these photographs suggest that the norm in all classes was for men to have several wives, which, as already noted, was not the case. On the other hand, some Western photographers chose to ignore the significance of the extended family in Middle Eastern society, and manufactured Middle Eastern family units which mirrored the Western concept of the bourgeois nuclear family. Malek Alloula, in his analysis of postcard images of Algerian society in the late nineteenth century, argues that models were often used to create this image of a nuclear *famille mauresque*:

> In the imaginary space of the postcard, where all social connections have been reduced and put out of sight, the ideal social unit in which the modern couple, itself an expression of a more rational order of which colonization is supposedly the purport, finally makes its appearance and takes the place of the 'anarchic', irreducible, traditional family.[10]

Anthropologists and ethnographers who spent time in particular communities were apparently in a better position to reflect the nature of family relationships. Most, however,

The photographer's presumed intention is to suggest that the single male in the picture has (at least) four wives. They could also be sisters, sisters-in-law, or other relatives – or not relations at all – simply people grouped together by the photographer. The fact that this can be regarded as a 'family' is presented as at best an oddity, or at worst, something which provokes disapproval in the viewer.

were more interested in patterns of kinship in the tribe and extended family, rather than in personal relationships within the family. Furthermore, their findings on family relationships were seldom evident from their photographic records. Even those women anthropologists, such as Hilma Granqvist, Winifred Blackman and Matthéa Gaudry, who were interested in these questions, rarely took photographs of family groups which included men and women. Their photographs tended to show only women relatives together, and occasionally brothers and sisters, or women with their sons. This reflected the sexual segregation which prevailed in most societies (see Chapter II), and therefore a marked reluctance on the part of many people to appear in a mixed photograph. On the rare occasions when photographs do show husbands and wives together, it seems likely that the anthropologist actually asked them to pose together.[11]

Mothers and Children

Among Western photographers, amateur and professional, the most common family theme was that of the mother and child. These images of motherhood sometimes had strong sexual overtones. Photographers were particularly attracted to scenes of women feeding their children in public which, especially among the poor of Egypt and North Africa, was a common practice allowing the photographer to create an image of earthy sensuality.

Many Western images of motherhood in the Middle East referred directly or indirectly to the iconography of the Madonna and Child, which had so coloured the portrayal of motherhood in the art and photography of the West itself. Sometimes the point was made simply by adding a caption to the photograph. For example, in a book published in 1910 describing women's role in missionary work from Palestine to China, entitled *Western Women in Eastern Lands*, there is a photograph of a woman, probably an Egyptian or Palestinian, with a child in her lap, with the caption 'A Muslim Madonna'.

19 Women of the Shammar tribe. Freya Stark, near Mosul, Iraq, 1930.

This photograph creates the impression that these women are quite at ease with the camera and its owner, and it also reflects something of Freya Stark's attraction to tribal life, a somewhat romanticized view perhaps, stressing the supportiveness and interdependence of the tribe as extended family. She wrote in a letter at that time: 'You would so love it here – the lovely free life of the tents, and pleasant family feeling of the tribe. I feel I should like to belong to a tribe, something so big and comfortable, and if you do come to grief you do it all together and there is none of the horrid petty bickering feeling of the towns.'[6]

20 'Arab Motherhood'. Reiser, Egypt, turn of the century.

This photograph emphasizes the earthy, sensual quality of the relationship between mother and child, while also evoking the image of Madonna and Child. The age of the child still at the breast is not surprising – children were usually breast-fed until they were about two years old.

21 'Down Will Come Baby, Cradle and All – if Mama Trips!' – Published in National Geographic Magazine, *December 1938, in an article entitled 'Change Comes to Bible Lands'.*

The rest of the caption to this photograph of a woman from Nablus in Palestine stresses the irresponsibility and irrationality of this method of carrying children on the head, and compares the woman's attitude to her child unfavourably with an American mother. 'With her child sound asleep in the basket, this Arab woman of Nablus goes on her way with apparent indifference. Fancy a fond young American mother facing traffic with her first-born balanced on her head!'

*22 'Degenerate Egypt –
Wretchedness of the People'.
Underwood & Underwood,
stereoscopic slide, 1896.*

This was part of a large series of
commercial slides distributed in
the United States and Europe.
That there was considerable
hardship and poverty in Egypt at
this time is undeniable, but the
image of raggedness and naked
children and the accompanying
caption is used to suggest that this
poverty is a result of moral and
cultural decline rather than
economic hardship, social
inequalities and the policies of
successive governments. By 1896,
Egypt was of course under British
rule.

Some photographers laid more stress on poverty, high-
lighting particularly the dirty and ragged condition of poor
children. These images may sometimes have been intended
to excite moral indignation, but this seems to have been
directed mainly against the parents, especially the mothers of
the children, rather than against the social and economic
conditions which caused poverty. Among missionaries in
particular, it was common to view lack of hygiene as solely
the result of the ignorance and low moral tone of women,
rather than something linked to a lack of clean water and
other basic necessities of life. Cleanliness and (Christian)
godliness were frequently viewed as inseparable.

Colonial officials, like missionaries, were prone to regard
women's treatment of their children as both negligent and
ignorant. Just as the supposed fecklessness of working-class
women in Europe was often blamed for high infant mortality
in their communities, so it was in the colonized world. Lord
Cromer, British Agent and Consul-General in Egypt from
1883 to 1907, commenting on a report of increased infant
mortality in Cairo in 1909, explicitly made this link:

> I have no doubt that the real reason [for the increase] is
> that Egyptian mothers do not in the least understand how
> to look after their children. You are probably aware that
> infant mortality in England and Wales is about 132 per
> thousand births, but that the rate is much higher, going up
> as much as 208 per thousand, in the manufacturing towns
> where women are largely employed in the factories.
> Moreover, it is a rather remarkable fact, which is not
> generally known, that when a strike takes place, and the
> women are therefore obliged to stay in their homes, the
> infant mortality at once decreases.[12]

23 'Fertility Rite with Jar'.
Winifred Blackman, Upper Egypt,
1920s, published in The Fellahin of
Upper Egypt.

In her book, Blackman devotes a
whole chapter to the fertility rites
practised by Egyptian peasant
women who, she noted, like
women in many parts of the world,
regarded these rites as vital to
ensure the birth of children. This
is one of a series of photographs
she took of a ritual performed on a
Coptic woman (lying down) who
had been married for some time
but had no children. Blackman's
desire to photograph the
procedure, however, led to certain
alterations being made. 'A
secluded spot behind the house
was selected, and a blanket spread
on the ground for the woman to lie
upon. Such a performance would
usually take place inside the
house, but, as the light indoors
was not strong enough for
photography, the woman
consented to it taking place
outside.'[7] Although Blackman's
description of the ritual may be
accurate enough, her presence as
an observer, especially with a
camera, had already converted
something which would have been
regarded as part of everyday life
into something more like a
theatrical performance.

Aside from poverty, however, there was another reason for this image of dirty, ragged children in the Middle East. This had nothing to do with neglect. There was a commonly held belief in the evil eye, source of malign influences to which babies and small children were considered particularly vulnerable. A smartly dressed child was thought by many to be likely to attract the evil eye, while a scruffy child might avoid these dangerous attentions. Although this practice could obviously be detrimental to the child's welfare, this belief in the evil eye also reflected women's consciousness of the fragility of life. Few women, rich or poor, had not experienced the loss of a child, or life-threatening illnesses in their children.

For this reason too, women in the Middle East tended to bear large numbers of children. Western middle-class images of women surrounded by hordes of children, whether in their own societies or in the Middle East, usually had derogatory implications: that these women were irresponsible in having more children than they could afford to look after. But in the Middle East constant childbearing had other implications. Not only was it due to the patriarchal pressure on women to bear as many sons as possible but, as in many other parts of the world, to bear many children was seen as a way of ensuring that a new generation of the family would survive into adulthood.

Certainly motherhood conferred a status on women of all classes in the Middle East which marriage alone did not give. To bear sons, ensuring the continuity of the male line, also gave women power and influence in the family in later life which it was difficult to achieve by any other means. Thus for most women, the role of mother tended to be more significant than that of wife. Ann-Marie Goichon, writing of urban middle-class life in Fez, Morocco, in the 1920s remarked: 'The woman of Fez is undoubtedly more mother than wife. Children hold an incomparably greater place in her thoughts than does her husband. If she wants to marry, it is primarily in order to have children.'[13]

Although Goichon is referring to a specific place and class, this observation seems to have reflected a widely-felt sentiment. Children conferred status on both their parents, reflected in the Arab custom of calling both parents by the name of their eldest son (or eldest daughter if there is no son) – thus Abu Khalid (father of Khalid) and Umm Khalid (mother of Khalid). Furthermore, motherhood usually enhanced a woman's status in her husband's family giving her considerable influence over her children's upbringing.

Family Memories

The dusty albums and folders of fading sepia photographs still in the possession of families today show four or five generations who have lived through a period of change and upheaval which affected the lives of people in many parts of the Middle East. Behind the new fashions in dress, the stolid or cheerful family groups, the affectionate snapshots lay, for some, more drastic changes.

The waves of migration from the Middle East, for example, beginning in the last years of the nineteenth century, scattered families across many parts of the globe. Migration in search of work and trade, both within the region

24 Armenian family, originating from Isfahan in Iran. Singapore Photographic Company, cabinet portrait, Singapore, date not known – probably before World War I.

This family may have been among the numbers of Armenians from Iran who emigrated to the Far East in the eighteenth and nineteenth centuries.

110

and beyond, was not confined to the nineteenth century. From at least the eighteenth century, Armenian families from Iran had been migrating to the Far East, to Indonesia and Singapore; in the nineteenth and twentieth centuries, Yemenis went to work in Java and Indonesia and travelled down the coast of East Africa; and small numbers of people from all parts of the Middle East had settled in Europe.

But at the end of the nineteenth century a combination of factors led to an unprecedented wave of emigration, particularly from the Arab provinces of the Ottoman Empire: mostly from Syria, Lebanon and Palestine to the United States, Central and Latin America and West Africa. These migrants were motivated mainly by economic hardship at home, the constant threat of conscription into the Ottoman army and the dreams of prosperity which attracted so many migrants to the Americas at this time. When transatlantic steamer fares became cheaper at the end of the nineteenth century, the trickle of emigrants became a flood. In the 1890s the numbers leaving Lebanon, Syria and Palestine were estimated at 5,000 to 10,000 a year. In the years before World War I they had risen to 15,000 to 20,000 a year.[14]

Some migrants risked taking their families with them, but the majority of men went on their own, hoping to summon their families when they had established themselves in the new country. Women therefore experienced a new kind of waiting, for news of their emigré husbands, brothers and sons – and it was often many years before the call came to join them. Meanwhile, responsibilities for family and property sometimes devolved on to mothers and wives, though usually under the supervision of male relatives.

Photographs as well as letters began to be used to communicate between members of separated families, to reassure those who remained at home of the migrant's wellbeing; and even to demonstrate, accurately or not, their successes in the new land. Photographs also began to play a

25 Portrait of Süreyya Ağaoğlu, her mother, brothers and sisters. Postcard, Istanbul, 1920.

Her mother had this picture taken to send to Süreyya's father Ahmad Ağaoğlu, a pan-Turkish and supporter of Atatürk, who was exiled to Malta by the British during their occupation of Istanbul from March 1920.

role in the long-distance arrangement of marriages: young men in the new country would often seek a bride from their home town or village, and photographs would be sent to show what potential fiancées looked like.

For those whose lives have been relatively calm and stable, family albums may give a sense of security and continuity, or sometimes nostalgia and an amused affection for old ways. The exact meaning of each individual photograph is often obscure, snapshots whose significance was known only to the participants, the meanings ascribed to them different for each generation, but they represent a past which can largely be taken for granted.

However, for families whose lives have been radically altered, often in a manner not of their own choosing, photographs have developed other meanings. The turmoil which has afflicted the Middle East since World War I has left many families separated by political strife, exile or emigration. Whole communities and nationalities, such as the Palestinians, and the Armenians who lived in Turkey,

26 Nihal Acar (see Caption 1). Istanbul, c.1920.

She is posed with a collection of framed photographs of her family, another means of suggesting the continuity of family life over generations.

A Lebanese Woman's Journey

The decision to make the journey to a new country and culture was often a hard one, especially for village women whose horizons were bounded by the district in which their family lived.

An Argentinian woman of Arab origin – her family came from a Christian village in Lebanon – recounted the story told to her mother by her grandmother of how she followed her husband to Argentina around the turn of the century. 'My grandfather wrote regularly [from Argentina] and sent money. He didn't talk of returning [to Lebanon] but of bringing his wife and daughter to America. At home, my grandmother [i.e. his wife] talked of this as a far-off event, but the very possibility was a source of anguish to her mother-in-law because for her [such a move] signified the certainty that she would never see her son (her grandfather) again. 'One of my grandmother's sisters whose husband, after eighteen years' absence in Argentina had just arrived in Lebanon to take his family back to Argentina with him, spent a long time talking to my grandmother to convince her to take advantage of this opportunity to travel with them. She was very insistent because she was afraid that her sister would end up as she had, spending most of her life alone [without her husband]. Grandmother, poor thing, wavered but then resolved to make the journey.'*

Their arrival in Argentina after the long journey was quite a shock and the journey to the small town of La Calandria where her husband had set himself up as a peddlar 'filled grandmother with doubts'. When they arrived, her first comment was, 'Thank God, at least there's a church.' Her husband was away travelling when they arrived, and when he returned, he and his daughter could not recognize each other.

*From Selim Abou, *Liban déraciné: immigrés dans l'autre Amerique*, Paris, 1978, pp. 48–51

have been uprooted and made stateless, physically cut off from the site of their past history.

In times of conflict, photographs have become a part of the ritual of mourning, and memorials to the dead. In present-day Lebanon, since the beginning of the civil war, all communities have 'immortalized' their young 'martyrs' by placing photographs with the flowers on their graves, and plastering their portraits on city walls. But in the dislocation of life, as well as in death, photographs can also play a symbolic role. They represent a kind of proof or assurance that the past, before the dislocation, really existed.

Roland Barthes, discussing the way photographs relate to the past argues that 'the photograph does not necessarily say "what is no longer", but only and for certain "what has been"'.[15] But perhaps for the dispossessed the photograph can bear both meanings: the people themselves know that their previous life no longer exists; and their photographs are, as Barthes puts it, 'a certificate of presence'. This is especially important, for instance, to the Palestinians, whose very existence as a people has so often been brought into question, so by implication denying them their past.

In a portrait of a respectable middle-class family in Jerusalem or Haifa before 1948, this past is reconstituted and can be counterposed against the popular contemporary stereotypes of the refugee and the terrorist. Of course, since family photographs from this period mainly depict the middle and upper classes, they can express this consciousness only for a minority. For the mass of the population, these memories had to remain in the mind's eye, and have been passed on to the next generation through often-repeated stories. In whatever class or national group, women have tended to be the repositories of family history, of an oral tradition into which photographs can be fitted. Looking at family photographs has become another way to evoke the past, its stories, personalities and myths.

27 Said and Aziza Racy, and their children Leila (far left), Felix (front), Stella, Carmen (far right) and Olga (in chair). São Paulo, Brazil, late 1920s.

Said and Aziza were cousins from Ibl al-Saqi in southern Lebanon, who married there and went to Brazil around the turn of the century. He was a textile merchant and, as the affluent air of this photograph suggests, was very successful. They returned to Lebanon for a visit and were caught there by the outbreak of World War I. They returned to Brazil via Manchester, where they had relatives, in about 1920.

Their daughters all married into affluent Lebanese families in Brazil, while Felix became a doctor and went to work in a poverty-stricken rural region of Brazil. Note that the younger children, born in Brazil, do not have Arab names.

Aziza Racy was one of five daughters of Wakim al-Racy, a Protestant clergyman. He became the first headmaster of the American Missionary School in Saida (Sidon) – known first as Gerard's Institute and later as Madrassat al-Fanoun.

Two of Aziza's sisters also emigrated from Lebanon. Soumeya married Fadlo Hourani, who had gone to Manchester in 1891 to join his cousin. The couple were married in 1902 and settled in Manchester. Nahia married Tawfiq Farhood, Fadlo's nephew, in 1911. They had met in Lebanon but were married in Manchester in Soumeya's home. They emigrated to the United States and settled in Brooklyn.[8]

Aziza's two other sisters remained in Lebanon: Nasima married Boulos al-Khauli, a professor at the American University of Beirut; and Khazma married Dr Iskander Nassif, a dentist.

All five sisters remained very close, despite the distances which separated them, and developed the habit of sending each other photographs of themselves and their families, like the one shown here, on special occasions.

28 Women from four generations of a Palestinian family. Jerusalem, c.1923.

Centre: Serene Husseini Shahid; *above*, her mother, Ne'mat Alami
Husseini; *to her right*, her grandmother, Zlikha Ansari Alami; *and to her
left*, her great grandmother, Asma Ghneim Ansari. Women kept their own
names after marriage: the first name is that of their family, and the second
that of their husband.

Asma Ghneim Ansari was brought up in the old city of Jerusalem in the
mid-nineteenth century and married Shaikh Abdel Qader Ansari, from a
family of hereditary Shaikhs (religious dignitaries) of the Haram al-Sharif.
She had a son, Shaikh Ibrahim, and a daughter, Zlikha. She died in the
1920s.

Zlikha married Faidi al-Alami, member of another prominent Jerusalem
family who became mayor of Jerusalem and a member of the Ottoman
parliament. He remained a deputy during World War I, during which the
family lived in Istanbul. Like her mother, Zlikha never received a formal
education. There was not strict physical segregation of the sexes in their
household, but until the 1930s or 1940s most women of this class veiled in
public and would withdraw when male guests came into the house. In 1919,
on a visit to Europe with Faidi, which included an audience with the Pope,
Zlikha wore an enormous picture hat which shadowed her face, rather than
a veil.

Zlikha also had only two children, Ne'mat and Musa. Ne'mat, born in 1895,
was the first female in the family to be sent to school, where she learnt
Italian and French as well as English and Arabic. In 1919 she married Jamal
Husseini, a member of one of the leading Jerusalem families. He was a
politician and although his family was wealthy, he was not personally well
off, and Ne'mat, who like her mother and grandmother was a wealthy
woman in her own right, helped out with the family finances.

Ne'mat was involved in the early women's movement in Palestine and was
the first president of the Arab Woman's Association. During the British
mandate Jamal's involvement in nationalist politics led to considerable
disruption in family life. Under threat of arrest, he fled to Lebanon in 1937,
followed by his family. From 1939–41 the family lived in Iraq, then returned
to Palestine, but Jamal was deported to Rhodesia for the duration of the
war. Grandmother Zlikha did not survive the return journey to Palestine in
1941, dying in the desert on the way. After the war, Ne'mat and Jamal
separated, she living in Beirut, and he in Saudi Arabia.

Serene, her daughter, grew up through the troubled 1920s and 1930s. She
was educated at private schools, including the liberal modernist Madrasa
al-Islamiyya in Jerusalem and the Quaker Girls School in Ramallah. When
the family moved to Beirut in 1937 she attended the American Junior
College and in 1939 enrolled at the American University of Beirut on a
scholarship. There she met a medical doctor Munib Shahid, a Palestinian of
Iranian origin whom she married in 1944. After 1948, they and other
members of the family lived in Beirut until the civil war again displaced
them.

An Armenian Family

These photographs of four
generations of women from a well-
to-do Armenian family from
Turkey can only begin to hint at
the changes which occurred in
their lives over this period. Their
history is recalled by Arshalouys
Zelvayan, whose life spanned both
the time of the family's residence
in Mersin, southern Turkey, and
the later years of exile.

*29 Akabi Lusazarian, Arshalouys'
maternal grandmother.*

She came originally from Kayseri
but later moved to Tarsus. She
lived until Arshalouys was about
eighteen; she remembers her
grandmother as a kind woman
who was good to her large family.

*30 Arshalouys' paternal
grandmother* (right), *who died
when she was very young, with her
father's brother Krikor Zelvayan,
who worked with Kevork in the
family business, and Krikor's wife.*

Note the elaborate, though severe
costumes and jewellery of these
well-to-do women. Their clothes
were distinctively Armenian, but
were often brought from Istanbul,
which was considered a centre of
fashion.

*31 Arshalouys and Arshak with
their two daughters and
Arshalouys' sister Vahanoush
(left) and her husband (far left).
Centre, Kevork Zelvayan. Cyprus
1927.*

In 1921 there was another series of
attacks on Armenians in Adana,
southern Turkey, which spread
alarm among the remaining
Armenian communities, and at
this point the Zelvayan family
took the decision to leave Turkey.
The family became widely
scattered: Arshak and Arshalouys
went to Cyprus with her parents.
Vahanoush, seen in the
photograph, subsequently went to
the United States with her
husband, who was already
resident there and had met her on
a visit to Cyprus. They settled in
Brooklyn. Arshak and Arshalouys
stayed in Cyprus until 1964 when
they emigrated to Britain because
of the Greek–Turkish conflict in
Cyprus.

29

32 Studio marriage photograph of Arshalouys Zelvayan and Arshak Tashdjian, Mersin, 1920.

She was just nineteen and he was twenty-four. Arshalouys recalls that her wedding-dress was made by a dressmaker in Mersin but the style was copied from a fashion book or magazine. This romantic studio photograph with its leafy backdrop gives no indication of the troubled times through which the Armenian community in Turkey had passed during World War I. Arshalouys remembers, however, that in Mersin during the massacres of Armenians throughout Turkey in 1915–16 things were very bad, especially for the poorer sections of the community. Her own family was partly protected by its wealth and influential position in the city. Even so, the men decided to take the precaution of sending the women and children out of the city for a time, hidden in a furniture van. Arshalouys went to a French school until she was seventeen although her schooling had been interrupted for a time by these upheavals.

Her husband, Arshak Tashdjian, however, had suffered much more, and had lost most of his family. Hence the family has virtually no pictures of his relatives. He came from Urfa in eastern Turkey and when he was a small child in the 1890s an earlier massacre of Armenians had brought the deaths of many of the men in his family. During World War I Arshak was working for a German company which was building bridges on the Istanbul–Baghdad railway. This afforded him some protection, though some other members of his family were killed. He finally fled with his aunt's two daughters, taking them first to Syria and then to Mersin, where they were later married. Arshak took up work as a carpenter. According to Arshalouys, Arshak first saw her through the window of her house and later came to ask for her hand in marriage. Her father at first refused, presumably because he did not know Arshak, who clearly could not match the social status of the Zelvayan family. Finally, however, he agreed to the match. Arshalouys does not seem to have been consulted about the marriage.

32

Chapter IV
Dressing the Part

This young woman is wearing the *tantur*, the spectacular headdress made of silvered copper, worn by high-ranking Druze women in Lebanon and Syria from the time of their betrothal, marking their status as married women. Bonfils and others took numerous photographs of women wearing the *tantur*, but by the 1880s it was already being abandoned in favour of less elaborate headwear, and by the turn of the century it had virtually disappeared. Hence the timeless image of the Druze woman, identifiable by her *tantur*, which appeared in commercial postcards and prints was in fact being undermined even as the photographs were being taken. Until the 1840s too, the *tantur* had not been worn solely by the Druze, but also by Maronite Christian women in the Lebanese mountain region. But after the wars between the Maronites and the Druze in 1841 and 1845, the Maronite clergy outlawed it as an item of Christian apparel.[1]

Looking at old photographs, one of the first things which strikes the eye is the style of the subjects' dress, and how this compares with our own. What people wore seems to have an important bearing on who they were, and what their lives were like. In early photography of the Middle East, however, costume, particularly the costume of women, became a form of visual identification for Westerners of races, 'types' and ethnic groups, and contributed to the imagery of the picturesque, the exotic and the erotic. But at the same time the imagery of dress played an important role within Middle Eastern societies. It could be used as a form of social control; or as a symbol of national identity. Equally, it could be used to signify the changing status of women.

Costume in an Era of Social and Economic Change

In the Western photographer's pursuit of the picturesque, the distinctive costumes of women in different regions of the Middle East, and the particularities of dress in various ethnic and religious communities were a constant source of fascination. Druze, Copt, Jew, fellah and bedouin could all be visually identified and labelled according to their styles of dress. The most spectacular women's costumes rapidly became popular subjects of photographic representation.

If women who wore these magnificent costumes could not always be found to pose for the camera, the resources of the photographic studio could always provide substitutes. Most professional studios had racks of costumes in which to dress their models, who could thus be instantly transformed into a 'Druze bride' or a 'Moorish type'. The actual origins of the sitter were irrelevant.

Many photographers were just as cavalier about the costumes themselves, creating their own confections of dress and ornament, while the caption on the resulting photograph would announce authoritatively that this was 'a bedouin girl'

2 'Femme arabe, femme turque' – Arab Woman and Turkish Woman. Zangaki, Port Said, 1870–80.

This studio portrait shows a woman (*seated*) dressed in 'the Turkish style', veiled in a semi-transparent *yashmak*. This was the dress adopted by the indigenous upper classes in a number of provinces of the Ottoman empire, especially in Egypt. Thus the costume need not mean that the wearer was of Turkish origin. The woman on the right wears the *burqu*, the face veil prevalent among urban Egyptian women. The women in this photograph are almost certainly models. The clothes they wear constitute outdoor dress, as suggested by the painted studio backdrop, of an improbable woodland scene. Note the usual array of studio props – the *narghileh* (water pipe), mother-of-pearl inlaid table, and the tambourine held by the Arab woman.

3 Armenian priest with members of his family. Garabed Krikorian, Jerusalem, 1907.

Random dressing up of subjects in photographic studios was not confined to models. In this portrait, the young Armenian girl, posed with a water jug, is dressed in clothes which approximate to a Palestinian peasant costume, quite unlike anything she might be expected to wear normally. The costume itself seems to be an imitation of the often elaborately embroidered peasant dresses of this region. On her head the girl wears an embroidered Turkish towel, usually used for bridal ceremonies, and certainly not as a peasant headdress. The costume and water jar were probably provided by Krikorian's studio, or borrowed for the occasion.

4 'Felah arabe' – Arab Peasant Woman. Tancrède Dumas, 1860–70.

Dumas was based in Lebanon but also took photographs in Palestine and Egypt. Where this bizarre concoction of a costume is supposed to come from is uncertain. Although the woman is described as a peasant, she is wearing the face veil of silver coins prevalent among certain bedouin tribes of Egypt, Sinai and southern Palestine, and not worn by peasant women. Whether she was a peasant or a bedouin, she would have been unlikely to wear her hair showing loose. If it had been allowed to show at all, it would probably have been tied in a plait. Both peasant and bedouin women frequently rolled up their sleeves to work, but this picture suggests that the photographer has deliberately posed his model with her veil pulled back and her arms exposed.

or an 'Arab peasant'. Large studios like that of Bonfils in Beirut sometimes used the same models and costumes to represent different 'types'. For example, a woman who appears in one Bonfils photograph as 'an Armenian woman of Jerusalem' appeared in a later photograph in the series in the same costume, but this time carrying a fan, as 'an Egyptian woman'.

Many of these photographs of women's costumes, whether taken in or outside the studio, were not only of dubious accuracy but tended to treat the people wearing them as little more than tailor's dummies on which to hang beautiful and exotic clothes and jewellery, and quaintly shaped headgear. The women seen in these photographs rarely seem to *live* in their clothes.

Yet these costumes did have very real significance in the lives of their wearers. They provided an indication of a person's community and status, and played important symbolic roles in daily life. To take just one example, the elaborately embroidered dresses worn by peasant women from certain parts of Palestine would instantly identify the region, and even the village they came from. There was a range of dresses for different occasions, the most important of which was marriage. For months and even years before her marriage, a young girl would spend her spare time embroidering items for her trousseau, usually in the company of other women. Songs like this one, from the village of Beit Dajan near Jaffa, sung by women friends of the bride (Halimeh) on the night before her wedding (the henna night), refer to the making of these clothes:

5 *'Type de jeune femme de Bethléem'* – Type of Young Woman of Bethlehem. 1870s–1880s.

The beautiful clothes of Bethlehem women are seen here in their most elaborate form, as they would be worn in a bridal costume, with elaborate embroidery on the breast panel and jacket, and the headdress of coins. But although women usually learned embroidery designs from their mothers, thus perpetuating long-used patterns, new elements also crept in. In a town like Bethlehem, by the late nineteenth century exposed to a good deal of foreign influence through the presence of missionaries and the tourist trade, new motifs gradually began to appear in embroidery as women incorporated floral and other patterns from fabrics or objects imported from the West. Among photographers the Bethlehem costume remained one of the most popular in the region. This photograph is one of a series of prints produced by the earliest process for colour printing, known as Photochrome.

for a long time have we embroidered the side panels,
remember Halimeh when we were friends,
for a long time have we embroidered the breast panels,
remember Halimeh when we were girls,
what did you wear little gazelle on your henna night?
they clothed me in silk coats, the clothes of kings![1]

To the trousseau would be added gifts from the future
husband, who would provide a stipulated number of dresses
of a particular type and design. Sometimes the bride's
maternal uncle would also give a gift of dresses, symbolic of
his lifelong obligation to protect his sister's children. In the
course of the wedding celebrations each of these dresses
would have its particular symbolism.

The bride's father would also buy her jewellery as part of
her trousseau. This often appears in photographs as a
spectacular form of decoration: silver necklaces, bangles and
coins on headdresses; but it was also an important economic
asset. It was a woman's own property and if she fell upon
hard times or her family was in financial difficulties, she
might, reluctantly, sell some of the coins sewn into her
headdress. In the late nineteenth century, Maria Theresa
dollars were the most popular coins with which to decorate
headdresses. At this time Ottoman currency was constantly
being devalued, while the Maria Theresa dollar, the Western
currency most widely used in the Arab provinces of the
Empire, held its value. It was known in Palestinian dialect as
Abu Risheh (the father of feathers) because of the outspread
eagle's wings on the back of the coin.

On the whole, Western photographs of costume, like
paintings of the same era, tended to lend it an archaic,
timeless quality. While it is undoubtedly true that dress was
important in defining a person's identity and status, this was
not, as these images often suggested, a definition based on
some unalterable natural order. Yet Westerners were not the
only ones to interpret these visual divisions of society as a
sign of social stability, or even stagnation. For the Ottoman
establishment, for instance, the maintenance of such visible
boundaries and definitions – between classes, sexes and
religious groups – was an important aspect of maintaining
social order and control.

In 1873, the Turkish painter, Osman Hamdy Bey, helped
to compile a catalogue of costumes of the Ottoman Empire
for the Universal Exposition in Vienna. He employed Pascal
Sébah, a photographer resident in Istanbul, to create a
uniform set of photographs of costumes by class and region.
The costumes were worn by models, male and female, who
were posed against plain studio backdrops. The resulting
photographs have more pretensions to accuracy of detail
than the average Western studio photograph, and in the
catalogue each plate is accompanied by a detailed commentary on the costumes.

6 'Young Girl in Huraidha
(Hadramaut, Yemen) in
Traditional Dress'. Freya Stark,
1938.

Freya Stark was greatly taken with
the beauty of Yemen and its
traditions, and took a large
number of photographs on her
travels there. In this and other
photographs she celebrates what
she saw as a changeless and almost
magical world entirely remote
from her own. She wrote: 'These
pictures hope only to keep the
remembrance of something very
complete, very ancient, very
remote and very beautiful, which
may pass for ever from our world.'
She obviously regarded such
traditional costumes as part of this
remembrance, but at the same
time she took a lively interest in
the way Yemeni women lived. She
also regarded concern for clothes
as something specific to women
and a useful bond of common
interest among women across
cultures.[2]

7 *'Types of Jewess. The Veiled Girl is Betrothed'. British Army photographer, Baghdad, 1917.*

It was not only commercial photographers who took pictures of 'types' categorized by religious or ethnic community, and identified according to their costumes. This is one of a series of photographs by this photographer showing 'types' of Iraqi women: Muslim, Jewish and Christian of various classes, mostly taken in the street rather than the studio. This photograph shows the distinctive costume worn by middle-class Jewish women in Baghdad, including the *hailiyi*, the hemp-stuffed, visor-like 'veil' worn by the woman in the centre of the picture. It was only later, in about the 1930s, that Jewish women began to dress in a style more akin to that of urban Muslim women. In both cases, of course, the well-to-do also began to wear Western clothes at home.[3]

Hamdy Bey's evident intention was to explain to a Western audience the nuances of Ottoman dress, but his commentary also strongly reflected a concern with social order, interpreting the clear division of people according to their appearance as the positive embodiment of a confident and orderly culture. In his introduction, he distinguished between 'costume' and 'clothing' (*vêtement*). Both, he said, had an object in common, to clothe the body, but while clothing was subject to constant change according to the vagaries of fashion, costume was generally constant and invariable, with only small changes and variations in ornament and fabrics. He further argued that clothing tended to create a universal uniformity, wiping out differences between classes and national groups. This, he implied, was the trend in the West, which he compared unfavourably with the adherence to 'costume' which typified the Ottoman Empire:

> There is no better way to understand the superiority of costume over clothing than by glancing through our collection of Turkish folk costumes . . .
>
> Thus it will be seen that costume fits perfectly the rational definition of what is good and beautiful, in the same way as does 'diversity within unity'. Neither of these terms can be applied to clothing, however, since, during the brief lifespan of each fashion, clothing allows for no variety; it is coldly, rigidly uniform . . .
>
> It is perhaps to no small extent due to the modern invention of clothing that European society must attribute . . . a previously unknown moral deformity – a new word has even had to be coined for it – *déclassé*.[2]

With the benefit of hindsight, there is a certain irony in Hamdy Bey's somewhat idiosyncratic defence of the Ottoman social order and its adherence to the principles of 'costume'. The 1870s, when the catalogue was published,

8 *Plate XXXIII from Hamdy Bey's catalogue* Les Costumes populaires de la Turquie en 1873
Figure 1 (right): Peasant woman from the Damascus area
Figure 2 (centre): Druze woman from the Damascus area
Figure 3 (left): Woman of Damascus

On the left (*Figure 3*) is a well-to-do lady of Damascus in indoor dress (and therefore unveiled). Her overdress and pantaloons were made of the striped satin material which was the speciality of the Damascus textile industry. The high sandals worn in the house and in the *hamam* (baths) were made of sandalwood or ebony inlaid with mother-of-pearl. In the centre is a Druze woman (*Figure 2*), wearing a *tantur* of rather smaller proportions than that worn in Lebanon at this time. She would also have veiled when outside her home. Hamdy Bey comments on the unusual richness of costume and jewellery of the peasant woman on the right (*Figure 1*), ascribing it to the affluence of many cultivators in the region around Damascus.

marked the beginning of a period of change in the Middle East which brought into question both that social order and the dress which reflected it.

The assumption made both by Western observers and Hamdy Bey that 'traditional' costume represented fixed and unchanging norms over the course of centuries has been challenged by the few serious studies which have been done on the history of costume in the region. Jeanne Jouin, who wrote on aspects of the history of women's costume in the Middle East and photographed dress styles in the 1920s and 1930s, suggested that costume had been slowly but constantly changing, adapting to new economic conditions and imitating styles from other regions. She took as an example the evolution of women's dress in Nazareth and the Galilee region of Palestine.

It was about 1760 that the women of Nazareth began to attract attention. They wear red and white striped blouses with red embroidery, and they cover their heads with a sort of flat bonnet made of several layers of Turkish tulle and long strips of red silk. This daring way of dressing was merely a prelude to the adoption of the Levantine fashions which were slowly to spread throughout the Galilee . . .

[but] today, the women of Nazareth conform to city customs. The country women have remained faithful to their long trousers and the *qombaz*, but the sequinned bonnet has disappeared, to be replaced by two small headscarves.[3]

In Turkey, Egypt, Syria and Palestine, the most marked changes in styles of women's dress were to be seen in those urban areas most affected by Western economic influence. By the early twentieth century, the upper classes in these cities were looking to Paris for their fashions. But as Jouin points out, among the well-to-do, the following of metropolitan fashions was nothing new: the focus had simply changed. 'Before they followed Paris fashions, the ladies of Syria and Palestine had followed those of Constantinople.' Fashion magazines, with drawings and, later, photographs of the most up-to-the-minute styles, began to circulate in affluent homes, and were copied by dressmakers. The wealthy paid visits to Europe where they bought clothes, and in large cities such as Cairo, Alexandria and Istanbul, department stores and dress shops opened, first to serve the European

Nummer 24.   Seite 1079.

Des Khediven Cousine in Monte Carlo:
Prinzessin Mohamed Ibrahim, die Tochter Ismail Paschas.

9 *'The Khedive's Cousin in Monte Carlo. Princess Muhammad Ibrahim, Daughter of Ismail Pasha'. Published in* Die Woche, *Berlin, 11 June 1904.*

The caption seems to be in error in describing this woman as Khedive Ismail's daughter. She was probably one of his granddaughters, Saliha, daughter of Ibrahim Hilmi Pasha and cousin to Khedive Abbas II who ruled Egypt from 1892–1914.
In 1903, a year before this picture was published, she married Prince Muhammad Ibrahim, a man who liked high living and travel, and was killed in a car crash in 1909. In common with other members of the Egyptian royal family and aristocracy at this time, the couple would certainly have spent time in fashionable resorts such as Monte Carlo, for which the Princess here dresses the part of the chic European lady.

community, then increasingly, the local elites.

Western fashions were generally adopted first among those groups which had most contact with Europeans, particularly urban Christian and Jewish elites. But it was not long before other well-to-do women followed suit. In such circles, dress *à la Franka* had become so much the norm by the 1930s that many younger women could remember little of previous styles. According to Jouin: 'Ask the women of Damascus, Aleppo or Jerusalem how their grandmothers dressed before the introduction of *Franka* [Western] fashions, and they will tell you they have no idea. The women of these families, in particular, have long been preoccupied with Paris fashions.'[4]

Until the 1920s and 1930s, however, much of this change was invisible to Westerners because the Paris styles were worn as indoor dress which was enveloped in a cloak and veil out of doors. In the photographic record only family albums reveal these changed appearances, though they were also commented upon by Western women who visited affluent harems. But on the whole, the dual vision of veiled women and picturesque 'folk' costumes continued to prevail in the West.

By comparison with the urban elites, changes in costume among most other sections of Middle Eastern society occurred more slowly and in a rather less dramatic fashion. Economic conditions, particularly the growth of Western textile imports, accounted for many of the changes which did occur. The impact of Western textiles on local markets varied very much from area to area, but certainly the import of large quantities of English and American cotton cloth from the mid-nineteenth century, especially in Egypt and the Ottoman Arab provinces, challenged locally produced cotton fabrics (see p. 157). Louis Lortet, for example, writing in the 1880s, noted that in the *souks* of Damascus, such cottons were cheap and readily available.

By the early twentieth century, photographs begin to indicate the incorporation of these fabrics into local forms of dress, even outside the main towns. Photographs of peasant women in areas close to the main cities show them wearing combinations of old and new garments: for instance, a 'traditional' embroidered or appliquéd overdress with a Western-style flowered cotton shift underneath. New materials and artificially dyed thread also began gradually to alter the appearance of 'traditional' peasant costumes. By the 1920s and 1930s, in parts of Palestine where embroidery was a highly evolved art, women began to incorporate in their designs motifs such as floral decoration quite different from the older, more geometric and stylized patterns.

This process of change was not, however, a straightforward progression from the use of local, traditional fabrics

10 'Aristocratic Court Women'.
Iran, c.1870s.

This costume – chemisette,
waistcoat, short skirt or culotte
with tights or socks – appears in
many late-nineteenth-century
photographs as the typical dress of
upper-class Iranian women. In
fact, the well-developed Persian
court tradition of figurative
painting demonstrates that until
the 1860s such women generally
wore ankle-length flared skirts or
pantaloons.

In this photograph, the women's
chemisettes are covered with a
waistcoat and stole, but some
Westerners remarked with
surprise that despite the strictures
on the modesty of women, it was
common for this garment to be
virtually transparent, revealing the
wearer's breasts. Ella Sykes, who
travelled in Iran in the late
nineteenth century, interpreted
this as a question of men's control
over women's visibility.
'Europeans cannot understand
why Persians consider a lady's
décolleté dress immodest, when
the costume of their own women
leaves so little to the imagination.
But the reason is that no male
eyes, save those of her husband
and relatives, ever rested on a
Persian lady's charms.'[4]

and styles to Western ones. Despite the threat posed by the flood of Western imports, some parts of the local textile industry showed remarkable resilience, seeking new markets and expanding old ones. For example, in Syria, the locally made silk fabrics used in the dresses of upper-class women retained their popularity until the early twentieth century when Western-style clothes became fashionable. At the cheaper end of the market, local cotton cloth in Syria, Palestine and Egypt retained a corner of the market until perhaps the 1930s. For example, in Damascus at the turn of the century, many women returned to purchasing local cloth for their long head veils in preference to English calico.[5]

But imported fashions and fabrics were not the only factors which affected the way women looked. From time to time, rulers, state and religious officials took a hand in regulating women's dress. Interference in this apparently personal matter reflected the view that the appearance of women was directly linked to the probity of their behaviour in public, a matter of honour for both the family and the state.

The degree to which this interference occurred varied from region to region. In most rural areas and more isolated small towns this regulation of women's appearance was left largely to family, the pressures of social convention and, perhaps, the religious authorities of the community concerned (see p. 133).

In nineteenth-century Iran, not only were such social and religious pressures exerted upon women, but the ruler of the country for the second half of the century, Nasir ed-Din Shah, imposed his own idiosyncratic ideas about women's dress on members of his harem, his court and sections of upper-class society. This somewhat bizarre costume is said by several sources to have originated in the Shah's fascination with the dresses of ballerinas whom he had seen performing in theatres during a visit to Europe. According to Wilfred

Sparroy, who was tutor to the children of the Iranian royal family during Nasir ed-Din's reign, on seeing these ballerinas 'he [the Shah] resolved there and then that their light fantastic dress should be thenceforward the only wear in his harem'. The photographs taken of the royal harem by Nasir ed-Din himself and others bear witness to the fact that he carried out his plan.[6]

How widely this costume was adopted in upper-class circles and what pressure there was to do so is less clear. Sparroy asserted that

> this irrational costume, thanks to the conservative
> principles of the race, is far from being so fashionable
> outside the court as European travellers would have us
> believe. A gentleman about the palace of Zill's-Sultan, to
> whom I had appealed on the vexed question of women's
> dress, tossed aside the photographs I showed him saying:
> 'There are two classes of Persian women who wear that
> unseemly European attire: those who can afford to lose
> their decency, and those who do not even know they have
> any decency to lose . . .'

For all this gentleman's disgusted dismissals, it does seem that some well-to-do women outside the court did adapt to the new fashion. Three Western women travellers of the late nineteenth century, Jane Dieulafoy, Isabella Bird and Ella Sykes who visited women in the harems of provincial officials, found them to be wearing this type of costume. Isabella Bird, giving another gloss on the semantics of costume, described the 'ballet' outfit of the wife of an Isfahan official as 'startling' in effect, 'a costume which is dress, not clothing'.[7]

While Nasir ed-Din Shah adapted Western clothing for Iranian women, to satisfy his own whims, the Ottoman authorities took a much broader interest in the regulation of women's dress. From the earliest days of the Ottoman Empire, the state had taken it upon itself to issue decrees and edicts on even the minutiae of women's dress. These rules had most impact on those living in the large cities of Turkey, where the state's influence was greatest. In the provinces of the empire the authorities were rarely in a position to impose such rules, except when they had a compliant local surrogate. The detailed nature of these regulations, affecting the thickness of the material used in the *yashmak* (face veil worn in Turkey), the length of skirts, and the degree to which women should be covered in public by *charchaf* (cloak) and *yashmak*, indicate the importance the authorities attached to the physical appearance of women in public.[8]

Minority communities in Turkey were also subject to these state pressures, and so-called 'traditional' costumes of the kind referred to by Hamdy Bey were in fact closely regulated by the state. Lucy Garnett in her book *The Women of Turkey*

11 'Twelve Years Ago these Faces would have been Veiled'. Kurt and Margot Lubinski, published with an article entitled 'The Transformation of Turkey' in the National Geographic Magazine, January 1939.

This photograph, probably taken at a public parade, is intended to show the variety of women's dress in urban Turkey at this time. Only a few of the women are reacting to the camera, the rest seem preoccupied with events going on behind the photographer. The caption comments that not only are the new styles of dress a sign of 'modern' sophistication, but so too is the acceptance of photography. The visibility of women in public had become an accepted fact. 'One more old-fashioned woman shields herself with her handbag, and warns a friend. Beside her, in a modish black turban and headshawl, is a younger woman to whom the camera is a matter-of-fact feature of parades and life.'

gives an example of this. During the vizirate of Reşid Pasha, the Chief Rabbi of Constantinople, on one of his periodic official visits to the Porte, received an intimation that the minister would like to see a reform of the distinctive headgear worn by the Jewish women of the city. This was the *chalebi*, a very tall padded headdress, enfolded in a shawl or scarf. Accordingly the abolition of the *chalebi* was announced in the city's synagogues, much to the distress of many women in the community.[9]

Official concern over women's dress did not disappear with the more liberal atmosphere of the period after the 1908 revolution in Turkey. Its symbolic importance in defining the status of women remained. But whereas during the Ottoman period this concern had been expressed in a conservative view of how women should be seen, in subsequent decades it became a device through which the state could signal its desire for change.

During World War I, when larger numbers of urban women began to go out to work, there was some debate in official circles as to whether their appearance should be allowed to change. As women began to discard the full veil and wear Western-style clothes in public, the authorities were thrown into a state of almost comic confusion over whether they should be allowed to dress this way.

In September 1917, the following announcement was publicly posted in Istanbul by the police: 'In the last few months shameful fashions are being seen in the streets of the capital. All Muslim women are called upon to lengthen their skirts, refrain from wearing corsets and wear a thick *charchaf*. A maximum of two days is allowed to abide by the orders of this proclamation.' This announcement met with a storm of protest, and more senior officials quickly retracted the order. A new announcement appeared: 'The General Directorate regrets that old and retrograde women were able to induce a subaltern employee to publicize an announcement ordering Muslim women to go back to the old fashions. We announce that the previous orders are null and void.' It is noticeable that the blame for these 'retrograde' attitudes is laid at the door of women, not men.[10]

In many cities of the Middle East, the decades after World War I saw some relaxation in the norms governing women's dress in public. In most cases this process was not formalized, and depended mostly on changes in fashion; on male ideas about what were respectable forms of dress for women; and on the efforts of women themselves to change these ideas. But in Turkey and Iran, the state once again took a direct role in determining changes in women's public appearance.

If the Ottoman authorities had usually played the role of guardian of conservative morality, the Turkish republican government sought a new, mobilizing role. Visual images, including photography, were used along with other forms of propaganda to encourage women to adopt new fashions. The veil was abandoned, though not formally banned, and Western-style clothes became the norm among city dwellers. The new fashions took much longer to penetrate to remoter rural areas, since they were mostly too expensive and not easily available. There was also resistance to adopting these new forms of dress from more conservative elements.

But the speed of change in Turkish cities was remarked in *11* other parts of the Middle East. An article in the Egyptian Feminist Union's magazine *l'Egyptienne* of 1 September 1925 was already commenting on the sharp change in public attitudes towards women's appearance in Turkey: 'In Turkey today a strong antipathy is evident against the practice of veiling among women. Turkish public opinion is so hostile to this outmoded form of dress that in the cities a veiled woman has become an object of both curiosity and criticism among passers-by.'[11]

Meanwhile in Iran, attempts by Reza Shah to follow the same path of reform met with less lasting success. In January 1936 Reza Shah's wife and daughters appeared unveiled in public for the first time when they accompanied him to a graduation ceremony for male and female pupils of the *danesh-serai* (primary school teachers' training college) in Tehran. This signalled the Shah's approval of unveiling, but

12 *'Teheran Emerges from Its Medieval Languor: Iran's Modern Capital Thrives under the Enlightened Policy of Reza Shah'. Published in* The Sphere, *25 September 1937.*

This photograph was taken only a year or so after the Shah initiated and enforced the abolition of the veil. The modernity of dress is directly equated with the new-found 'modernity' of the Iranian state and society. The rest of the caption stresses the relegation of 'the old Persia' to a 'fragrant memory' while the new Iran is 'a land of enlightenment' embodied in the 'modern' Western clothes seen in this street scene.

13 'Turkish Girls under the Republic'. From an album published by the Turkish Government Information Office, 1930–40.

The Republican government in Turkey laid stress on organized physical activity for women and frequently published photographs which extolled this kind of well-ordered exercise. This also helped to legitimize a form of dress which would not otherwise have been socially acceptable in public for girls of this age.

once this signal had been given, the authorities enforced it in a much more heavy-handed and authoritarian way than had been seen in Turkey.

For women who were endeavouring to lead an active life, working or studying, this policy was doubtless welcome, but for many women who still lived in a secluded milieu, the change came as an unwelcome shock for which they were not prepared, arousing great opposition. Thus when Reza Shah left the country in 1941, the combination of male conservatism, hostility to the regime and the sense of social unease experienced by many women brought the return of veiling and former styles of dress in some sections of society.[12]

In areas where there were official efforts to promote changes in women's role and appearance, photographs were used to create a new image of women as active participants in public life, rather than as passive and secluded. They also played a part in reinforcing the legitimacy of new forms of dress. Illustrations in magazines such as that of the Iranian Ministry of Education (*Taalim o Tarbiyat*) in the 1930s used photographs to stress the importance of sports and gymnastics in girls' schools, clearly activities which required clothes quite unlike those customarily worn by young women.

The promotion of the scout and guide movement in a number of Middle Eastern countries also presented a new image of female activity and dress. Both sexes wore uniforms similar to those worn by scouts and guides in the West. In Egypt, the Ministry of Education published a manual for girl guides in 1934 entitled *al-Fatayat al-Zahrat* (literally, blossoming young girls) in which the photographs portrayed neat, competent-looking guides presented in very much the same way as their Western counterparts.

People in the Middle East were conscious of the meanings of these changes in women's appearance, and certainly ascribed to them more importance than that given to equivalent changes in male dress. Westerners also regarded

14 Cartoon by 'Sayyah' in the weekly magazine Ettelaat, *1322 (1942/3).*

It was published at the time when the *chador* was being reintroduced after the exile of Reza Shah and the caption reads sarcastically: 'Dear women of Iran, whatever you have learnt from the enlightened women of the world, you can put into practice even inside the *chador*.' The pictures illustrate women wearing the *chador* and in various 'modern' pursuits: as a girl guide, playing tennis, horse-riding, skiing, dancing and swimming.

them as significant, though from a rather different perspective. For the new breed of Western photo-journalists, the sight of women in the street in Ankara, Cairo or Tehran wearing frocks and hats was considered newsworthy. In 1925 the London illustrated magazine *The Sphere* published a number of photographs showing recent changes in male and female headgear in Turkey under the title 'Changing ideas in Turkey'. The caption describes the reforms which did away with the fez (*tarboush*) and the relaxation of the rules on women's dress. It concludes, 'Since Mustafa Kemal Pasha [Atatürk] decided to allow Turkish women to follow the lead of their European sisters in matters of dress, thousands have discarded the veil and taken to wearing Paris creations. The rare beauty of the Turkish woman, which until now has been merely a tradition, is now verified.'[13] The three head-and-shoulders portraits show women wearing stylish variations of the turban or scarf.

Other Western observers seemed less certain whether they preferred the 'new woman' to the older images. Mystery unveiled could also smack of banality. In 1939 the *National Geographic Magazine* in an article on Turkey printed a very contrived photograph of a woman wearing a kind of 'harem' costume posing with a water jar. The caption sounded a certain note of nostalgia. Such 'gold-braided "local colour"', it said, 'will soon be a memory beside the Bosporus. Visitors buy such glittering costumes for fancy-dress balls, picturing harem life *à la* Arabian Nights. Turkey's women have turned from Turkish trousers to ski pants, sports shorts and backless bathing-suits – from the seclusion of the Seraglio and haremlik to a full share in world life.'[14]

Among Westerners who approved of these changes, modernity of dress was often taken to mean that the women who wore 'modern' clothes had automatically become 'just like Western women'. But although style of dress had considerable importance as an indicator both of people's self-image and of their aspirations, it did not necessarily translate simply into a desire to be 'westernized'. Its meaning also varied from one situation to another. Where women had taken it upon themselves to change their style of dress it might be taken as an assertion of freedom, a defiance of convention, or a flouting of family authority. But where the wearing of a Western-style dress and hat had been sanctioned by community or state, it could just as well imply conformity and was certainly not a reliable guide to a woman's freedom of choice or action.

In an era of rapid change the meaning of particular forms of dress could also vary from one social class to another, and from region to region. In Turkey in 1890, the wearer of a *yashmak* and a *charchaf* would have been assumed to come from a well-to-do elite family. In 1930, a woman from that class would have been recognizable by the fashionable cut of her dress and coat or suit.

Yet in other areas, Western styles were not always

15 *An Egyptian teacher dressed in Guides' uniform, Cairo 1930s/ 1940s.*

indicative of the highest social class. Jeanne Jouin, examining styles of wedding dresses in North Africa in the 1920s, found that although in some cities the elite had taken to wearing Western-style white wedding dresses, in Algiers, the aristocracy at this time still retained the rich velvet wedding gowns embroidered with gold thread. White wedding dresses were worn by sections of the bourgeoisie which could not aspire to such finery.[15]

Modes of dress outside the main cities remained very much affected by ideas about social status and the probity of women, and it seems that male members of the community played a leading role in deciding the rules. In some parts of Syria veiling of women remained closely associated with social status. In the 1930s, informants from the towns in the interior of the country, Palmyra, Deir az-Zor and Dera'a, told Kazem Daghestani that they could remember the time when veiling of women had not been customary: 'Rich people among us began imposing the veil on their women who did not need to work in the fields or outside the house,' said a shaikh from Palmyra. An informant from the Hauran said that it was Damascene women married to Hauranis or the wives of Ottoman officials who had started this trend in Dera'a.[16]

In village society, the appearance of new fashions in women's dress might mean that the family concerned had made money or moved up the social ladder, but it seems that if it was women who took the initiative to change their appearance, it could be interpreted by men as a challenge to their authority. One example of such an incident was given by Ammar in his study of a village in Upper Egypt at the beginning of the 1950s. The men, who often travelled outside the village, had altered both their language and dress, while the women, who travelled little, had not been much affected by city ways in either respect. But it seems that the men were sensitive even to minor innovations which appeared in women's dress. On one occasion, Ammar wrote 'there was a commotion in the village over the spread of city headgear among the women. This led to their nightly itinerary to the Nile to fill their water jars being stopped for a while because the men complained that the women made it an occasion for displaying their colourful headgear.'[17]

A woman from Yatta, a small and fairly isolated village in the Hebron district of Palestine, recalls that when she was young in the 1930s, ideas of modesty in women's dress were quite different from those which prevail today. Her view of the past may be somewhat idealized, but it does suggest that the relationship between women's dress and concepts of their moral probity is not fixed or static. Attitudes to 'modesty' in dress seem to have altered only when more outsiders began to come to the village.

We never wore an underdress or long-sleeved undershirt like people do now, just our *thob* [overdress] and nothing underneath. Those old dresses had big, wide long sleeves; you tied them up on top of your head and carried your shopping in them, and walked along or worked with your arms bare. We didn't think about it being immodest. This idea of shame is a modern thing. We all knew each other, no strangers ever came to the village, why should we be ashamed? We lived among our family, men and women working together and sleeping together. There were no moral problems. Nobody looked at anyone else with the eye of sex like they do today. We were too few and too busy.[18]

Thus in an era of quite rapid social change, neither social status nor the degree of personal freedom allowed to women could simply be read off from visual evidence without taking into account a range of social, economic and political factors which may not always be clear from the photographic record. In this context, there was another unseen consideration which particularly affected those parts of the Middle East which came under direct colonial rule: the symbolic but often ambivalent role which modes of dress came to play in anti-colonial nationalist struggles. To understand some of the assumptions which underlay this symbolic aspect of the struggle, one needs to examine first how Westerners viewed the significance of the veil, which lay at the centre of this debate.

Western Images of Veiling and Exposure

No single item of clothing has had more influence on Western images of Middle Eastern women than the veil. This covering of the face was taken to symbolize Islam's special form of patriarchal subordination of women, despite the fact that veiling had been practised to various degrees in a number of other cultures: in pre-Islamic Arabia, as well as in ancient Assyria, Greece and Byzantium. Veiling was also practised in some Jewish and Christian communities living in countries where Islam was the dominant religion. Like seclusion, veiling – which could be described as a portable form of seclusion – was largely an urban phenomenon. It was not generally practised in peasant societies, and only among some bedouin tribes.[19]

The majority of Westerners, however, took little account of social nuances in the practice of veiling. They were simply fascinated or shocked by the sight of veiled women in city streets, visible yet invisible. For Western men in particular, the veil presented a challenge to the imagination. Writers, artists and photographers dwelt on the 'mysteries' which lay behind this piece of cloth. In his travel narrative *Voyage en Orient*, Gérard de Nerval began by expatiating on these excitements:

Ladies of distinction veil their forms beneath a *habbarah*

16a (above), b (opposite) Two photographs from a series taken by the French neuro-psychiatrist G.G. de Clérambault of the technique of donning the haik (the voluminous cloak and veil worn by women in Morocco and Algeria). Fez, Morocco, 1917.

During World War I, de Clérambault was sent to Morocco to recuperate from a battle injury, and while he was in Fez during 1917 he took a large number of photographs of the process of veiling, with models posing to show every stage of donning the *haik* to the final point of total concealment. De Clérambault seems to have shared the fascination with things 'Oriental' common enough in France at that time, but added to this was his intense interest in the subject of the relationship beween women and clothing.

He had conducted case studies in

of light silk, and women of the people wear a simple tunic of wool or cotton (*khamiss*) with all the grace of an ancient statue. There is scope for the imagination in this disguise, and it does not extend to all their charms. Beautiful hands adorned with talismanic rings, and silver bracelets; sometimes alabaster-like arms escaping from the broad sleeves pulled back over the shoulder [probably in order to work]; bare feet, laden with rings, which leave their slippers at every step – all these we may admire, divine, surprise, without annoying the crowd, or causing any embarrassment to the woman herself. Sometimes, the folds of the veil, with its blue and white check, which covers the head and shoulders, may get slightly out of position, and the light, passing between it and the long mask which they call the *borghot* [or *burqu*] gives us a glimpse of a charming brow over which brown hair falls in closely bound ringlets, like those we have seen in busts of Cleopatra; or a tiny, well-shaped ear, from which clusters of golden sequins, or a jewel of turquoise and silver filigree, dangle over the cheeks and neck. It is then we feel impelled to ask a question of the veiled Egyptian's eyes, and that is the moment of greatest danger . . . it would be impossible for a woman to make more of that small part of her person which she is permitted to show.[20]

For the photographer directing his camera on the veiled women, the gaze he received in return could be disturbing as well as seductive. Malek Alloula, writing of the commercial photographs of women which appeared on postcards of colonial Algeria suggests that:

These veiled women are not only an embarrassing enigma to the photographer but an outright attack on him. It must be believed that the feminine gaze that filters through the veil is a gaze of a particular kind: concentrated by the tiny orifice made for the eye, this womanly gaze is a little like the eye of the camera, like the photographic lens that takes aim at everything.[21]

Frustrated in the city streets, the photographer might turn to less concealed subjects, for instance, peasant and bedouin women who did not usually veil and who, when they were working or feeding their children, often had few inhibitions about exposing legs, arms and breasts. Westerners found this habit puzzling but eminently photogenic. Another way to break the taboo of the veil was to go back to the studio where the photographer, using models, had the power to decide what should be exposed and what covered.

Marina Warner has suggested that there are four approaches to the portrayal of the female nude in Western art: the nude as an erotic symbol, usually associated with sin, danger, corruption and death; as the symbol of spiritual innocence; as a symbol of asceticism, the stripping away of

France of women he found to be sexually aroused and obsessed by the touch and feel of fabrics, especially silk. He published two articles in 1908 and 1910 under the title 'Passion érotique des étoffes chez la femme'.

His Moroccan photographs, which seem to be an extension of this fascination into another realm and another culture, certainly have a marked feeling of eroticism, not only in the poses but in the way the fabrics are presented in relation to the women's bodies. The gradual concealment of the woman's face and figure under the white drapes and folds seems never to forget the body beneath, producing imagery just as erotic in intention as that of the gradual stripping away of clothes.[5]

135

States of Undress

*17 'Fellahmädchen, nacht' –
peasant girl, naked. [?Egypt]
Printed in an unknown German
publication, 1908.*

Just as the juxtaposition of veiled
face and naked breasts in the
previous picture gives it a violent
quality, so here the fact that the
woman still wears a head covering
makes her total nakedness more
stark.

17

18

136

18 *'Scenes and Types – Arabian Woman with the Yashmak'. Probably Nuredin & Levin, Cairo. Postcard, late nineteenth century.*

A number of commercial photographs were taken playing on this theme of concealment and exposure. It was a logical extension of a common Western observation that women from the popular classes in Egypt often appeared more concerned to conceal their faces than their breasts. Yet the starkness of this image suggests a form of violence, in the power of the photographer to lay bare parts of this woman's body at will. The caption also strays very far from accuracy. This type of face veil, the *burqu*, was characteristic of Egypt, not Arabia. It is certainly not a *yashmak*, which was the Turkish style of veil, shown in Caption 2.[6]

19 *'Sudanese Woman, Fully Dressed'. Late nineteenth/early twentieth century.*

This studio photograph makes a rather different point about the exposure of a woman's body. Semi-nakedness is, it is implied, for such women the norm, something Westerners usually identified with what were described as 'primitive' cultures.

20 *'From Veiled Women to Life Classes with Nude Models'. Turkey, published in* National Geographic Magazine, *January 1939.*

This photograph and its caption link the idea of unveiling with the novelty of this 'life class' at the Academy of Art in Istanbul. The nude model is not shown, only the various images of her painted or drawn by the students. Implicit is the sharp contrast between the exposure of the model – which, the caption says, would still shock 'Turkey's farmers' but not these women students – and the image of the veiled woman symbolizing Turkey's past. The caption also contrasts this figurative art with the largely abstract art of Islam. This is a striking example of how Westerners perceived the 'novelties' of modernism in countries like Turkey and Iran through a simplistic juxtaposition of images, with the culture of the past assumed to have faded away without trace.

137

material trapping and spare flesh; and *nuda naturalis*, the nude representing the primal state of humanity.[22]

Certainly most of the photographs of nude or semi-nude women taken in the Middle East in the nineteenth century stand within the first tradition. But the eroticism and danger which this genre aims to convey does not depend on the simple act of stripping off clothes, but rather on the juxtaposition of clothed and unclothed parts of the body, with the veil or headcovering often remaining as a motif. Above all, these photographs are assertions of sexual and cultural power, exposing, selectively and at will, parts of women's bodies, sometimes with an almost tangible sense of violence. The frequent suggestion of sexual danger in the semi-nude figure of the odalisque is, however, not accompanied by quite the same connotations of sin as can be found in comparable images of the seductress in the West. These photographs, like many Orientalist paintings, are a transgression not of Western morality but of the rules and taboos of another culture, viewed as inferior to that of Europe.

The Politics of Dress: Nationalism and Feminism

The question of whether or not the veil should be worn also became a symbolic issue among advocates of change in the status of Middle Eastern women. These included some missionaries and colonial officials, as well as both Western and indigenous feminists. One of the questions which underlay the debate was whether the veil was to be viewed as a symbol of male oppression of women, or a crucial part of indigenous culture which was threatened by Westerners' attempts to strip it away. Thus campaigns by Westerners to abolish the veil encountered resistance because they challenged indigenous cultures. But the issue was clouded by another consideration – that the removal of the veil could appear as a challenge to indigenous men's control over the sexual and social lives of women. Resistance to such cultural change on the part of nationalist movements could therefore create a very ambivalent situation for women who, while they might support nationalist goals, also sought emancipation and removal of the veil.

In Algeria, where the Orientalist image of the veiled seductress had been developed from the beginning of the French occupation for the benefit of soldiers, colonists and tourists, the struggle over the social and political implications of the veil was sharpest. From the 1930s until the 1950s, the French made concerted efforts to engineer a variety of social changes in Algerian society, including the abolition of the veil. These efforts reinforced the growing nationalist movement in its belief that this was an attempt to sabotage and destroy the remaining cohesion of Algerian society, already undermined by colonial economic and settlement policies. The veil in this period therefore became a symbol of the continuity of national culture, a view forcefully expressed by

Frantz Fanon, who combines the metaphors of cultural and sexual violence in his condemnation of French colonial policy:

> The occupying forces, in applying their maximum psychological attention to the veil worn by Algerian women, were obviously bound to achieve some results. Here and there it thus happened that a woman was 'saved' and symbolically unveiled.
>
> These test-women, with bare faces and free bodies, henceforth circulated like sound currency in the European society of Algeria. These women were surrounded by an atmosphere of newness. The Europeans, over-excited and wholly given over to their victory, carried away in a kind of trance, would speak of the psychological phenomenon of conversion. And in fact, in the European society, the agents of this conversion were held in esteem. They were envied. The benevolent attention of the administration was drawn to them.
>
> After each success, the authorities were strengthened in their conviction that the Algerian woman would support Western penetration into the native society. Every rejected veil disclosed to the eyes of the colonialists horizons until then forbidden, and revealed to them, piece by piece, the flesh of Algeria laid bare.[23]

Fanon added, however, that if unveiling had been a tool in the hands of the colonial power, the veil later became a weapon for the oppressed – 'hiding a face is also disguising a secret' – as in the years of the liberation struggle in the 1950s and 1960s women became couriers for the resistance, using the voluminous *haik* (enveloping cloak worn by Algerian women) to conceal messages, guns and bombs.

Elsewhere in the region, the veil did not acquire quite such powerful connotations in nationalist movements as a symbol of defence against colonial efforts to undermine indigenous culture. In some cases, male nationalists advocated reforms of women's status, including the abolition of the veil. But everywhere there were also conservatives, nationalist or not, who were violently opposed to any such changes.

The knowledge that there was strong opposition helps to explain why even the most active feminists proceeded with caution on the question of unveiling. As Margot Badran, a historian of the Egyptian feminist movement, points out, the upper- and middle-class women in this movement were very much aware of the dangers which attached to unveiling. In personal terms they risked harassment and even violence if they appeared unveiled in the streets. In a wider sense it would also be regarded as a sign of lowered social status, leaving them open to the attentions of predatory males who regarded 'free' women as sexual prey.[24]

Some women also saw the necessity for caution in political terms. Leading feminists in Egypt in the first part of the

21 'Young Armenian Woman in Her National Dress (from Erzerum, Turkey) before World War I'. Postcard, published during or just after World War I by the Armenian support committee in Kotzschenbroda, north of Dresden, Germany.

Although this is a posed studio photograph, it is probably a genuine portrait of an Armenian woman. The national dress here appears as an emblem of an entire culture under threat.

twentieth century, such as Malak Hifni Nassif and Huda Shaarawi, regarded issues such as education and improved legal status for women as more important than removing the veil. They feared that too hasty unveiling would jeopardize the campaigners' credibility as 'respectable' women.

Remaining veiled certainly did not stop women from becoming politically active and, in some cases, it probably helped to overcome resistance from husbands and families. As one Egyptian woman activist recalled, 'Wearing the veil did not stop us doing things.' Thus, during the Egyptian nationalist uprising of 1919–22 women appeared in the streets fully veiled to protest, and even address meetings. In Palestine, where social mores remained more conservative than in Egypt, in the 1930s upper-class Muslim women appeared veiled to demonstrate and present petitions to the British authorities as part of the nationalist campaign against Zionist settlement.

Palestine also provided another example of the way women's dress could become part of national symbolism. Although the question of the veil was the most 'political' aspect of women's dress because it was so closely bound up with questions of male authority, women's costumes too could be elevated to become symbols of national pride. One instance of this has been Palestinian peasant women's dresses. Today, the most elaborate of these have become a source of motifs in nationalist art, and examples of this handiwork from the early part of the century are preserved, or bought at high prices, as part of the national heritage. What was historically the dress of a particular class, linked by its designs to specific parts of the country, has become, since the dispersion of the Palestinians in 1948, symbolically the property of the nation.

Removing the Veil

In 1927 Anbara Salaam spoke at the Women's Renaissance Society in Beirut without her veil, the first Muslim woman in greater Syria to make this political gesture in public. She was addressing the meeting on her experiences of living in England, from 1924–26. When she returned to Lebanon, she found that wearing her veil when speaking in public 'hampered her and blocked her thoughts'. Her action caused a great furore, especially since she came from one of the leading Sunni Muslim families in Beirut (her brother Saeb Salaam later became Prime Minister of Lebanon). Those women who dared to imitate her were insulted and even violently attacked. She herself had to withdraw temporarily from public life. The pressure was the worse because she was not married at the time, and she was accused of unveiling herself in order to attract a husband.

Anbara was born in 1897, the second daughter of Salim Salaam, a prominent Lebanese politician, and grew up in her grandmother's strictly conservative and religious household. She was very close to her father, who was much more liberal than her mother on the subject of her upbringing. She was sent to nursery school with one of her brothers and was then educated at home until she was ten, when she was sent to a Christian school in order to learn French. At this time the issue of proper dress already loomed large. She recalled that on her way to school people shouted at her: 'Go back to your people and tell them to veil you.' Her family then insisted that she wear a face veil, but she refused to wear the *milaya* (an enveloping cloak) and instead wore a black coat.

Yet these constraints did not prevent her becoming involved from her early teens in the new nationalist currents affecting Syrian intellectual circles in the years before World War I. Her ideas on the position of women were much influenced by reading the work of the Egyptian reformer Qasim Amin, who advocated the emancipation of women (see Introduction p. 32). In 1913 she wrote an article calling on women to play their part in seeking Arab rights in the Ottoman Empire. In 1914 she attended a public lecture in a political club – something unheard of for a girl of seventeen – and a headline subsequently appeared in the newspaper *Arabeel*: 'Muslim Girls in Nightclubs'. Under French rule in the 1920s she continued to campaign on women's rights.

In 1929 she married Ahmad Samih al-Khalidi, a Palestinian who was principal of the Arab College in Jerusalem and deputy director of education under the British Mandate administration. The couple lived in Jerusalem until the declaration of the state of Israel in 1948 and formed a remarkable literary partnership, collaborating on works of history and educational theory. In 1948 they were forced to move to Lebanon where Ahmad al-Khalidi died in 1951. But Anbara lived to see the horrors of eleven years of the Lebanese civil war, dying in June 1986.*

*Sources: Tarif al-Khalidi, obituary in *The Times*, 18.6.1986; and Hanan al-Shaykh, in a series of articles which appeared in *Al-Nahar* supplement, Beirut, 1974–5

22 Anbara Salaam

Dressing Up

Women's dress is often loaded with social and even political symbolism, but there have always been a few people in every culture who, whether in earnest or for fun, have tried to escape these labels of class, community and gender by dressing up as someone else. A handful of photographs can be found from the Middle East to witness these transformations.

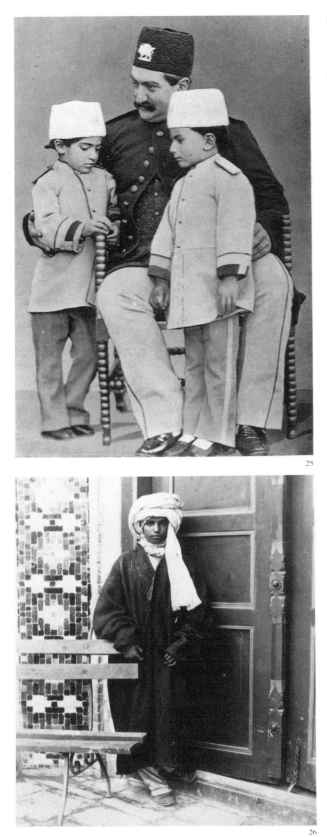

25

26

23 *Egyptian woman from a well-to-do family wearing a peasant costume. Studio portrait, 1920s–30s.*

24 *'Young Christian Woman from a Lebanese Bourgeois Family Dressed up as a Bedouin to Honour a Visitor'. R. Montagne, 1920s–30s.*

It is not unusual to find photographs of women from the elite dressed up in peasant or bedouin dress, or in 'picturesque' regional costume. Sometimes this was improvised at home, but studios often had a stock of such costumes for their clients to wear.

25 *'Zillu's-Sultan, His Favourite Daughter in Boy's Clothes and a Son who is Now a Priest [sic]'. Photograph given to Wilfred Sparroy, Iran, 1889.*

Sparroy, who was a tutor in the court of Nasir ed-Din Shah, tells the following story about this photograph: 'So devoted was he [Zillu's-Sultan, elder brother of Nasir ed-Din] to his favourite daughter . . . that he could not bear her to be out of his sight; accordingly she was requested to dress herself in male attire so that she might accompany him whithersoever he went; and this she did until she was ten years old, when the harem claimed her budding womanhood as its own. A photograph – a charming souvenir of those tomboy days of hers – was given to me on the eve of my leaving Persia.'[6] The daughter, on the left, has her hair cut short and is wearing, in miniature, the uniform of a Persian general.

26 *Young woman dressed as a man, Iran. Jean-Baptiste Feuvrier, between 1889 and 1893.*

According to Feuvrier, a French doctor who worked in Iran from 1889 to 1893, the woman had adopted this costume as a disguise in order to elope with a man of whom her parents disapproved. He added that she was then 'condemned to continue wearing male clothes', presumably because she was terrified of being discovered by her family.

143

Chapter V
Working Women

Women and Agriculture

The women are proud of being able to carry heavy burdens. They train themselves to be strong and competent. It makes them respected personally. They are conscious that everyone is watching them and expressing their opinions.[1]

1 Making a clay cooking brazier, Artas, Palestine. Hilma Granqvist, late 1920s.

Granqvist did not publish this photograph but she commented on it in her study *Birth and Childhood among the Arabs*. She stressed the way women learned skills from their mothers and other older women. 'I was especially interested in the girl who still has the wet clay on her fingers [*standing*]. How closely she watched, intent upon catching every detail of the women's work. No doubt she would manage next time.'[1]

Hilma Granqvist's account of how the Palestinian peasant women she knew viewed themselves and their work runs counter to two common images of Middle Eastern women. One, based on the life of the upper-class harem, stresses the indolence of women's lives, their boredom and lack of occupation. Paintings and photographs depict them sitting or reclining in attitudes of lassitude, eyes staring into space. Not only does physical activity seem beyond them but their mental faculties appear equally atrophied. On the other hand, for the rest of womankind – peasants, bedouin and the urban poor who did work both inside and outside the home – is reserved the label of drudge. These women are portrayed as ignorant, enslaved by 'hard and degrading physical labour' while their husbands take it easy. These simple dichotomies in which, either way, the woman is a passive victim were also applied by Western observers to other parts of Asia.

But women such as those whom Granqvist knew do not seem to have regarded themselves are mere drudges. While they may have been oppressed in many ways, they appeared confident of their ability to fulfil an active role in life, a view for which the stereotypes do not allow. Unfortunately there are very few other studies from the period before the 1950s which offer clues to how women regarded their work.

Photographers, however, found images of men and women at work in agriculture or crafts very appealing subjects. In the Middle East, Asia and Africa 'native crafts', agricultural tasks and even food processing were presented in photographs and *tableaux vivants* to visitors at the great exhibitions, and they formed an important part of the repertoire of images on postcards and in illustrated travelogues.

These pictures of 'native life and customs' show people performing those tasks easily visible to the camera. The simple technologies of agricultural production and craft industries had, for photographers and viewers alike, pleasing echoes of biblical or Pharaonic times, and suggested that nothing much had changed in the lives of the peasant, the bedouin and the craftsman or -woman for thousands of years.

By the early twentieth century, material details in photographs had begun to subvert this notion: new fabrics and styles of clothing appear; kerosene cans replace pottery jars for water-carrying; and new kinds of agricultural equipment can occasionally be seen. But the major economic changes – the commercialization of agriculture, changes in ownership and control of agricultural and pasture land, land hunger and migration – are not apparent. The surface of rural life as seen in photographs goes on much the same, reinforcing the idea of an unchanging seasonal round.

Anthropologists and ethnographers concerned to document methods of production often took photographs which showed in great detail the techniques and equipment used in

2 *'Women at the Well'. Bonfils, Bethlehem, late nineteenth century.*

One of the commonest of women's tasks, fetching water from the river or well, was also one of the most photographed. In the context of Palestine, pictures of women at the well usually have an implicit or explicit reference to the various biblical scenes in which women go to draw water. In Egypt especially, photographers were frequently attracted by the sight of women carrying water jars on their heads. Their graceful posture was also imitated in posed studio photographs of women carrying a water jar on their head or shoulder.

3 'Bedouin Female at a Camp South of Metlili Mountain' (Jebel Metlili, south of the town of Batna, Algeria). Hilton-Simpson, c.1914.

Hilton-Simpson was a British ethnographer who travelled extensively in the Aurès region of Algeria with his wife between 1911 and 1918. According to his own account, it was his wife who took many of the pictures of women. The woman seen here, like most peasant and bedouin women, has to combine her domestic tasks with childminding. Hilton-Simpson took the view that women were the repositories of ancient tradition in these cultures and this photograph's intended focus is the woman nursing her baby while she crushes seeds with a wooden pestle and mortar in the time-honoured way. Yet certain other aspects of the picture are not noted, even in the list of ethnographic details given in the Royal Anthropological Institute's catalogue entry for the photograph. Even in a bedouin encampment there are signs of the changes taking place in the wider economic context: the sack of grain, probably from a commercial distributor, marked Ravin Bleu, Batna; the Western floral design of the material from which the women's dresses are made; and the tin on the left, probably of oil or fat, with a French label.

agriculture and crafts, and the divisions of labour in particular communities, but they too tended to reinforce this timeless image. Although anthropologists might be aware of the economic or political changes which affected village or nomadic economies and their relationship to the wider society, they did not necessarily choose to document these changes. In fact, they would often seek out 'traditional' practices in the consciousness that they were already starting to disappear.

This was evident, for instance, in much of the work of French anthropologists on Berber cultures in Algeria. An example is Matthéa Gaudry's account of the economic and craft activities of the women of the Aurès mountains. She consciously selected an area where wider economic changes had not yet had a visible effect, and her photographs showed women performing traditional crafts and tasks. She went so far as to stress that the women could be viewed as the repositories of these traditions while the men began to respond to changing economic circumstances:

In some respects, the ancient Berber stronghold of the Aurès is an example of a civilization frozen in its primitive state. Thus, at a time when local industries were disappearing in many parts of the Maghreb, and when the Sidi Khalil code [French codification of Berber customary law] threatened to supplant local customs, it was interesting to study the habits of these mountain women who had remained shielded from outside influences to a far greater extent than the men.[2]

The impression created by most photographs of rural life in the Middle East, whether by travellers, commercial photographers or anthropologists, was of societies which were not only changeless but unaffected by the world around them. Yet landowners, moneylenders and agents of the state were constantly intruding upon the lives of the peasantry. By the twentieth century wider economic changes also had an impact, direct or indirect, on village life in all but the most isolated regions (see pp. 25–6).

When colonization or indebtedness caused a peasant family to lose access to land; when a bedouin tribe's access to pasturelands was cut off by the enforcement of border controls; when war devastated village lands; or when the price of grain or cotton fell in response to world market pressures, women as well as men felt their effects and women were sometimes thrust, if only temporarily, into new roles. These roles were usually modifications of an existing division of work between men and women.

Divisions of Labour

In both peasant and nomadic societies there were clearly defined divisions of labour between men and women, but the rules on how this division was made varied from one community to another, and it could also change over time.

In virtually all cases, women's primary responsibility was reproductive – the bearing and rearing of children – and managing the home, in which domain they often had a good deal of autonomy. A study of an Upper Egyptian village in Aswan province made by H.D. Ammar in the early 1950s found that the woman was 'almost absolute manager of the

4 Women carrying river mud from the Nile to enrich the soil. Egypt, early twentieth century.

Though Egyptian peasant women might perform tasks like this, they were excluded from key jobs relating to the production of cotton – the most important cash crop – including the crucial control of the irrigation system.

house. She is the treasurer of the crops, money and legal documents and holder of the keys to the various chests in the house.'[3]

In work outside the home, however, practices varied greatly with region and the socio-economic status of the family. For example, in the village studied by Ammar, women apparently did not engage in agricultural tasks outside the home after they reached puberty; whereas Winifred Blackman's study of villages in other parts of Upper Egypt, conducted in the 1920s, suggests that women did participate in some agricultural work, especially at harvest time, and also engaged in a number of crafts including pottery, weaving and basketwork.

In Lebanon, Palestine and Syria women frequently worked in the fields, especially at harvest time, when the whole family turned out to help. In Palestine, where it was common for peasants who owned little or no land to enter into sharecropping arrangements with landowners, these contracts sometimes stipulated that the sharecropper should bring a woman, usually his wife or a female relative to look after the ploughing animals and other tasks.

Women's role in the family's work also varied according to status. A relatively affluent family with land or trading interests would be less likely, for reasons of social prestige, to allow its women to work outside the home. Such families could also afford to hire outside workers, rather than using all its able-bodied members for its labour needs.

It was common for both bedouin and peasant women to have certain productive activities which were considered their domain: for example, rearing domestic animals – chickens, goats or sheep, and in the more fertile regions cultivating fruit and vegetable gardens. Sometimes this produce would be sold at market, but usually most of it was kept for family consumption. food processing – making butter, cheese, and *laban* (yoghurt), as well as grinding grain and making bread – also took up a lot of women's time.

On the other hand, most jobs involving any mechanical implement, such as the plough, the potter's wheel, or irrigation machinery, were normally monopolized by men, unless the absence of male workers made it necessary for women to perform these tasks.

In most cases, the division of labour in the family would be determined by the male head of household who would interpret the accepted patterns of work according to economic conditions and family circumstances. But the importance of women's role in the family's survival and reproduction, especially in poorer communities, may sometimes have offered them more opportunity to influence male decision making than those women with higher social status who played a less crucial part in the family's economic life.

Hilma Granqvist's studies on Artas are among the few to examine women's own attitudes to themselves as workers,

5 *Husband and wife picking figs, Artas, Palestine. Hilma Granqvist, late 1920s.*

Fruit – figs, grapes, olives and apricots – were important crops in the hill regions of Palestine and for the harvest whole families would turn out to help. The men and boys usually retrieved the fruit by climbing the trees or shaking the fruit from the boughs with the long pole seen in the photograph. The women and girls would then collect the fruit from the ground. Here, the couple are posed in a way that suggests their sharing of the work, though whether this was spontaneous or whether they were asked to stand like this is not recorded.

and their economic relations with men. Although it is clearly unsafe to generalize from the experiences of women in one small village, her observations certainly reveal attitudes more complex than the usual stereotypes suggest. Granqvist's informants seem to have regarded their work as a potential means of influencing their menfolk. Because of the rules men laid down about the division of labour, they could not easily overstep the accepted line between men's and women's work. Thus despite the women's essentially subservient position, they perceived that their husbands' dependence upon them for services could give them a kind of leverage. One woman expressed this as follows: 'Who shall bring him water from the well? Who shall go and gather wood for him? Who shall bring grass and leaves for the animals and who shall take milk, fruit and vegetables to the market? Who shall grind his meal and make his daily bread? Who shall make and repair his clothes and clean his room?'[4]

Of course the other side of this picture was that women

Work in the Village

Umm Issa is a woman in her sixties from a poor village in the Hebron district of Palestine. She recalls her life as a young woman: 'I'd start early in the morning with milking my three cows, then I'd make bread, then I'd carry my baby down to my father's fields and work there. At the end of the afternoon I came back, cleaned the house, looked after the children and cooked. Then I milked the cows again, made butter if it was the season, and laid out my bed and slept . . .

'We had to work together in the old days. We didn't have money to hire people to do the work for us, and everyone knew how to do things that needed doing, so it was natural to help each other. Plastering roofs, for instance. We had to stop the rain getting into our houses, and there was no one else to do it, so we learned to do it ourselves. You might find as many as fifty people, family and close friends working together roofing a new house or plastering an old one . . . The men's job was to mix the straw and soil and water, while spreading the plaster on the roof was the women's work. It was women who plastered the walls inside the house every few years too . . .

'Another thing I used to do was building *khabi*, the bins we had in our houses for storing wheat and lentils and barley. It's easy. You bring earth from your fields and mix it with straw and water. Then you build a little and leave it to dry for a few days, then you build a little more, and so on. A *khabi* is too big a thing to build all at once; the wet plaster wouldn't stand up. Most people used to know how to do it. I learned from my mother. I did it for myself, and sometimes for relatives, but never for money. The few young people who still use *khabi* have to pay old women to build them now, they don't know how to do it themselves.'*

*Account recorded in the West Bank in 1985 by Kitty Warnock and used with her permission

6 *'A Native Churn in Use in Upper Egypt'. Owen Tweedy, 1926.*

Tweedy was a British journalist who was at this time Middle East correspondent for the *Daily Telegraph* and the *Financial Times*. He took a large number of photographs of his travels in the region. He gives the following commentary on this picture: '[The churn] consists of a goatskin attached by three ropes to a rough tripod of three palm sticks. The milk is put into the empty skin and it is the duty of the daughter of the house to swing it to the accompaniment of an Egyptian folk song until the butter forms. The system dates from Pharaonic antiquity and holds its own in spite of the competition of modern churns which are considered to make inferior butter.'

7 Women winnowing grain after the harvest, Huraidha. Freya Stark, Hadramaut, Yemen, 1938.

The grain is tossed in the straw trays to separate the kernels from the chaff. In most places, the whole community would turn out to help with threshing and winnowing, which was usually done on a flat space near the village.

8 'A Woman Coolie [sic] Feeding Her Cow'. Kagehisa Haruyana, Hadramaut, Yemen, 1924–26.

One of a series of photographs of rural Yemen taken by Kagehisa Haruyana, a Japanese businessman or engineer who was installing water pumps in the area. Note his use of the word 'coolie' to describe this peasant woman, transferring the concept from his own culture. The woman appears to have enjoyed being photographed.

9 Two women grinding corn in a hand mill, Palestine. C.A. Hornstein, 1920.

There are many photographs of women doing domestic tasks of this kind, partly because they often sat outside their houses or in a courtyard where they were more easily visible to outsiders. The theme of grinding wheat or corn with a millstone was particularly popular in photographs of Palestine, because of the numerous allusions to this process in the Bible.

10 'Arab Women [and one man] Selling Fruit to British Soldiers on Their Way Upriver'. British Army photographer, during the British occupation of Iraq, 1917.

In many parts of the Middle East, women routinely took produce to market to sell, either with other women or with their menfolk. Only in certain areas, for example in parts of Morocco, was it considered improper for rural women to appear in the marketplace. Here, the circumstances of war brought a new, if transitory, clientele to the Iraqi countryside.

151

were frequently overworked and this, combined with frequent child-bearing, often put a severe strain on their health. Yet these women clearly did not regard all their work as mere demeaning drudgery. Relief was also provided by women's collective activities: making food, drawing water, gathering wood and herbs, doing embroidery, sometimes going to market. Despite family and communal rivalries and jealousies, co-operation in certain kinds of work was a necessity. This has even led some (mostly male) observers to assert that in peasant and bedouin societies, the workload placed on an adult woman was such that she would sometimes welcome her husband taking a second wife to lessen her burden. Granqvist collected the following saying in Artas which expresses more plausibly and succinctly women's ambivalent feelings on this issue:

> How sweet it is to have thy husband to thyself (alone)
> and how sweet in the handmill between the two (wives)[5]

Although the image of the peasant household dominated by father and husband may have been the norm, there were plenty of exceptions. In the Ottoman Empire, conscription would periodically wreak havoc in both urban and rural communities, stripping them of able-bodied men for unpredictable lengths of time. Conditions for conscripts were harsh: they could be away for years and some did not return

---

A Weaving-song

In pastoral and nomadic societies it was quite common for men to be away from their families, sometimes for quite long periods of time, moving herds from pasture to pasture or fighting and raiding other tribes. Peasants too sometimes had scattered lands which they left home to cultivate. The following is a Berber women's weaving-song from the Aurès mountains in Algeria. The woman laments her husband's absence 'with the tribe' and complains of the burdens he has left her to shoulder.

> Hush Ala, hush my little son;
> We are making a *kechabi* for your father;
> He has gone away and left you,
> Leaving only cares for your mother;
> Hush Ala, hush my little son;
> We are making a *burnous* for your father;
> He has gone away and left you,
> Leaving only sorrow for your mother;
> Hush Ala, hush my little son;
> We are making a *burnous* in many colours.
> Your father has gone away to the tribe,
> Dry your eyes
> and leave your tears for your mother.*

*Quoted in Naziha Hamouda, 'Rural Women in the Aurès: a Poetry in Context', *Oral History Journal*, Vol. 13, No. 1, spring 1985, p. 43

at all. Women in rural households were, in these circumstances, obliged to take over some male roles in production and management of family affairs, unless there were remaining male relatives to take control. In Egypt from the 1830s until the 1890s Muhammad Ali's policy of using *corvée* or forced labour on public-works projects and large agricultural estates also caused a great deal of disruption in the patterns of agricultural work and division of family labour.

Lastly, when men decided to migrate, whether abroad or to the city in search of work, women were often left to cope in the village. These alterations in the sexual division of labour, however, were not always quite what they seemed. In many cases women could take over work previously assigned to men only when it became less prestigious and less central to the family's livelihood.

Women and Work in Urban Environments

The images of women's indolence in Middle Eastern societies stem from the assumption that those who were confined to the harem were totally inactive. While the institution of the harem undoubtedly restricted the scope of women's activities and did not encourage intellectual development, this did not necessarily mean that all women were idle. An Egyptian writer, Afaf Lutfi al-Sayyid Marsot, argues that while this life of idleness might have been true for some in royal harems, it was not the case in most households: 'Life in the average affluent harem, as described to me by the women who lived it, was a very busy and gregarious one. The lady or ladies of the household had to exercise a number of executive and managerial decisions to ensure the smooth running of the household.'[6]

Just as in the West, the fact that upper- and middle-class women managed their homes and servants was not considered to merit acknowledgement as 'work' any more than housework itself. In well-to-do harems, most of the physical labour and service roles would have been filled by slaves or servants, and to a lesser extent by younger members of the family, while the older members would tend to have roles in the organization of the household. Of course, the larger and more affluent the home, the more thinly work of all kinds would be spread. In middle-class households with few servants the women of the family would usually have more work to do.

In most areas where the harem system was practised in the nineteenth century, it also generated various kinds of employment for women of other classes in the provision of services for secluded women. There were women pedlars and traders who sold goods in harems, dressmakers, marriage brokers and *hakimas* (female medical attendants) and female *hamam* (public bath) attendants. In many instances it seems that the women who performed these roles were members of

Christian or Jewish communities, though this was not always the case. Freed slaves might also set up in this type of business. However, the fact that these women did their work inside the harem means that there are hardly any photographs of them or their activities.

Slaves formed a large part of the domestic labour force in upper-class harems until the late nineteenth century, especially in North Africa, Egypt and Turkey. Yet there were clear distinctions between the roles and status of slaves, male and female, of different origins. The Circassians (people from the Caucasus who migrated into the Ottoman Empire in large numbers in the mid-nineteenth century) formed an upper echelon of slaves in the upper-class harems of Turkey and Egypt who usually did not engage in manual work of any kind. Slaves of African origin, on the other hand, normally performed manual domestic tasks which varied according to the size of the household and the number of slaves and servants attached to it.

The trade in black slaves was officially prohibited in the Ottoman Empire in 1857, though in practice, it continued for some decades. The decline in Circassian slavery in the late nineteenth century seems to have been due mainly to economic factors: in the worsening economic conditions, these expensive slaves became more and more of a luxury. The end of the Hamidian regime in 1908 and the break-up of the imperial harem, which had served as a model for upper-class harems, also marked the end of the era in Turkey when slaves played a major domestic role. In Egypt, the Khedive signed an anti-slave trade convention with the British in 1879 and from then on the number of slaves gradually dwindled. In parts of North Africa, especially Morocco, however, slavery continued well into the twentieth century.[7]

The gradual decline of slavery brought an increase in the numbers of paid domestic servants and the influx of Europeans into many of the cities in the region generated a further demand for domestic service. As in Europe, domestic service became one of the few forms of paid employment available to poor women though it was often very badly paid and female servants, like female slaves, were sometimes subject to cruelty and sexual abuse from the men of the household. However, the other side of the coin was that servants, like slaves, sometimes became almost part of the family, despite their inferior status.

Like other women who were associated with the life of the harem, slaves and servants were rarely photographed. Apart from the 'slaves' who appeared in Western studio reconstructions of the harem, female slaves or servants were occasionally seen in family-group photographs. Now and then a Westerner would actually photograph an individual who was a slave or a former slave, sometimes with an accompanying story of her life.[8]

Women and Property

Another aspect of women's involvement in economic life which visual records cannot show was ownership of property. In contrast to most Western women until the end of the nineteenth century, under Islamic law women were legally entitled to their own property both before and after marriage. Although there might be a considerable gap between theory and practice, and many variations in the way the law was interpreted, it did give women of all classes the opportunity to achieve a minimum of independence, or at least room to bargain with husbands and male relatives.

Even a poor peasant or bedouin woman would usually own at least some pieces of jewellery. This was usually part of the *mahr* or brideprice paid by the husband at the time of the marriage. *Mahr* payments could also be made in money, land, livestock or other kinds of property. Its composition varied considerably from class to class and region to region, but it was fairly common for the wife to retain a portion of the *mahr* as her own property, the rest going to her father. Some women would invest their share of the *mahr*, if it was sufficient, in land, livestock or property. Others simply kept it as a nest egg against divorce, financial hardship or the death of their spouse.

Women were also entitled to inherit, though only half of the share which went to the male heirs. But it was not always easy for women to claim their share of an inheritance unchallenged. If a woman inherited land or property it was not uncommon for male relatives to try to persuade or intimidate her into waiving her rights in the interests of consolidating family property. This kind of battle seems to have occurred at all levels of society. In Egypt examination of the records of *sharia* courts (religious courts which dealt with matters of property, inheritance and personal status) indicates that numbers of women, including better-off peasant women, fought to keep their own property and sometimes won.

If the majority of women who had any kind of property regarded it as an insurance against hard times, a few used their assets in more active ways. Some lent money to their husbands to help with family or business needs, but would even go to court to ensure that they were paid back. In the following case recorded in an Egyptian *sharia* court in 1830, the court supported the demand of a relatively wealthy woman that her naval-officer husband should pay up what he owed her:

> . . . the esteemed Ahmad Mahmud, naval lieutenant from the ninth battalion of Hasan Agha bin Bashi, gave legal testimony . . . that he possessed and he owed by legal right and observed legal practice to his wife, the *hurmah* Zahrah, the woman, daughter of the esteemed Haj Ahmad al-Faris, the Egyptian, the sum of 7,000 *nisf*

155

fiddah: 6,000 *nisf fiddah* from the balance of her bridal gift and 1,000 *nisf fiddah* from a debt to her, and he has paid her three copper plates and a dipper worth 49 *ghrush rumi*, an Arab *kilim* [rug] worth 40 *ghrush rumi*, the sum of this being [89] *ghrush rumi* that he has paid her, or 3,200 *nisf fiddah* and he undertakes its legal discharge. Of this 3,000 *nisf fiddah* is from the balance of her bridal gift and the rest is from his debt.[9]

Apart from tangles over family finances, some women who were independently wealthy undertook business dealings through a *wakil* (agent) or a male relative. Records of property transactions from Egypt and Syria show that women not only owned land and houses but bought and sold them, invested in trading deals and bought and sold female slaves. From the early days of Islam wealthy women as well as men made religious endowments on property, known as *waqf* (pl. *awqaf*): such endowments might be religious schools (*madrassas*) or shrines dedicated to their memory or they could be family *waqf* properties whose revenues would be distributed among designated members of the family – usually women as well as men.

Husbands had no legal control over how their wives disposed of their own money or property, though they might try to influence their wives' decisions. But a study made by Ann-Marie Goichon of the bourgeoisie of Fez in Morocco in the 1920s came to the surprising conclusion that even in this conservative milieu, women were generally free to decide how to use their own money:

> She [the wife] is free to invest her capital as she likes, selling one building and buying another, constructing or repairing properties, and so on. If she consults her husband at all, it is out of pure affection. It is clear that in this context, women have considerable scope for initiative, and they do not hesitate to make use of it, especially in building work and major improvements to their homes. Their husbands leave them to fulfil these aspirations for themselves.[10]

Crafts

Women both in cities and rural areas had also been involved to some degree in productive activities through the practice of craft skills. In rural areas, peasant and bedouin women often specialized in particular crafts: pottery, weaving, basket making and so on, in addition to food processing. Most of the products were for family consumption or sold in the local community, but in certain regions, especially close to major cities, some of these crafts became more commercialized. In urban areas, women were generally less visible in craft production but they were quite frequently involved as part of a family unit of production.

Abianeh is a mountain village some sixty kilometres south of Kashan, in central Iran. The family group in the photograph is engaged in making soles out of compressed rags for *giveh*, a type of shoe worn in this part of Iran. They have cotton uppers and soles made out of rags, mainly from *karbas*, a type of material made by local weavers. This was the kind of work done by the poorest families in the village. The men would travel round buying the rags from which the women would make the soles. Other women made the cotton uppers and the finished product would be bought by peddlars in exchange for goods which the families needed – sugar, tea, utensils. Sometimes the men in the family would take the shoes to market themselves.[2]

The photographic record of craft industries involving women was very uneven. In rural areas, it was popular to take pictures of women weaving, spinning, making pottery or baskets. There were also certain centres which became internationally famous for particular crafts, such as carpet making in parts of Iran and Turkey. In the cities, traditional crafts did attract the attention of photographers but since women employed in such crafts usually worked from home or in back rooms, it was the male-dominated skills which appear most often in photographs.

Small-scale craft production underwent many changes in the century after 1850. Changing patterns of trade in the Middle East affected the demand for the products of these craft industries. Household goods – pottery jars and bowls, straw trays and baskets, rugs and carpets, wool and cotton fabrics for clothing – all began to face competition from imported Western goods. This was a slow and uneven process, affecting first the immediate hinterlands of the cities and only much later the more isolated regions. But over time, this process gradually eroded demand for locally produced goods, including those which women made. And with each generation that passed, there were fewer women who taught these skills to their daughters.

In the cities and towns the impact of Western imports on craft industries was sometimes more dramatic. For instance, one of the most important craft industries in Egypt, Palestine and Syria had been the production of cotton cloth. In the nineteenth and early twentieth centuries these small-scale industries were overtaken by imports of British and American cloth. Although some parts of the old craft tradition managed to adapt and find new markets, many weavers were put out of business. The weavers themselves were almost exclusively men, but much of the spinning and carding had been done by women, so that when there was a sharp decline in demand they too lost their livelihoods.

On the other hand, certain specialized crafts in which women played a role not only survived but flourished – for

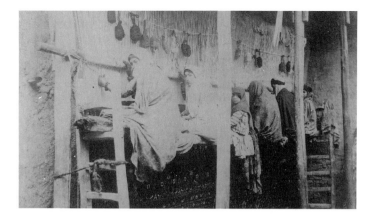

*12 Young women making carpets, Sultanabad, Iran. Major P.M. Sykes,
early twentieth century.*

This was one of a number of centres of carpet weaving in Iran, where this
craft was practised by both settled and nomadic communities. Until the
mid-nineteenth century carpets had mainly been a form of investment, in the
absence of banks, but in the century which followed they became a major
international export.

Both urban and rural weavers were drawn into this commercial network. In
both settings, the majority of weavers seem to have been women. In the
rural areas, in settled and nomadic communities where weaving was
practised, the women used designs passed down through generations,
varying or embellishing them according to taste. It was not until the 1930s
and 1940s that other patterns were introduced to meet commercial demand.
In the cities, however, where both men and women participated in
production, carpet designs were usually decided by the merchant or agent,
who gave the master weaver a set pattern for his or her weavers to follow.
The role of women in urban carpet making seems to have been very varied.
A.C. Edwards, who wrote a history of the Persian carpet industry in the
1940s, gives one example from the town of Hamadan of a woman who
became a prominent figure in the carpet industry. There were no looms in
Hamadan town until 1912. Eight looms were then set up in a house,
supervised by Korbra Khanum, an expert woman weaver who had moved
into town from a nearby village. By 1948 she was technical superintendent of
a factory of 120 looms, the largest in Hamadan. Though most of the weavers
in Hamadan seem to have been women, the prominence she achieved was
probably exceptional.

By contrast, in Meshed, the master weavers all appear to have been men,
and in Kerman, where most of the weaving was done in private houses with
a family labour force of women and children working under a male master
weaver. Edwards remarks on his surprise when, in Tabriz in 1948, he saw
men and women working side by side on the same looms: 'a few years ago
such a thing would have been unthinkable'. In rural areas weaving also
became increasingly commercialized though units of production remained
small-scale. Weavers were normally women, though men tended to control
the commissioning and sale of carpets.

For a rural family, the decision whether or not to weave a carpet was
influenced first by the labour demands of agriculture and second by the state
of the market. Edwards gives an example from the villages in the Hamadan
region. Villagers, he says, would sell in the local bazaar only when the
market was 'sweet' (i.e. favourable to the seller). The family also had to
have sufficient ready money to finance the inputs for a carpet and the
women who would weave it had to have time to do the work between
bearing and rearing children, household work and helping the men in the
fields at harvest time. The money earned from the sale of carpets seems to
have gone into the household coffers and not directly to the women. Labour
conditions in factories and workshops, whether in towns or villages, were
often appalling. It was common to employ young children, mainly girls, and
although child labour under the age of fourteen was banned in Iran in 1938,
ten years later Edwards still found under-age children working in carpet
factories. The weavers worked long hours in the kind of cramped and
contorted positions shown in the photograph.[3]

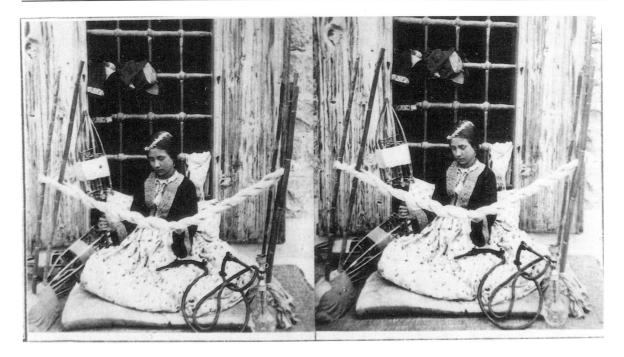

example, the silk industry in Lebanon, carpet weaving in Iran and Turkey and crafts which catered to the growing demand for souvenirs from pilgrims and tourists, such as the mother-of-pearl inlay work in which Bethlehem craftsmen specialized.

Changing Roles for Women in the Workforce

In the nineteenth century it was not uncommon to find women working as part of a family labour force, but for a woman to go out and work for wages was quite another issue. Those who did work for wages, with the exception of seasonal agricultural employment, which was usually sanctioned by the family, were generally viewed with disapproval. Such work was seen as lowering women's social status, both because it was a sign of poverty and because it indicated that they did not have men to provide for them. Poor women who were divorced, widowed or repudiated by their families often had little choice but to work. But evidence from nineteenth-century Egypt suggests that they could be penalized for doing so. A woman who was forced to go out to work to support her children was quite likely to have them taken away by the courts which deemed that paid employment made her unfit as a mother. The woman's primary role of childcare conflicted, in the view of these male judges, with working for wages, however desperately needed.[11]

The general male attitude towards women working outside the home at this time appears to have been that they would 'go astray' especially if they were allowed to work with men. Even in areas where there was some history of female employment in factories or workshops, such as in the

13 'Jeunne Fille de Zouk filant la soie. Maronite' – Young Maronite Woman of Zouk Spinning Silk. Ludovic Hart, from Charles Lallemand's Galerie Universelle des Peuples. *Stereoscopic slide, Lebanon, 1860s.*

Although the individual details in this photograph showing silk spinning as a domestic craft may be accurate enough, it seems possible that the scene has been 'arranged' for the photographer, particularly with the *narghileh* placed prominently in the foreground of the picture. From the 1850s onwards the Lebanese silk industry had begun to expand rapidly as a number of spinning factories were established, mostly under foreign control. These factories also generated work in the mountain villages for peasant families who grew the mulberry trees and for women who reared the silkworms. By the 1870s foreign interests in the Lebanese silk industry had diminished but the number of locally owned factories had increased. At this time about one third of silk was hand-spun (as shown in this picture). But for factory production, owners had from the beginning favoured employing women, usually on a seasonal basis for up to 200 days a year, though the owners often met resistance from local families who did not want their women to work.[4]

159

Lebanese silk industry, there were periodic attempts to prevent this, both by families and local authorities. For example, the *Mutessarifate* of Lebanon (covering the central mountain areas) issued a decree in 1874 forbidding women to work in the same silk factories as men.[12]

In Egypt under Muhammad Ali who, in the early part of the century, pursued policies which aimed to industrialize the country, there seems to have been some ambivalence about the role of women in the workforce. Should they become part of a vast cheap labour force in the interests of economic development, or should they perform their more accustomed role of servicing the men who do this work? Judith Tucker quotes an instructive anecdote on the subject of the employment of women in *corvée* (forced) labour:

> Most contemporary observers remarked, often with horror, on the numbers of women and children engaged in forced labour on irrigation projects, carrying away the earth dug up by the men. Abbas Pasha, in a conversation with Hekekyan, recalled his opposition to Muhammad Ali's policy of utilizing forced female labour: 'One day in Shoobra His Highness [Muhammad Ali] said to me, "Abbas, we must make the women work," and I replied boldly, for I could not contain myself: "I have seen women delivered on the dykes and forced the following day to recommence their work of carrying earth and mud clods. The men are made to work by us – without remuneration – who will cook for them and make their bread?"'[13]

Until well into the twentieth century, large-scale industrial enterprises were few and far between in most parts of the Middle East; but there were two notable exceptions: Egypt and Turkey. In Egypt some factories had already been established by the 1830s, and more were set up as part of Muhammad Ali's efforts to develop and diversify the Egyptian economy. Although women's employment was often ignored in the records, there is evidence that in Muhammad Ali's reign women were already working in the textile workshops of Mahallah (still a centre of the Egyptian textile industry today). It seems that these women workers were usually peasants employed during slack periods in the agricultural season. There were even instances of factories being established entirely with female labour. In a *tarbush* factory in Fuwwah, Tunisian women workers were brought in to train an Egyptian female workforce.

In Egypt the decline of small-scale craft production of textiles was quite rapidly succeeded by the growth of factory production – both for the processing of raw cotton and for cloth making. This contrasted with the situation in Syria where an overall decline in small-scale cotton cloth production was not matched by a growth in large-scale factory production.

14 'Femmes publiques arabes' – Arab Prostitutes, Jaffa, Palestine. Paul Castelnau, 16 August 1918.

Castelnau was one of the photographers working on Albert Kahn's photographic documentation project (see p. 50). Though some of the models seen in commercial photographs may have been prostitutes, it is rare to find a photograph where this is made explicit, as it is here. This photograph was taken at a time when Palestine was full of British and other soldiers of the Egyptian Expeditionary Force, which had captured Jersualem in December 1917. It was also a period of considerable hardship for the local population, with severe food shortages and dislocation of normal life. Though there is no reason to suppose that this caption is not genuine, it is revealing that Castelnau chose this as a subject in his pursuit of 'social documentation'.

Note the proprietorial pose of the man standing in the background. The photographer himself may have placed the *narghilehs* – so often seen in studio scenes of harems – in the foreground as an exotic touch.

By the end of the nineteenth century factory employment in Egypt for women and children had settled into a pattern, establishing a division of labour generally similar to that in Europe, with women confined largely to the most labour-intensive aspects of textile manufacture, food processing and packing. In the first half of the twentieth century, similar developments took place in other countries of the region, accompanied by an overall decline, for women as well as men, in the practice of craft skills.

Those women who did unskilled manual jobs for wages were frequently overlooked in the records, as both employers and census takers showed a tendency to ignore their existence. Judith Tucker writes of women doing manual labour in nineteenth-century Egypt: 'Although women . . . shared in the onerous conditions of the later-nineteenth-century workforce, including a ten- to fifteen-hour day six or seven days a week, we encounter official blindness to women's work.'[14]

She adds that the 1907 official census listed a total of three women working in construction, and contractors consistently denied employing women, but an independent researcher in the same period counted twenty-seven women working on just one site he visited at random. Just as women working in agriculture have often been 'invisible' to the statisticians, so were those who did manual labour. Occasionally, however, women performing these unusual tasks caught the eye of photographers, providing a few fragments of evidence. For example, in several instances, photographs of archaeological digs in Palestine show numbers of peasant or bedouin women

15 A cotton ginning factory at Sakha in the Egyptian Delta. Lehnert & Landrock, early twentieth century.

This photograph provides a rare glimpse of women doing factory work in Egypt, separating the cotton fibre from the seed or boll for spinning. This work was quite often done by peasant women on a seasonal basis during slack periods in the agricultural cycle. Women were in demand in the textile industry because they could be paid very low wages.

working on sites, clearing and gathering rubble from the excavations (see p. 67). In 1938 the *National Geographic Magazine* published a photograph of women working on the construction of an irrigation system near Homs in Syria, part of the French mandate government's public-works program-me. Here the motive for printing the picture seems to have been to stress the 'modernity' of the sight of women working alongside men. But in fact, if these were peasants hired as seasonal labour, there would probably be nothing very unusual in these women working with men.

It was in Turkey that the most visible and dramatic changes occurred in patterns of work in the early part of the twentieth century. Two factors account for this development, and for the fact that it is unusually well documented: first, the chronic shortage of male manpower in the civilian economy from 1913 until the mid-1920s; and second, the economic and social policies pursued by the Republican government of Kemal Atatürk from 1922 onwards.

In the last years of Ottoman rule, efforts to modernize Turkey's ramshackle economy, mostly under pressure from the Great Powers, made slow progress, and industrial employment did not increase dramatically. But by the beginning of the twentieth century, women in some regions were already working in factories. On the whole they were drawn from the minority communities, particularly in Bursa where there were forty-one small factories by 1913/15 employing numbers of women. As a result of a law passed in 1915 the female labour force in the textile industry expanded considerably. A new stocking factory set up in Urfa employed 1,000 women. In the provinces of Izmir, Sivas, Ankara and Konya 4,780 women were employed in carpet production. In Kutahya, Eskişehir and Karahisar provinces, 1,550 women were employed in textile production. In Diarbekir women replaced men at 1,000 looms.[15]

During the period from 1908 to 1914 women's groups campaigned successfully for women to be allowed to work in

17 Girl working at a new building, Khartoum, Sudan. R. Turstig, 1907–08.

Turstig was working in Sudan as a meteorological inspector and took a number of photographs, some of which were subsequently published in books on Sudan. Certainly the sight of a woman working on a building-site would have been unusual enough to catch his eye.

16 Women working in a silk factory, Bursa, Turkey. Published in Şehbal magazine, 1910.

There was some public interest and discussion on the issue of whether women should work outside the home at this time, though only a very small proportion of urban women had paid employment such as factory work. Wages and conditions of work were usually poor. Note that most of the workers in this photograph are quite young.

162

the post office and the telephone exchange (see also Chapter VIII). These developments went some way towards lifting the taboo on urban middle-class women working in public places, but it was the war which brought women into the urban labour force in substantial numbers. From the outbreak of the Balkan wars in 1912 until the end of the war against Greece in 1922, the mobilization of men to fight caused an enormous drain of manpower from the civilian economy. One of the results was that the state found itself obliged to support the idea of urban women working outside the home as substitutes for men. In the countryside, this process of replacement probably happened automatically as it had in the past.

Some war work was done by women on a voluntary basis through organizations such as the Red Crescent (the Muslim equivalent of the Red Cross), but numbers of women also took paid employment, both clerical and manual. A women's work corps was established within the army and women were used to do heavy manual work such as making roads and collecting rubbish.

The impact of these developments on the economic and social position of urban women was considerable. Whereas in the rural economy, periodic shortages of manpower had been met by temporary redivisions of workroles between men and women, in the cities this shortage brought into the workforce women who had never previously worked outside their homes.

After the war, the labour shortage continued because the casualty rate from disease and battle had robbed the country of a substantial part of its young male workforce. This made it necessary to retain some women in the labour force. At the same time, the new Republican government launched a package of legal and social reforms of women's status (see Chapter VIII for details). Some Turkish historians argue that the continuing need for women workers in the economy was one of the key motives for these reforms.[16]

19 Pages from a book published in Turkey around the beginning of World War I, with drawings showing some of the kinds of work being done by women – including street sweeping, and clerical work in the post office. The latter had been one of the jobs which the Organization for the Rights of Women had demanded should be open to women.

18 Woman working with her husband in a petrol station in Egypt. Published in Al-Dunya, 1938.

According to Al-Dunya, Sayyida Kerimeh jointly operated this petrol station with her husband, a position considered unusual enough to make a news item. Here she is being interviewed by a journalist from the magazine.

20 *Kuwait Oil Company. Women secretaries. Miss Wandi and Miss Leila Ibrahim, now working in the [KOC] secretariat – formerly of Jaffa, 1950s.*

Many of the inhabitants of Jaffa, like other Palestinians, fled or were driven from their homes in 1948 and were not permitted to return. As refugees, trying to survive in the surrounding Arab countries, women as well as men were often obliged to take on new roles. The beginning of oil-led economic development in Saudi Arabia and the Gulf in the 1950s offered new opportunities for Palestinians to find work. Some women as well as men, especially those with education and skills, began to find employment there.

After World War I there was also an increase in the availability of white-collar employment in many parts of the Middle East: in the provision of services, clerical and professional jobs. Work which entailed direct contact with the public was not generally popular with women, nor encouraged by men. In those countries under colonial rule or with large foreign populations, such as Egypt and Algeria, it was mainly foreign women or members of minority communities who worked, for example, as assistants in shops and department stores.

Turkey, where women were officially encouraged to work, was a partial exception. Demetra Vaka Brown, a Turkish woman of Greek origin, born in Istanbul, who had lived abroad for many years, returned to Turkey after World War I and was astonished to discover a dress shop owned and run entirely by women. However, the story she told in her book *The Unveiled Ladies of Istanbul* suggests that the women in the shop were not motivated by a straightforward desire to go out to work. The proprietress was an Arab whose husband, like a number of prominent Arabs from the Ottoman provinces, was arrested during the war when the couple were in Istanbul visiting relatives. He was deported and died on the journey. His wife, though not destitute, said she started the shop to keep her mind off her grief. The twenty-eight employees, seamstresses, designers, embroiderers and accountants, were all the daughters of minor officials who were mostly supporting not only themselves but other members of their families, possibly in the absence of male breadwinners. They had all been educated in Turkish rather than foreign schools. Despite the fact that they went out to work, Demetra Brown noted that they were not at all happy about having their photographs taken. 'No!' they exclaimed, 'what will our men say?' And when they finally consented to be snapped, they wanted to cover their faces, saying, 'Our men would not like our being photographed without our veils.'[17]

She was clearly puzzled at this apparent evidence of conservatism among women 'emancipated' enough to be family breadwinners. Certainly the relationship between women's access to work, the norms of social behaviour and Western notions of emancipation was far from straightforward, even in Turkey where these changes were officially encouraged.

Women and the Professions

It was among the upper and middle classes that the most dramatic changes in women's lives occurred. Among liberal families of these classes from Egypt to Iran, though not to the same extent in North Africa, education of women, whether at home or in schools, had become accepted by the 1920s. This trend was accompanied by a gradual opening of certain professions to women. All over the region women became teachers and even administrators in the segregated women's education systems and a handful of women also became lawyers and journalists (see p. 206 and pp. 215–17).

Medicine was the most problematic of the so-called 'caring professions' which began to open up to women in this period. Women had acted as midwives and healers in the past in all strata of society. Some undoubtedly had minimal skills and probably did a good deal of damage, but others had wide knowledge of herbal healing and other techniques which, with the professionalization of medicine, became devalued. This professionalization first began in Egypt in the early nineteenth century and, some argue, narrowed the work of the *hakima* (female healer) to midwifery alone.

The early years of formal medical training of midwives in Egypt were not altogether auspicious. When Clot Bey first opened a medical school in Abu Zaabal in 1827 it included a school for midwives. But no pupils came forward, and Ethiopian and Sudanese slavewomen were brought in to fill the places. Later the school moved to Cairo and became better established. According to Naguib Bey Mahfouz, a historian of medical education in Egypt, 'As soon as the graduates of this school began to work in private homes and were employed by aristocratic families, all prejudices against the school rapidly disappeared and it became possible to select more suitable candidates.'[18] But in the late nineteenth century the midwifery school went into decline. Admissions fell and many pupils left the school as a protest against working as nurses during their training. While midwifery and associated work involving only the treatment of women, often in their own homes, had been established as an acceptable profession, nursing remained more dubious because it might involve both contact with men as patients and menial work.

The professionalization of midwifery gradually spread to

21 Süreyya Ağaoğlu, the first woman in Turkey to qualify as a lawyer, coming out of court in Ankara in the 1930s.

Encouraged by her father, she became one of the first women to read law at Istanbul University (see Chapter VII, Caption 12) and she began to practise law in 1929. She recalls that at her first appearance in court, in a divorce case, a woman in the courtroom, seeing her black coat and short hair, asked, 'Is this really a woman?'[5]

In Egypt the first women lawyers began practising at the end of the 1930s. Mufida Abdul Rahman (see Chapter VIII, Caption 19) and Atiya Husain al-Shafa'i took their first case together at Minya al-Qamh in the Delta in 1939, successfully defending three men accused of unlawful possession of drugs. A large crowd gathered outside the courtroom, such was the sensation that their appearance caused.

22 A group of nurses, probably students at Kasr al-Aini school of medicine in Cairo. Early twentieth century.

Despite efforts to encourage nursing as a profession, it has remained the least popular of the so-called 'caring' professions thought appropriate for women.

other countries. In the 1920s, for instance, Damascus university's school of medicine opened a school of midwifery and between 1924 and 1928 twenty Syrian women received the midwifery diploma after a three-year course. None the less, these new trained midwives were still few and for the most part the services of traditional birth attendants and other healers remained important in most rural areas of the Middle East until the 1950s and 1960s when state health services began to bring professionalized medicine to the countryside.

Although the new echelons of professional medicine were dominated by men, the few women who did manage to become doctors enjoyed high status. In fact, in all the major professions, women who succeeded were held up as shining examples of progress by some governments (especially that of Turkey), by professional organizations and by women's movements. But nowhere did women reach these positions in sufficient numbers to pose any threat to overall male domination. As privileged exceptions, some became celebrities, and their portrayal, in both the local and foreign press, was in striking contrast to that of the anonymous women engaged in picturesque or burdensome labour which had dominated much early photographic imagery of women's work in the Middle East. They were presented as named individuals, respectable, self-confident, and even triumphant in their achievements.

Women's movements too were keen to publicize and promote the achievements of professional women, whether or not they subscribed to feminist ideas, to stress women's competence and intellectual capabilities. They also took an interest in the achievements of women in other countries of the region. In 1927 the Egyptian Feminist Union magazine, *l'Egyptienne*, carried a small item congratulating 'our Turkish sisters' on the appointment of Bedrie Hanoum (probably Bedrie Veyessi Nejmedin) as chief of the Bureau

23 'Midwife Carrying Her Wages on Her Head'. Winifred Blackman, Upper Egypt, 1920s. Published in The Fellahin of Upper Egypt, *Figure 38.*

In village communities, midwives played an important social role, even though they may have had limited medical skills. Villagers who did not have cash paid for their services in kind. Here, according to Blackman, the fee consisted of maize, bread, dates and various nuts. Sometimes a little money was also included.

of Hygiene. She was a graduate of Istanbul Girls' College and had studied medicine in Munich.

But the high profile of this small group of mostly well-to-do women who succeeded in breaking into professions still considered difficult of access even for Western women, often obscured the fact that for the majority of women, even in this social stratum, education did not necessarily lead to work outside the home. For most, marriage and family remained the first priority.

For other social classes, opportunities for women to work outside the home did not necessarily improve progressively over time. When peasants found themselves without land, women lost many of the economic roles they had played. They might, however, be obliged to take up some kind of paid employment in order to survive, even though this might represent a lowering of their social status. The decline in

24 Sabiha Gokçen, the first woman pilot in Turkey, 1930–40.

One of those 'firsts' for women often celebrated in photographs of Turkey at this time. She is presented as capable and confident, the glamour and drama of flying enhanced by the way the machine looms into the sky above her.

*25 Bedia Afnan naming a ship built by Palmers Shipbuilding & Iron & Co.
Ltd, at South Shields, Newcastle, 1930s.*

Bedia Afnan was born Bedia Nuri al-Husri in Istanbul in 1901. Her father
came from an Arab family from Aleppo with a tradition of service in the
Ottoman administration. The family had settled in Istanbul and Bedia's
early education was at a French convent school there. Her father, a
prominent writer, who at a young age had been appointed *mutasarrif* of
Nasiriyyah in southern Iraq, was the victim of a political assassination in
1913, and her mother, a Turkish lady of Circassian descent, died soon after
him. Bedia was subsequently cared for by her uncle Sati al-Husri (see
Chapter VII, p. 202) and his sister Bedia.

They sent her to Istanbul College for Girls to learn English and complete her
education. She had started to write and had her work published in several
magazines in Istanbul, but then she went with her aunt to join Sati in
Baghdad in 1923. In 1925 she married Hussein Afnan, Secretary to the
Council of Ministers of the Iraqi government, who subsequently became a
member of the Iraqi diplomatic corps and served as chargé d'affaires in
London and later in Ankara. In 1933, on their return to Iraq, Bedia became
involved in social work and was appointed head of the Iraqi Red Crescent.
After her husband's death in 1940, she was appointed Inspector of
Education for girls' schools. Her years of training in her uncle's school in
Istanbul and her life-long interest in education, as well as her years spent in
the West, had imbued her with progressive ideas on education. In 1946
Bedia was sent by the Iraqi government to work in the newly established
Arab League office in Washington, DC. When the League offices closed
down in 1949 she remained in the US and joined the Iraqi Embassy. For
many years she represented Iraq in the United Nations on the committee on
social and economic affairs and was elected as a member of the human rights
committee in her personal capacity. She later moved to the Iraqi mission to
the UN in Geneva where she remained until 1969. She lived in Beirut until
her death in 1975.

traditional crafts and services diminished opportunities open
to some strata of urban women, and these were not always
replaced by other, comparable opportunities for work. On
the other hand an increase in the wealth and social status of
the head of household might cause him to forbid his wife and
female relatives to work outside the home.

Despite the ambivalence of these changes, attitudes to
women and work certainly altered considerably between the
end of the nineteenth century and the 1950s. By that time,
women who tried to pursue a career would not meet with the
universal disapproval they would have faced fifty years
earlier. The main problem remained that, despite the hopes
of the women's movements, the fact that women were
permitted to work rarely had any radical effect on the roles
which men expected them to play in the family.

Chapter VI
Women in the Public Eye

Women as Entertainers

The Middle Eastern 'dancing girl' is an indispensable part of the Orientalist repertoire of images, appearing in paintings, postcards, peepshows and later in Hollywood movies. The poses she adopts, and her profession itself are used to suggest lasciviousness and sensuality, exciting both enjoyment and disapproval in Western viewers. Oriental dance is also associated with the biblical story of Salomé, a frequent theme in Western paintings, literature and music, investing it with sinister undertones of destruction and sexual revenge.

In commercial photography of the late nineteenth and early twentieth centuries, the caption 'dancing girl' or *almeh* and the suggestive poses of the photographers' models signalled their sexual availability, which was often emphasized by the exposure of breasts, shoulders and arms. These photographs presented dance as a manifestation of 'Oriental' sexuality which, unlike the life of the harem, was to some extent visible to outsiders.[1]

Westerners were fascinated by the female dancers, who were often described as coming from a 'tribe' of entertainers. For example, E.W. Lane refers to the women dancers known as *ghawazee* as a tribe from upper Egypt though it is more likely that this had become a generic term for female public entertainers. His description of these women, like most photographs in later decades, stressed the identification commonly made between public dancing and prostitution:

2 'Pint-Bitter-Bottled'. G. Lekegian, Cairo. Published in Black and White, 13 November 1897.

The photograph is used to illustrate a narrative of an Englishman's adventures in the 'fleshpots' of Cairo. His description of the dancer is reminiscent in its ribald tone of similar accounts of encounters with nightclub dancers in Europe, yet with an added touch of the alien and exotic. The woman is assumed to exist entirely for the amusement of this clientele.
'One black-eyed Arab, of ugly but amiable countenance, sat down beside the Doctor and myself after her performance, and we conversed to the extent of our powers. She knew three words of English and about four of French; we a little more French and English, but no Arabic, which was her native language.
'The Doctor said: "Well, my dear, how's your poor tummy now?"
'This in the Doctor's French was rather funny.
'And she said: "Anglais – pint – bitter – bottled" [i.e. English beer].
'Thus you see how truly expressive is our language even in the mouth of a Cairo dancing girl. She drank a pint of beer, then another half-pint; and no doubt her tremendous exertions required exceptional quantities of liquid support. Then she sent the empty bottles on to the stage, and they were set on a little table beside her place there that all men might see she had been entertained in the audience and so put money into the pocket of the proprietor. She smoked cigarettes for some time, failed to make much conversation or understand ours, then bade us farewell. My brother said that these girls generally die young, as their business is calculated to put a tremendous and unnatural strain upon their systems. I was sorry to hear that poor "Pint-Bitter-Bottled" could not hope to enjoy a long innings, and trusted the Doctor might be in error here. At any rate, her life, if short, will be merry, and she will probably pass away in the sure and certain hope that an eternity of wriggling awaits her in a better world, where the "bitter-bottled" will be plentiful and free.'

I need scarcely add that these women are the most abandoned of the courtesans of Egypt. Many of them are extremely handsome, and most of them are richly dressed. Upon the whole, I think they are the finest women in Egypt . . . Women as well as men take delight in witnessing their performances, but many people among the higher classes, and the more religious, disapprove of them.[2]

A similar example of this association of dance with prostitution was to be found in the Western image of the Ouled Nail, a 'tribe' of women dancers who worked in and around the town of Biskra on the edge of the Algerian desert. In the early years of the French occupation of Algeria, large numbers of French soldiers were billeted in this area, and Biskra became a lucrative centre of trade, entertainment and prostitution. By the late nineteenth century it had become established as a tourist attraction, and a starting-point for trips into the Sahara. Interest centred on the *cafés mauresques* in which the Ouled Nail women danced, decked in their spectacular costumes and jewellery.

These women were singled out for attention because they performed mainly in front of European audiences. It is

3 'Dancing in the Sand', Biskra, Algeria. Published to accompany 'Here and There in North Africa' by Frank Edward Johnson, National Geographic Magazine, January 1914.

The rest of the caption reads: 'Europeans come into contact with the famous dancing girls of the Ouled Nail tribe of desert Arabs chiefly at the city of Biskra, in Algeria, where two whole streets are inhabited by women of this class. They resort thither to earn dowries which will enable them to return to the desert and marry men of their own tribe.' Note the French officers in the group watching the two Ouled Nail women dancing.

unclear whether all the dancers so described actually came from the Ouled Nail tribe or whether this too became a generic name for any woman who danced in public. There seem to have been a number of other tribes in the region whose women danced in public, though not necessarily for Westerners.

The Ouled Nail woman, loaded with jewellery and smoking a cigarette, became one of the stock images of both commercial and travellers' photographs of Algeria. The connotations of the image were again excitement and exotic sexuality. For those with a biblical turn of mind, the Ouled Na'il dancer could also be seen in the role of the fallen woman. For example, Frank Edward Johnson, author of a long rambling article on his travels in North Africa in the *National Geographic Magazine*, published in 1914, uses the following quotation as a caption to one of the numerous photographs of Ouled Nail women which he includes in his story:

4 Cover of a French tourist brochure from the Tourist Office in Algiers featuring cigarette-smoking Ouled Nail women as the star attraction. Probably late 1940s or early 1950s.

The fate of the Ouled Nail, or dancing girl, of Biskra is often that described by the prophet Jeremiah: 'Though thou clothest thyself with crimson, though thou deckest thee [*sic*] with ornaments of gold, though thou rentest thy face with painting, in vain shalt thou make thyself fair; thy lovers will despise thee' (Jeremiah 3:30).[3]

The role and status of the woman entertainer in her own society was, however, much more complex than this popular Western view suggests. The status of such performers varied very much from area to area. While dancing or singing in public, especially in front of men, was not viewed as a highly respectable profession, it did not inevitably make its practitioners social outcasts. Their status depended very much on the kind of society in which they worked; the audiences for which they performed; and the attitudes in that society to women appearing in public.

In areas where social control over women's appearance in public was most strict, women entertainers would have had least status, but they may also have had a larger measure of freedom from male control. Research on the so-called *huriya*, or 'free woman' in Morocco suggests that society's view of women who did not conform to the norms of marriage and respectability was not a simple one. The *huriya* category ranged from those who had been rejected entirely by their kin, or who were without kin, to those 'once-married women' who temporarily did not wish to tie themselves to one man in marriage. The public dancers, known as *shikhat* in Morocco, were usually considered in the 'unmarriageable' category. But in certain respects they could profit from the fact that they lived on the margins of patriarchal society: although in some ways they were exploited by it, they were not obliged to conform to all its rules. The popular definition of the *shikhat* as 'women who do not want men to tell them what to do' is indicative of this.[4]

Lane said that the *ghawazee* were despised by the upper classes and by those of a religious turn of mind, but this does not mean that such people would entirely shun women performers. The question of women entertainers' respectability and acceptability in society was also determined by the class from which their audience was drawn. For a female singer who worked for upper-class patrons, it was possible to avoid the stigma which attached to the public entertainer. Many commercial photographs of singers and dancers have the caption '*almeh*' which was usually taken to mean the same as 'dancing girl'. But as better-informed observers noted, this usage was based on a misunderstanding of the meaning of the word. Although it later took on the connotations of 'dancing girl', *almeh* (pl. *awalim*) in Arabic meant a learned or instructed woman and was applied only to women singers (and sometimes dancers) who worked in the upper echelons of society.

5 '*A Professional Dancer from Wad Abdi in Beni Suig*'. M.W. Hilton Simpson, Algeria, 1914.

The professional dancers of Wad Abdi in the Aurès mountains seem to have worked, in the main, for a local rather than a European clientele, dancing at weddings and festivals. Hilton Simpson, an ethnographer and traveller, with his wife Helen, made a number of journeys to the Aurès region (south west of Biskra) between 1912 and the 1920s. His comments on these dancers again associate their style of life with the 'looseness' of their morals and those of their society. 'These women are very numerous indeed in Wad Abdi, and also seek their fortunes much further afield, and as far as I can see at present, their existence is due to a naturally voluptuous disposition combined with the very great ease with which divorce is obtainable in the Aurès.'[1] The caption added by the Royal Anthropological Institute in London stresses the ethnographic details of the dancer's costume, her coral and silver jewellery to avert the evil eye and the talismans in silver boxes around her neck to protect her from *jinns* (spirits).

6 *Almaz (Sakhna al-Maz), a famous* almeh *of the late nineteenth century, in an engraving by a German artist named Lorie.*

Ebers gives an account of al-Maz's performing style, based on an account by Lorie and by Gentz, a friend of his who also heard her sing. For a male audience she sang from behind a screen but was said to be acutely conscious of the audience's reactions, singing only a few verses at a time. The more eager the sympathy and applause of the audience, the more impassioned her singing. According to Gentz, 'The agitation reached its highest pitch when the singer declaimed the story of her life. When she was young and fair, she met a Persian, a physician, fell violently in love with him and hoped to share the joys of affection by a marriage with him; but this beautiful dream was dispelled. She parted from the man she had so ardently loved, and became an *almeh*. Even now the remembrance of that time of first love fills her soul with anguish; her unsatisfied longing and love are the source of her inspired song.'[2]
It would be interesting to know if she sang the same kind of songs for a female audience, but it seems there is no record of this.

At the apex of this world of entertainment were those who performed in the royal courts of Turkey, Iran and Egypt. Sometimes these women were professionals brought to perform in the royal harems on special occasions; sometimes they were members of the harem, usually slaves, who received training in the arts of singing, music and poetry. Male members of the court could also watch these performances. This tradition of women entertainers, often concubines of rulers and their male relatives, and highly trained in these performing arts, goes back to the court harems of the Abbasid and Ummayad eras when caliphs were frequently the main patrons of the arts. Even women slaves could rise to the highest rank in the court harem through the practice of these skills.

In nineteenth-century Egypt, *awalim* were very much in demand in the harems of the elite for entertainment at weddings, festivals and parties. They were not touched by accusations of 'exposing themselves' to men and, because they were largely invisible to Westerners, are not to be seen in photographs. One of the few detailed descriptions of the professional life of the *awalim* is given by Georg Moritz

Ebers, in his book *Egypt, Descriptive, Historical and Picturesque*.

This class of musician in Cairo, he says, 'if they are really distinguished performers, are held in high esteem, and often make a rapid fortune. Here, as in Europe, among these favoured mortals, the women hold their own against the men in number and estimation.' Clearly a successful *almeh* could become wealthy as well as famous. This was substantiated by Lucie Duff Gordon, who heard a performance by an *almeh* named Sakhna al-Maz whom she described as 'a Muslimeh and very rich and charitable'.[5]

But Ebers implied that both at the beginning and end of their careers these women needed male patronage in order to maintain their status, though it is difficult to ascertain whether this was generally the case. According to his account, the *awalim*

> begin their career in the house of some great personage, and when the first bloom of their charms is faded, and they are discarded by their master, they adopt his name, and remain connected with him, to a certain extent, as his clients [*sic*], they sing in public with more or less profit. They are in request [*sic*] at all festivities, particularly at weddings and sing to the ladies in the harems, and even to men, but then they are usually concealed behind a curtain or lattice. When they have a good reputation they are highly – nay even extravagantly – paid; frequently marry, and have the advantage of a man's protection; and when the freshness and charm of their voice is worn out they retire into private life, and end their days in comfort and peace.[6]

For those who were less successful, however, the only alternative was to fall back on singing and dancing in public places frequented by men, such as cafes, and rely on contributions from the audience for a living. This may have been the fate of Kuchuk Hanem, the dancer Gustave Flaubert met in the small Egyptian town of Isna in the late 1840s and described having sex with. Judith Tucker suggests that from Flaubert's account 'she danced, played and sang with a grace and skill bespeaking a past with the *awalim*'.[7]

But her presence in Isna may have been the result of another of the hazards which faced women who made their living either as public dancers or prostitutes: the interference of the state. She probably lived in Isna because in one of the periodic 'clean-ups' of Cairo in 1834 Muhammad Ali had banished all women in public entertainment to the provinces. Certainly in the 1830s and 1840s, both Lane and Gérard de Nerval noted that male dancers had replaced women in public performances. This ban did not end until 1866 with Muhammad Ali's death, and by then another obstacle had appeared. A new tax was levied on 'dancing girls' to be collected from each individual by tax farmers.[8]

In the cities of Turkey, women working as dancers seem to have derived a certain amount of protection from the strong guild system which existed in the nineteenth century. *Cengis*, professional female dancers who appeared in places of public entertainment as well as in the palaces and harems, were quite highly organized. They usually worked in a *kol* or company, a troupe which consisted of older women as managers, with dancers, musicians, a singer and young assistants. The managers acted as business agents for the troupe, arranging their hire for performances. They also trained recruits who were often young women who, for one reason or another, were rejected or cut off from their families. Most of the female musicians in Turkey tended to be from minority communities – Armenians, Greeks, Jews or gypsies – partly because of the relatively low status of the entertainment profession and also because in these communities the taboos against women performing in front of men were generally less strong.[9]

In all these entertainment roles, whether they were regarded as more or less respectable, women had a somewhat ambivalent position. Sometimes they enjoyed more freedom of movement and association than was usual in their societies and those who became wealthy as a result of their work further strengthened their position. But finally their status, whatever the class, was precarious and frequently depended on the patronage of men, if not on sexual relations with them. A very few women seem to have managed to establish reputations as independent beings, but examples such as the following are few and far between.

Huda Shaarawi had a childhood memory of one such woman who came to their house in Cairo. She was an itinerant poet named Sayyida Khadija al-Maghribiyya. Poets who recited in public generally had a higher status than singers and she was clearly a woman of some erudition. When she visited Huda's home in the 1890s, the young girl was amazed at Khadija's confidence and freedom.

> Sayyida Khadija impressed me because she used to sit with the men and discuss literary and cultural matters. Meanwhile, I observed how women without learning would tremble with embarrassment and fright if called upon to speak a few words to a man from behind a screen. Observing Sayyida Khadija convinced me that, with learning, women could be the equals of men if not surpass them. My admiration for her continued to grow and I yearned to be like her, in spite of her ugly face.[10]

On a less socially elevated level, C.J. Edmonds, a British political officer in northern Iraq in the 1920s, tells of a Kurdish woman entertainer he encountered known by the name Faqa Marif. She was 'a sort of professional jester' who, in order to have freer access to male society, dressed as a man. She would spend her days wandering from guesthouse to guesthouse, talking with men and entertaining them, and receiving payment – anything 'from a horse to a pair of trousers'. She had a horse which she rode and sometimes went out hunting with the men. But at night, wherever she was, she would return to the women's quarters to sleep. 'I asked her once why she did not marry and she replied simply that it was not in her nature to.'[11]

Entertainers in the Community

Although most of the photographic images we have of Middle Eastern women performers show, or purport to show urban-based professional entertainers, dancers and musicians, male and female, played an important role in the everyday life of many communities, whether urban or rural. Music and dancing were part of most festivities – religious festivals, weddings, circumcision ceremonies and so on. Sometimes richer families or communities would hire professional musicians, or among the poor, the women would dance or sing themselves.

Compared with the many photographs of the 'belly dancer' or the *almeh*, it was relatively rare for the camera to record glimpses of these other aspects of women's role in entertainment.

7 Musicians and dancers at a village festival, Jubbat al-Safa, Syria. Probably P.S. Coghill, 1945.

This photograph seems to have been taken by Sir P.S. Coghill, a British official who was visiting this village, though the reason for his visit is not known. Here the women of the village are dancing to the music provided by men, who may also be villagers themselves.

177

8 *Wedding festivities at al-Gherek in Upper Egypt. Winifred Blackman, February 1925.*

Blackman focuses the camera on the response of the male audience to a professional dancer entertaining them at a wedding. In another photograph (from a different village), she shows such a professional dancer sitting outside a house talking to a group of men, something which a village woman would not usually be seen doing.

9 *Musicians and dancers. Probably Ghilan province, Iran, c.1870.*

From the costumes of the male audience, this is probably a village in Ghilan province close to the border of Azerbaijan. These were probably travelling dancers and musicians from the large Christian community in Azerbaijan. In parts of Ghilan Muslim women did dance, but only in their own communities, not on a professional basis, and they would not have appeared with bare heads, like the dancer in the centre of the picture. The tent in the background was probably a reception tent for a wedding.[3]

The Export of 'Oriental Dance'

Western images of Middle Eastern music and dance are dominated by the *danse du ventre* – the 'belly dance' – which was generally thought of as obscene or shocking. Sophia Lane Poole, watching the entertainments in the harem for the wedding of Muhammad Ali's niece, described the dances performed by a group of young Turkish girls as 'quite charming' but found what she described as 'Arab dance' 'extremely disgusting'. Eugènie le Brun, who lived in Egypt, considered this type of dance was questionable enough when performed in public in France but was even less suitable for the Egyptian family circle:

> You are already familiar with this Egyptian dance whose shameless nature is all too clear from its name. You have seen it performed on the boards at the Champs de Mars and at the Trocadèro. But you cannot imagine the impression it makes when performed in such a different setting from that to which we are accustomed in Europe.

10 'Concert d'Alger'. Photograph in the collection of Prince Roland Bonaparte of the Paris Exposition of 1889, showing the live performance in the 'Moorish cafe'.

The girl who is dancing wears an Ouled Nail-style costume. She is said to have been seventeen years old, born in Setif, Algeria. The black woman seated on the left is given as twenty, born in Algiers, 'a dancer and breadseller'. This presumably meant that at home she did not dance for her living, but performed as a sideline. This is part of a series of photographs in the collection depicting the dancers and artistes, Egyptian and Algerian, who appeared at the Paris Exposition. In most of the individual portraits in the album the sitters have been posed full-face and side-face, in the 'anthropometric' style (see pp. 48–50).

Here, on the contrary, at family gatherings and watched by children and pure young girls . . . well, quite frankly, it's disgusting![12]

By the late nineteenth century the Oriental dancing girl was not just an image in a painting or photograph, but could be seen in the flesh at many of the great exhibitions held in Europe and the United States in this period, where 'live' displays of 'native arts' became popular features of the entertainments on offer. At the 1889 Paris Great Exposition, there was a *Café Algèrien* with '*danseuses algèriennes à l'établissement dit de la Belle Fatima*' and '*l'Almeh Aiousche du Café Égyptien de la Rue du Caire*'.

An Egyptian dancing troupe appeared at a number of these exhibitions: including the Antwerp International Fair of 1894, as part of the Cairo Street; and in the Midway, the entertainments section of the Columbia International Exposition in Chicago in 1892. Here, in a theatre decorated with hieroglyphs and Pharaonic figures located in the Cairo Street, Americans could watch the 'genuine native muscle dance'. Not all of the audience was amused. Julia Ward Howe, one of the early feminist campaigners in the United States, obviously found these performances as repugnant as she would a stripper in her own culture. She wrote: 'The Cairo dancing was simply horrid, no touch of grace about it, only the most deforming movement of the whole abdominal and lumbar region. We thought it indecent.' At the Panama Pacific Universal Exposition in San Francisco in 1915 the Law Enforcement League complained against the 'lewd acts' performed at the Mysterious Orient Dance Hall. The authorities at the exposition subsequently closed the dance hall of the Streets of Cairo concession. Placed in the context of quaint 'native customs' these dancers mostly served to

11 'Egyptian Dancing Girls' on parade, part of a collage of photographs by Grantham Bain of the opening of the St Louis Exhibition, published in the Illustrated London News, *21 May 1904.*

confirm all the stereotypes Westerners already had of Middle Eastern women and their dances.[13]

By the early twentieth century, the music hall and then films and night clubs took the Oriental belly dance into their stock of stereotypes. But by this time the 'belly dancer' had begun to take on a different look, as the costume evolved from the short waistcoat and undershirt, wide pantaloons and low-slung belt which made up the usual attire of the urban dancer in Egypt and North Africa to the spangled bikini top, bare midriff and low-slung skirt which are the stock in trade of the Hollywood or night-club 'Oriental' dancer.

Exactly how this evolution occurred is not known. One writer speculated that the change may have been influenced by the costume of the Indian *nautch* dancers (public dancers who also had the reputation of being courtesans or prostitutes) which may have been introduced by the British into Egypt, where they ruled from the 1880s, and thence into the world of Western entertainment.

Colonial rule in a number of Middle Eastern countries brought an increased demand for night-club-style entertainment in cities like Cairo, Algiers and Beirut. In this context, women singers and dancers were particularly associated with vice and prostitution, both by Westerners and by their own societies. The Egyptian singer Umm Kulthoum described the boom in highlife and night clubs in the years just after World War I when Cairo was full of British soldiers. While rich Egyptians as well as foreigners might engage the services of public entertainers, male and female, she reflected the disdain in which they were held:

Cairenes became worried over the bad influence on youth and a Committee of Honour was formed to spread virtue and fight vice and corruption. But the Committee of

Honour had a difficult time with the cabarets and other pleasure palaces which lined the streets bounded by Maydan al-Opera, Sharia Imad al-Din and the Fajjalah . . . Drink, dancing music, entertainment of all kinds was to be found in this area. Along both sides of Muhammad Ali Street stood the little shops, with musical instruments hanging from their walls and signs: 'al-Usta Hamidah, Oud player'; or 'al-Usta Zubah, belly dancer'; or 'Naimah al-Misriyyah, artist' (a name which was a general cover term for a female entertainer, one whose morals were not above reproach). Inside each of these little shops sat one of the Mutaybatiyah (the good-time makers) who dealt with customers needing entertaining and who shared the fees.[14]

Women and the Development of the Theatre and Mass Media

As bowdlerized versions of Middle Eastern entertainment were being exported to the West, so Western genres of entertainment began to gain a foothold in parts of the Middle East. In Istanbul and Cairo, with their substantial European communities, Western-style theatre and opera had become established by the end of the nineteenth century. Although many of the performances were by touring European companies, in Turkey and Egypt they began to attract local audiences, including well-to-do women.

There was also the beginning of a local theatrical movement. In Istanbul, local theatre companies in the second half of the nineteenth century were dominated by the Armenian community which provided most of the actors and actresses; and Armenians owned many of the theatres. But in an effort to widen their audiences, Armenian professional companies put on plays which would also appeal to the wider community. For example, one of the most successful of these theatres, owned by Güllü Agop, put on plays by Turkish writers, including the nationalist Namik Kemal, though his work rapidly fell foul of the state censors.

Women gradually became an important component of the audiences, and Agop's theatre encouraged women spectators by charging them less for tickets – at first he even offered free tickets – and providing latticed boxes to conceal them from the rest of the audience. For women to appear on stage in a play, however, was another matter. Even the first Armenian professional actresses who began performing in the 1860s were criticized by the Armenian patriarch and conservative members of the community. For Muslim women the acting profession remained taboo until the end of World War I.

In 1920, Afife Jale appeared in a play at a theatre in Kadiköy, Istanbul, to a storm of protest. The fact that she appeared at all had been made possible because the Darulbedai (House of Arts – the theatre school founded in

1914) had admitted women as students. After Jale's appearance on stage the school lost its status as an educational institution but continued as a professional acting company which included women.[15]

In Egypt, too, indigenous theatre had become established by the early years of the twentieth century and entered its most lively period after World War I. Even before this time, there were a few women such as Mary Ibrahim, an Egyptian who gained a reputation as a 'serious' actress, but until the 1920s it still remained difficult for Muslim women to appear in plays. After the war, however, the status of actresses was improved by the emergence of a number of Egyptian playwrights and impresarios of considerable talent, such as Najib al-Rihani, Yusuf Wahbi and Amin Sidqi, who built up their own theatre companies. For an actress to belong, for example, to the company of Yusuf Wahbi, himself from an aristocratic family, would give her a social status greater than that usually accorded to female performers. It also offered an entrée to that part of the upper class which patronized the arts.

Many actresses in Egypt also worked as singers, either as solo performers or in the fashionable musical theatre shows. By 1930s, new opportunities opened up in films, radio and the record business which transformed the most famous of these women performers into 'stars'. Egypt became, and remained, the centre of the entertainment industry in the Arab world, and a pole of attraction for talent from all over the region. There was a boom in mass media of all kinds: records, radio, illustrated magazines and later cinema which allowed the artists to reach a much wider audience, in Egypt and the rest of the Arab world.

These singers and actresses were seen, and their voices heard far beyond the walls of the theatre, concert hall or home. With this development went the trappings of stardom familiar in the West at this time: the posed photographs, the gossip, the public appearances. These stars, almost without exception very self-conscious about their public images, none the less took differing attitudes towards their reputations.

Obviously those performers who, like Umm Kulthoum, Munira al-Mahdiyya, Fathiyya Ahmad and Asmahan, became famous because of their considerable talents, had most opportunity to create the image they wanted. Umm Kulthoum, who was to become the most famous of all Egyptian singers, always took care to project the image of a respectable lady, and throughout her long career she kept her private life firmly private. In contrast, Asmahan (the stage name of Amal al-Atrash, from a leading Druze family from Jebel Druze in Syria), who became famous as a singer in Cairo in the 1930s, appeared uncaring of the lurid rumours which surrounded her career and private life, perhaps because she was living outside her own country and community.

كتالوج لأغاني فقيدة الفن

المطربة اسمهان

12 Asmahan, as she appeared on a catalogue of her records, Cairo, early 1940s.

Asmahan was born Amal al-Atrash in Jebel Druze, Syria in 1912. The Atrash family played a leading role in the Druze communities of Syria and Lebanon. In 1925 she went to Cairo with her mother and two brothers, to escape the fighting during the Druze rebellion against the French, who ruled Syria under the Mandate system at this time. One of her brothers was the singer and composer Farid al-Atrash, who became a major figure in the Egyptian entertainment world. She first sang in public in Cairo in about 1930, taking the stage-name Asmahan at the suggestion of her mentor, the composer Daoud Husni. Her career was interrupted in 1933 when she married her cousin, Prince Hasan al-Atrash – according to her own account, in order to get away from her mother. She returned to Jebel Druze and remained there for the six years that the marriage lasted. When it broke up, she returned to Cairo and resumed her career. She had a beautiful and well-trained voice and was considered one of the leading singers of that period. At the same time, she seems to have lived at a whirlwind pace, and had affairs with a succession of well-known figures in Cairo, apparently including the journalist Muhammad al-Taba'i, editor of *Akhir Sa'ah*; the banker Tal'at Harb; and Ahmad Hasanayn, an aide to King Farouq. She was also briefly married in 1940 to the film director Ahmad Badr Khan. But in 1941 she returned to Prince al-Atrash in Jebel Druze, it was rumoured because she was doing intelligence work for the British there. In 1942 she returned to Cairo and married Ahmad Salim, general director of the film company Studio Misr. She was killed in a car crash in 1944.[4]

Those women performers who became famous gained the patronage and protection of sections of the elite interested in the arts and access to the literary circles of Cairo. Leading singers and actresses like Umm Kulthoum, Munira al-Mahdiyya and Fathiyya Ahmad all benefited from this. During her early years in Cairo, in the 1920s, Umm Kulthoum enjoyed the support of the poet Ahmad Ramy who wrote many songs for her and who was crucial in introducing her to influential Cairenes who appreciated her talent and helped to promote her career.

By no means all the women who had successful careers in acting or singing were from well-to-do backgrounds. For all the social opprobrium which might be attached to the night-club singer or dancer, the upper reaches of the entertainment world did offer a few women a kind of individual social mobility seldom otherwise open to them. Umm Kulthoum, for example, was from a poor village family

13 Women in a show at Badia al-Masabni's theatre, Cairo. Published in
al-Dunya *magazine, 1938.*

Badia al-Masabni first came to Egypt from Syria in about 1906, but she
subsequently went back to Syria and returned to Cairo only around 1921.
She worked with the actor and playwright Najib Rihani in the early 1920s,
becoming an accomplished dancer and comedienne, and his leading female
star.
Like most female entertainers at this time she had a series of male
'protectors'. Jacques Berque repeats a story from her memoirs about the
period before she joined Rihani's company: 'During one of her tours
through the Sa'id [Upper Egypt], she took the fancy of an important
personality, who followed her around from town to town. One day he
invited the whole company to his estate. By dint of munificence, he at last
became her official protector. Others succeeded him, including a leading
Cairo lawyer. Eventually, and not without bargaining, she joined Najib
Rihani's company.'[5]
She married Rihani in about 1923 and left both him and his troupe in 1926
amid a blaze of publicity and speculation about a reconciliation.
Badia then opened her *salah* (a music hall, featuring a variety show with a
female singing star every night as well as comedians and dancers) in Imad
ed-Din Street. This was a highly successful venture and she initiated novel
events such as the very popular weekly matinee at around six p.m., for
women only. She also employed some of the rising young female stars of the
day, such as Leila Murad, and she seems to have trained her own dancers.
The Salah, which moved in the summers to an open-air site in Giza,
remained in business until after World War II when Badia retired to Syria.
She controlled the business side of the Salah herself, either owning it or
holding a long-term lease, probably with financial support from some of her
male admirers. She was known as a tough businesswoman and is even said to
have threatened some intrusive journalists with a gun.[6]

in the Delta and Munira al-Mahdiyya seems to have come from a modest background in the provincial town of Zaqaziq.

Some of the women who succeeded in the entertainment world also became shrewd businesswomen. Umm Kulthoum, for instance, recalled that when she and her father first came to Cairo in the early 1920s they were identified as country bumpkins and many people tried to swindle them. She increasingly took over the management of her own affairs which by the 1930s included record and film contracts. By the end of the 1930s, she was apparently negotiating record contracts for a percentage of sales, a rare practice at this time.

Apart from appearances on stage and screen, records and radio shows, these women's photographs and stories of their activities appeared in numerous illustrated magazines which catered to the growing market of literate men and women of the middle and upper classes. There were more specialist publications, such as *al-Masrah* (*The Stage*) which, as its title implies, was devoted to theatrical news. But there were also picture papers such as *al-Musawwar* which carried photographs on subjects ranging from current affairs to entertainments and the activities of the royal family. *Ruz al-Yusuf*, which became the most famous magazine of political satire in the 1930s, began its existence in 1925 as a general-interest paper with a strong bias towards the arts and entertainment because its proprietor, Fatma al-Yusuf, was formerly an actress (Ruz al-Yusuf was her stage name).

These papers not only contained photographs and stories about local stars but also followed the doings of Western stars, particularly from the beginning of the movie era. The photographs of Western female stars which appeared in these magazines as early as the 1920s were much the same as those which appeared in European publications. They emphasized the '*femme fatale*' or vamp image, and sometimes showed these women in various stages of undress or in passionate embraces. These images would hardly have been acceptable in Egyptian society at large, but at this time most ordinary Egyptians did not have access to such magazines which were aimed at the 'chic' elite.

Some Egyptian actresses and singers also assumed this vamp image but were rather more cautious about their presentation. This chic, westernized image was curiously mingled with what seemed to be parodies of 'Orientalist' poses and costumes. Usually these were costume photographs taken to advertise the appearance of a performer in a particular role. But they add a strange twist to the imagery of women, apparently internalizing some Western ideas of how Middle Eastern women looked.

There was considerable self-consciousness about the use of photographs on the part of both publishers and performers. Fatma al-Yusuf, with her strong connections in the

14 Fatma al-Yusuf, proprietor of Ruz al-Yusuf, *on the cover of the magazine, 14 July 1926.*

Fatma al-Yusuf was a Lebanese Muslim who, orphaned as a child, was taken to Alexandria in Egypt, and brought up by a theatrical family. She went on the stage before launching *Ruz al-Yusuf* in 1925. It became a very successful magazine and from the late 1920s was famous for its bitingly satirical cartoons, but by the 1930s Fatma herself had ceased to wield effective editorial control.[7]

15 Munira al-Mahdiyya in theatrical costume, with a guitar. On the cover of Rashaq al-Hasan magazine, 27 February 1926. Photograph taken by 'M. Charles'.

Munira al-Mahdiyya was born in Zagazig in about 1885. Though she was often said to have been uneducated, she does appear to have been sent to school. She was apparently interested in music from childhood and she particularly admired a female singer known as al-Lawandiyyah from Tanta, whom she saw in concert as a child.

At around the turn of the century she went to Cairo and began to sing in the cafes of Imad ed-Din Street before turning to the stage. She became a protegée of Salamah Hijazi, one of the best-loved stars of the Egyptian musical theatre, and she sang his songs and played roles created by him until his death in 1917. By that time she had become one of the first really famous female theatre stars in Egypt. Like many actresses of the 1920s and 1930s, she was also a well-established singer, and from about 1910 until 1930 her voice was greatly admired. She had begun recording for Odeon records in 1912 and then switched to the Lebanese recording company Baidaphone and became one of its major artists.

In her heyday in the 1920s and 1930s she appeared in some thirty musical plays and Arabic adaptions of operas such as *Carmen* and *Madame Butterfly*. She also performed as a solo artist and did concert tours in Egypt, Syria, Palestine, North Africa and Turkey. Her career dwindled in the 1930s.[8]

entertainment world, was particularly aware of the fact that women performers liked to keep control over the images they presented. Captions in *Ruz al-Yusuf* sometimes commented directly on the origins of the photographs published. In an edition of March 1926 there was a page containing several photographs of entertainers among which was one of the singer and dancer Badia al-Masabni dressed up as a bedouin man. The caption informed readers that the photograph, taken in 1912, had been given to the magazine by Badia herself. It concluded nastily, 'she was thinner in those days'. On the same page was a photograph of the singer and actress Munira al-Mahdiyya, taken, according to the caption, in 1919, with the comment that she was very careful to whom she gave photographs. 'She was angry about the use of this one,' it concluded gleefully.

But sometimes even Fatma al-Yusuf was more careful. When she wanted to publish a photograph of the poet and writer May Ziyadeh (see p. 216) she wrote the following respectful, even obsequious request:

To May Ziyadeh   16 March 1926

Esteemed lady,

  Please accept the greetings of one previously unknown to you, although the tie of literature and art binds us together. Accept the greetings of one who admires your elevated position in the world of journalism and literature, one who has served, and still serves the arts. I was formerly an actress and now serve journalism through the magazine which carries my name, of which I hope you have heard. If you would grace the cause of art by sending your picture to be published in my magazine, I should be grateful, though I know you might not be willing to publish your photograph since you are not an admirer of advertising and publishing. This is simply a request from

16 *Fathiyya Ahmad, shown working with a theatrical company, in a photograph published in* Rashaq al-Hasan *magazine, February 1926.*

Fathiyya Ahmad was born around the turn of the century, into a family with an interest in music and performance. She was the niece of Bamba Kashr, a very popular *almeh* of the nineteenth century. Two of her sisters also became singers, though they were less successful than she.

She began working in the theatre in 1910, appearing with Najib Rihani in 1918. In the 1920s she switched to concert singing, ostensibly because of the low quality of much theatre music. She became a very well-established singer and had recording contracts with several companies including Mechian, Columbia and Odeon Records. She made a particular name for herself singing 'in the Turkish style' in which she had received coaching. The appearance on the musical scene of Umm Kulthoum, with her repertoire which emphasized classical and religious music, induced Fathiyya to hire teachers to instruct her in these forms as well.

In the late 1920s she married a wealthy man and retired for a few years while she had children. In 1931 she returned to work in the *salah* (music halls) particularly in the Salah Badia Masabni. In 1933 she ran the Salah herself for a brief period while Badia was away in France making a film.[9]

an aspiring colleague to an established one and I hope it will be well received. Please accept my thanks, admiration and respect.

Ruz al-Yusuf[16]

While women performers could become stars of the mass media, and could gain genuine respect as musical performers, to become a composer of music was more difficult. Where Arabic music was concerned, women had long been excluded from playing in and composing for orchestras and instrumental ensembles. While singers like Fathiyya Ahmad and Umm Kulthoum studied music and read poetry to improve their techniques and performance, they did not compose the music they sang.

The story was told in the Egyptian Feminist Union's magazine of Bahija Hafiz, a woman who had tried to become a composer of Arabic music, but had encountered resistance from the male musical establishment and ended up becoming a film actress. She explained how this happened in an interview with Saiza Nabrawi, editor of *l'Egyptienne*, published in 1928.

She appeared in a photograph illustrating the article in an 'artistic' pose, her abundant hair loose down her back and one shoulder bare. She came from an aristocratic and very musical family in which all the children had played as part of a family orchestra. So she grew up a competent musician, knowing something of the traditions of Arabic classical music, and she began to try her hand at composition. Her style seems to have been an attempt to combine the Arabic classical tradition with Western harmonic values, something which was tried by a number of composers at this time. The result, 'languid and melancholy', was said to have pleased European audiences, but she had many more difficulties in convincing the Arab musical establishment.

At the time of this interview she was starring in a silent film, *Zeynab*, based on a novel by Muhammad Hussain

Heikal, in which the heroine was a peasant girl from the Delta. Bahija Hafiz explained to Saiza Nabrawi why she had ended up making films:

> Many people have criticized my choice of profession as scandalous! But have they for a moment considered the many difficulties encountered by a woman on her own who is not well-off, yet wishes to remain independent? What pushed me into films was not a mere whim or the desire to make an exhibition of myself, but freedom . . . [sic] Moreover I only took these decisions when I had finally despaired of obtaining the least encouragement or support from my fellow-citizens.

She added that the conservatoire of Arabic music, which had been established with government help, had refused to accept her work, as had the privately-sponsored Oriental Music Club. While it is impossible to know whether she was excluded entirely on the grounds of her sex, it was certainly true that the conservatoire remained a bastion of male privilege despite subsequent efforts by Saiza Nabrawi and the Egyptian Feminist Union to end this exclusivity. By the mid-1930s music institutes were established for the training of women music teachers, but these concentrated mainly on Western music. Meanwhile, as it turned out, Bahija Hafiz was not entirely frustrated in her musical ambitions: a 1931 catalogue from the Odeon record company includes six records of background music she composed to accompany *Zeynab*. She later went on to found a film company.

The period from the 1920s to the 1940s was one of considerable creativity in the performing arts in Egypt. Some of the results were frivolous, some serious, but they had great influence throughout the Arab world and the music of the stars of that era reached a wider audience than ever before. This had its influence on more hidden aspects of popular culture, especially the songs and dances performed at home by women and children. Gradually the older oral traditions became mingled with the new popular songs from the radio, films and later television.

It was not, however, just the music which was influential. So were the images of the stars, particularly the women. Photographs took on a new role in creating visual images of women for mass distribution, which, combined with films and advertising, created new stereotypes and ideals for women's appearance, and new images of women's sexuality. In the Middle East, as in the West, women stars – whether local or foreign – came to represent glamour and excitement as well as a guide to the latest fashions. Though these images might meet with disapproval in some quarters, their influence gradually spread beyond the rich and privileged elites.

The visions of womanhood which they presented were always ambivalent. Sometimes they referred directly to

Western ideas of the chic, the modern or the sexually daring – by implication in behaviour as well as in appearance; sometimes they created virtual parodies of Western Orientalism; and at other times they began to evolve new images which reflected aspects of a newly self-conscious national culture.

The Changing Image of Umm Kulthoum

Umm Kulthoum, the most durable of these women stars, avoided the image of Western chic and of Orientalism, and also shunned any projection of sexuality. Because she took great care how she was presented to the public, it is interesting to trace the evolution of her photographic image from the raw country girl of the early 1920s to the symbol of the Egyptian and Arab nation which she came to represent by the 1960s.

Umm Kulthoum was born in the early 1900s in the small village of Tammay al-Zuhaira in the Egyptian Delta. She began singing as a child under the supervision of her father, Shaikh Ibrahim, who was the shaikh of the village. She studied at the local *kuttab* (elementary religious school) and her father, recognizing her remarkable talent for singing, began to take her to perform the traditional religious music with which she had been brought up at *mawlids* (saints' feast-days) and other religious occasions. She became quite widely known in her home province and began to sing also at parties held by landowning families in their country houses. Thus she also came to the notice of members of the Cairo elite interested in the arts who came to spend their summers in the countryside.

Her fees for performance gradually increased, and her father acted as her 'impresario'. By her own account, an important landmark in her career came when, still a young girl, she met Shaikh Abu al-'Ila, one of the leading exponents of *maqam*, the classical tradition of Islamic religious singing. She and her father met him by chance at a railway station and having listened to her sing, the shaikh was sufficiently impressed to urge her father to take her to Cairo.

After an initial resistance to the idea, her father finally agreed that they should go to Cairo where they seem to have first arrived at the beginning of the 1920s. Under the guidance of Shaikh Abu al-'Ila she developed her repertoire of religious music which remained the heart of her art, though she did from time to time bow to audiences' demands for more popular secular songs. She asserts in her memoirs that it was the shaikh who taught her not just to sing but to convey the meaning of the words she was singing. 'Until I met him,' she says, 'I was still a parrot . . . repeating words I was learning without really understanding them at all.' Although she was already well-established as a singer in Cairo by the time of his death, it was clearly a great loss.

17 Umm Kulthoum in her early days in Cairo, c. 1925. *Published in* Radio Misriyya, *25 June 1938.*

18 The image of Umm Kulthoum in the early 1930s, rather similar to her photographs for HMV advertisements at this time. Published in Ruz al-Yusuf, *November 1931.*

Umm Kulthoum's public image gradually evolved from the village girl to the stature of a national symbol. These changes were reflected in the way she was presented in photographs. In the early days her image seems to have been entirely determined by her father, who had his own difficulties over her role as a singer. In her memoirs she recalls that as she grew up, the fact that she was a girl performing in public began to trouble him.

> So he began to dress me in boys' clothes, a *zibun* or long vest, over the *jallabiya* [full-length garment] and on my head the *iqal* and the *kuffiyeh* [headrope and headcloth]. I sang in this garb for several years. I realize now that my father wanted to deceive himself, to postpone in his mind what he was doing, letting his daughter sing in public. And he also wanted to deceive the audience and convince them that the singer was not a young girl but a young boy.

But when they came to Cairo in the early 1920s, Shaikh Ibrahim soon 'saw that this garb was no longer appropriate and he was the first one to suggest that I might wear dresses (still long, modestly cut, and with long sleeves) to sing in instead of the coat and *tarhah*'. By the late 1920s Umm Kulthoum was beginning to take charge of her own image. By the 1930s, her dress became that of a conservative, well-to-do woman of sober tastes. In her HMV record advertisements of the late 1920s she still appeared in a head-and-shoulders portrait with her forehead, neck and hair completely covered, in a style which still hinted at her rural origins. But by 1932 HMV was using a new photograph of Umm Kulthoum bare-headed and wearing a dress with a modest V-neckline. In the 1930s she also began to appear in films and photographs show her wearing more glamorous clothes to suit the parts she played. Most of the films in which

19 Umm Kulthoum with her first teacher, Shaikh Abu al'Ila, posed at the Pyramids. Published in Ruz al-Yusuf, *1926.*

190

20 *Umm Kulthoum in the post-World War II era, a postcard image still on sale after her death. The sense of her fame and importance is highlighted by the halo-like lighting behind her head.*

she appeared were built around her songs, and they were extremely popular. They were ideal vehicles for Umm Kulthoum, focusing on her great musical ability, for unlike most of the other leading female singers of that era, she had never trained or worked as an actress.

From the end of World War II until her death in 1975 she became a legendary figure, not just in Egypt, but in the Arab world as a whole. During the years of turmoil in Egypt from 1946 until 1954 she began to sing songs with nationalist and political overtones, but her music always continued to draw upon the classical traditions with which she was raised. She came to embody the hopes and aspirations – so often dashed – for a bright future for the Arab world, while at the same time retaining her appeal as a woman rooted in the traditions of the Egyptian countryside. How far she herself generated this image and how far it was the result of people's need for such a symbolic mother figure is difficult to tell, but when she died in 1975 after a year's illness, Radio Cairo made the dramatic gesture of reciting the Quran in her honour after the news, an accolade usually reserved only for a head of state.[17]

21 *Umm Kulthoum in the more glamorous costumes of her film-making years. Published in* Radio Misriyya, *June 1945.*

Chapter VII
The Spread of Education

Attitudes to Women's Education

In the late nineteenth century, portrait photographs began to show sitters old and young, male and female, holding books. Old men who could not read, middle-aged matrons and young children were portrayed clutching this symbol of education and literacy. It might indicate that the people in the photograph were educated; that they wished people to think they were educated; or that they wanted to advertise the fact that they were educating their children. For a man, literacy and education had always been a social asset, but the same was not true for women. Until the nineteenth century it was comparatively rare to find women of any class in the Middle East who had more than an elementary education. The only kind of formal schooling available was the *kuttab* (elementary religious school) to which many families, even among the poorer classes, might send their sons, but much less often their daughters.

Among the upper classes, private instruction was some-times given in the harem, and there had always been a few women who had used this opportunity to its utmost and through their own tenacity had achieved not only literacy but had even become writers and poets. In the imperial harems of Turkey, Iran and Egypt there was a tradition which stretched back to the Abbasid and Ummayyad caliphates of the early Islamic era that both free women and some favoured slaves received an education in the arts of recitation and singing. For example, in nineteenth-century Iran there were some female *rowzeh-khwans* (reciters) who recited the story of the martyrdom of Hussain (one of the central events in the canon of Shia Islam) before the ladies of royal and upper-class harems. There were also educated women who taught religious studies and writing in these harems (see the story of Nasir ed-Din Shah's mother: p. 212).

But on the whole the chances for women to obtain anything more than the most elementary education were few and far between. A young Turkish woman named Zeyneb from an upper-class family who corresponded with Grace Ellison described this state of affairs:

> When our grandmothers could sign their names and read the Koran they were known as 'cultured' women . . . compared with those who had never learned to read and write; when a woman could dispense with the services of a 'public letter writer' she was looked upon as a learned woman in the town where she lived, and her time was fully occupied writing correspondence for her neighbours.[1]

1 Portrait of a Turkish woman. Kamal Yanik, Photo Hilal, Salonica, before World War I.

She is the grandmother of the Turkish writer Tomris Uyar, and as the book before her suggests, she had been educated. By this time books had become quite a regular part of studio props for portraiture.

In the latter half of the nineteenth century more upper-class women gained access to an education as it became fashionable to employ Western governesses in the harem. This trend was supported by Muhammad Ali in Egypt after the failure of his efforts to start a system of public education for females. Sultan Abdul Hamid was also said to have encouraged the importation of governesses to Turkey. As Zeyneb told Grace Ellison: 'With the craze for the education of the West, French governesses came to Constantinople in great numbers; for it was known what high salaries the Turks paid, and how hospitable they were.'

This reflected a general increase in interest in formal, Western-style education. Governesses offered a means of giving young women the elements of 'culture', modelled on the attainments considered suitable for a young lady in the West, while retaining control over their movements and whom they associated with. Yet the importation of European governesses could result in a very culturally confused education as young women living in strict seclusion were exposed to a quite different set of social and cultural assumptions. Zeyneb's experience of learning from governesses was, she claimed, very unsatisfactory. She did not object to Western culture or education as such, but she argued that as it was conveyed via these governesses, it created ideas and expectations based largely on the content of French novels, which bore little relation to the lives of still-secluded Turkish women.

The introduction of an education based on Western ideas of suitable cultural attainments for women – learning to speak French, reading European novels and playing the piano – had very contradictory effects. At least until the end of the nineteenth century this was considered in some elite circles as a harmless education for harem women, having little relevance to the 'outside' world. But among the women who received this 'safe' education, there were some in whom it simply aroused a desire for more knowledge, and for learning which was more relevant to their own society.

One of the few detailed accounts of an upper-class woman's difficulties on this score is to be found in Huda Shaarawi's memoirs. She was educated at home, under the eagle eye of one of the family's eunuchs. First she studied the Quran with her brother and had memorized it by the age of nine. But when she expressed the wish to study Arabic grammar, she encountered opposition. French grammar would have been acceptable, it seems, but not Arabic. Written classical Arabic, as the language of public affairs, was considered the province of men and therefore a dangerous thing for women to learn. When she managed to get a teacher to agree to give her Arabic grammar lessons, the eunuch Sayyid Agha forbade it, and his reaction gives a clear indication of how a 'suitable' education for women was defined at this time. He told the teacher contemptuously,

'Take back your book, Sayyidna Shaikh. The young lady has no need of grammar as she will not become a judge!'[2]

Huda's education was interrupted by her early marriage at the age of thirteen (see p. 100). But when she and her husband were separated only fifteen months later she was able to return to her studies. She had a governess who taught her French and to play the piano, which met with no objections. But her renewed attempts to study Arabic grammar brought more frustration. When she finally found a teacher, an elderly shaikh from the Azhar University, he was soon driven away by the opposition of Sayyid Agha.

In the late nineteenth century many still considered the education of women a dangerous business and were certainly reluctant to allow women to be educated outside the home, fearing a loss of control over their ideas and activities, but there were two major developments which affected the future of women's education at this time. The first and more equivocal of these was the influence of Christian missionaries on the spread of women's education. The second was the gradual development from the late nineteenth century onwards of state education systems, in reaction both to these Western pressures, and, in some parts of the Middle East, to an internal debate on the role and status of women.

The Missionary Influence on Women's Education

Arguably one of the most important influences on the development of women's education in the late nineteenth century was the spread of Western missionary activity. Well before the Great Powers exerted direct influence in the Middle East through colonial rule, missionary organizations, both Protestant and Catholic, from Britain, Europe and the United States were dividing up the region between themselves.

The missionaries' primary aim was to achieve conversions, among Muslims, Jews and local Christian communities. But their success rate was generally low, and it was rare to find examples of 'rice Christians' compared with, for instance, China and parts of Africa. Such successes as they had in this endeavour were mostly in local Christian communities: for instance, among Armenians in southern and eastern Turkey and in Iran; Copts in Egypt; Chaldeans in Iraq; Maronites, Greek Orthodox and other Christian groups in Lebanon; and the Greek Orthodox community in Palestine. In most cases, conversions were closely tied in with the provision of education and health services, which added to those already provided by local religious organizations – Muslim, Christian and Jewish.

The impact the missionaries had on education was therefore unevenly distributed in geographical terms, focusing mainly on regions where they had a core of converts or

*2 'Ecole juive' – Jewish (Girls')
School. Photo Garrigues, Tunis,
c.1910*

There was considerable interest in
education, including the education
of girls, among Jewish
communities in North Africa from
the nineteenth century onwards.
These communities often
established their own schools, as
here, but they also sent their
children in considerable numbers
to both state schools and those
established by Christian
organizations.[1]

*3 Armenian schoolchildren
dressed up for a play. Jerusalem,
1913.*

This school, run by the Armenian
Patriarchate, was very unusual for
its time, since both boys and girls
attended it.

sympathizers. Schools were established in the main cities as
well as in these selected rural areas. But the education the
mission schools provided was not confined to Christian
communities. They actively encouraged those of other faiths
to come to their schools, including those for girls. In
Lebanon, Palestine and Egypt, for instance, it gradually
became more common for well-to-do Muslim families to
send their daughters to these missionary schools, at least
until the age of seclusion, not because they had any intention
of converting to Christianity, but because they thought the
education the missionaries provided was worth having (see,
for example, Anbara Salaam pp. 140–1; and Nazira Zein
ed-Din p. 232).

In these circumstances, many of the organizations running
these schools gradually toned down their evangelism to the
more general aim of instilling 'Christian principles'. There
remained a few, however, who were convinced that the
provision of education, especially for girls, would in the end
lead to conversions 'by the back door'. These dedicated
evangelists argued that if literacy were instilled through Bible

Calesthenics at Miss Arnot's Mission, Jaffa, Palestine.
Copyright 1900 by Underwood & Underwood.

reading, the influence of a Christian education would eventually do its work.

One of the most fiercely determined of these evangelists in Lebanon and Syria was Mrs Bowen Thompson who first set up a school and workshops for Christian women who were survivors of the Druze/Maronite war in Lebanon in 1859–60 and of the massacre of Christians in Damascus in 1860. Later she started a number of girls' schools in Lebanon, and one in Damascus, which at its inception was designed to serve the city's Jewish community. She imported large numbers of Bibles in Arabic from which the women and girls learned to read. By the 1870s and 1880s the pupils in the schools included Druze and orthodox Muslims who were interested in education, though rarely in Christianity. But Mrs Bowen Thompson believed that conversions were possible:

> We have been specially encouraged by the faint streaks of morning which are dawning athwart the darkness of the Mohammedan horizon, giving fair promise of shining more and more unto the perfect day . . . God's ancient people [the Jews] also in these lands are wakening from the long night of darkness and seeking for their children that enlightenment which a scriptural education alone can give. The Gospel, seen in the hands of a Muslim or Jewish child, carried into the harem or the home, while at first only tacitly admitted, may imperceptibly drop into the mother's heart, and yield the fruits of repentance and hope.[3]

None the less, by no means all those who came to teach under the aegis of missionary organizations shared this kind of philosophy. For example, Istanbul College for Girls, an

4 'Calisthenics at Miss Arnot's Mission, Jaffa, Palestine'. Stereoscopic slide, Underwood & Underwood, 1900.

Commercial pictures such as this, by one of the largest producers of stereocards, served both to amuse tourists and to edify the suporters of missionaries in the West. Calisthenics were very fashionable in Europe in the early twentieth century, and here their practice helps to emphasize the virtues of a Christian education: order, discipline and cleanliness. Generally speaking, missionaries tended to view the societies in which they worked, in the Middle East and elsewhere, as lacking in these virtues. To instil them was part of the work of redemption.

"Search the Scriptures"—a Bible Class of Christian Mothers in Bethlehem of Judea, Palestine.
Copyright 1900 by Underwood & Underwood.

American school founded in 1871, took a more liberal approach to the education of students from other cultures and religions. Among the teaching staff were members of the earliest generation of university-educated women from the United States who, while they undoubtedly intended to instil Western 'Christian values', seemed to have little interest in active proselytizing. Mary Mills Patrick, headmistress from 1875, resisted pressures from the school's sponsors, the Woman's Board of Missions in Boston, to pursue a sectarian policy in the school.[4]

The college's first pupils came mostly from the European nationalities in the Ottoman Empire – Bulgarians and Greeks – along with a substantial number of Armenians. But by the late 1880s some well-to-do Muslim Turkish families had also enrolled their daughters. One of these was Halide Edip, who started at the college in 1893 or 1894. But her schooling was interrupted when Sultan Abdul Hamid forbade Turkish Muslims to attend foreign schools, and she had to be taught at home for several years. She later returned to the college and graduated in 1901. The first Turkish Muslim to graduate (in 1890) was Gulistan, daughter of General Tawfiq Bey. The general seems to have faced considerable criticism for his decision to educate his daughter, not only outside the home but at a foreign school. Mary Mills Patrick recalled that when Gulistan graduated, she appeared at the ceremony 'closely veiled, sat with her mother in the audience and did not go to the platform even to receive her diploma which was passed to her over the heads of the people'.[5]

The philosophy of the college seems to have been to encourage women towards independence of mind and the ability to command others. This approach was not entirely welcomed by the state education authorities of Turkey

5 ' "Search the Scriptures" – a Bible Class of Christian Mothers in Bethlehem of Judaea, Palestine'. Underwood & Underwood, 1900.

Bethlehem was a largely Christian town, but missionaries of various denominations made numerous converts, particularly among the large Greek Orthodox community. This was mainly the result of the strained relations between the Palestinian laity and the predominantly Greek clerical hierarchy, which led to some disenchantment with this creed. People were also attracted by the education offered by the missionary organizations, Protestant and Catholic. Most missionaries regarded education as part of the process of conversion. Here they seek to teach the still largely illiterate female population to read the Bible, probably in the hope that this will also influence their children.

during Abdul Hamid's rule. Patrick recounted in her memoirs that in the 1890s a Ministry of Education official who came on a tour of inspection and saw students acting as classroom monitors, remarked, 'Alas, alas, are you teaching our daughters to govern us?'

From the time of the Young Turk revolution in 1908 enrolment at the college widened to include more Muslim pupils and it soon became one of the most prestigious schools to which the elite sent their daughters. Graduates of the college made up a substantial proportion of the first generation of Turkish professional women in the 1920s and 1930s.

In Cairo, Beirut, Jerusalem and Tehran, similar kinds of colleges and secondary schools for girls established by Christian missions, Protestant and Catholic, also became popular schools for the well-to-do of all religions. In educational terms, these schools obviously promoted ideas about academic achievement and cultural values which were prevalent in the West, as well as notions of how women should behave and their role in society. It is hard to make any generalizations about the impact this had on the future outlook of their pupils, by no means all of whom accepted these ideas in their totality. But it does seem that in some individuals considerable tensions developed as a result of the conflicts between the outlook instilled by their schooling and that of their own families and society.

These schools also had another, more directly political impact. Each nationality – British, German, French or American – created schools modelled on those in its own country and instilled not only its own culture but its language and its political perspectives in their pupils. The significance of this has to be seen in context of the Great Power rivalries in the region and the way in which these educational institutions created or reinforced loyalties and ties to particular external powers.

Sometimes the schools also contributed to the divisive

6 Catholic convent pupils, Istanbul, before World War I.

In most major cities of the Middle East Catholic schools played an influential role in the education of women at both primary and secondary levels. Many women from different religions and denominations who attended these schools, recall particularly their strict discipline, which the rigid poses of this photograph clearly evoke.

7 *American College for Girls at Istanbul, the class of 1901.*

Halide Edip is in the centre of the front row. This was the year she graduated from the college.

trends within society. In Palestine the constant battles between the various Christian denominations and their Great Power backers cannot have failed to influence the atmosphere in the schools run by these denominations. But in Palestine these conflicts had little effect on Muslim–Christian relations, as Muslim elite families also sent their children to these schools, and therefore they had little long-term effect on social cohesion. The same, however, was not true in Lebanon where the dividing lines in the education system came to coincide with sectarian and linguistic rifts in the wider society and often served to reinforce them: French education for the elite, particularly the Maronites; British or American for other elite groups, and later, the Arabic-language state system for these who could not afford anything better.

The appearance of foreign schools in Turkey in the late nineteenth century was very much associated with growing foreign interference in Ottoman internal affairs, and suspicions were aroused, whether justified or not, that these schools were involved in promoting separatist nationalisms, particularly among Armenians and Bulgarians. In the Armenian case these suspicions of foreign involvement were a contributory factor in the massacres of Armenians during World War I and the expulsion of the majority of Armenians from Turkey.

Memories of a Catholic Education, Lebanon

In the following reminiscences, the Lebanese writer and poet Etel Adnan, now resident in the United States, looks back on her education at a French convent in Beirut during the era of French colonial rule in Lebanon (1920–46).

'When I speak about these French nuns I am not generalizing about all nuns. These were under French power so they were colonizers, they were instruments of French politics. It doesn't mean that they necessarily behaved the same way in their own country. As a child, of course, I didn't know all that. But now I see how their political role made them even more authoritarian. They looked down on everything local. They used the word Arab as an insult. Of course, it bothered me: I knew something was fishy. There were Muslim children in the school and still they [the nuns] were anti-Semitic. They called themselves missionaries in the very place where Christianity started. They threatened us when we spoke Arabic, telling us that we should be learning to speak good French. So Arabic was associated with punishment. They kept telling us that you could not think in Arabic and that Arabic was not a national language . . . Because of these French schools I didn't study Arabic. At the school there were all different kinds of children – Lebanese, French, Italian, White Russian and Greek. But the French nuns looked down on the Lebanese as natives. They considered me halfway between the Europeans and the natives because my mother was Greek. Because I admired my father very much – and he was certainly not the way they described Muslims – I kept aloof from the nuns. But not all the children did and some got terrible inferiority complexes.'*

*Memoirs told to Margot Badran, Sansalito, California, December 1984, reproduced with her permission

The Development of State Education

Whatever doubts there may have been about the effects of foreign missionary-inspired education on local politics and culture, these schools certainly played an important part both in providing educational opportunities for women and also in raising internal debates on the issue of whether, and to what extent, women should be educated.

From the middle of the nineteenth century, the subject of education in general and women's education in particular had been on the agenda in intellectual circles in Egypt and Turkey. It was taken up a little later in Iran and greater Syria, and rather more slowly in North Africa. In general, it was liberal male intellectuals who became the first public advocates of women's education. Thinkers such as Qasim Amin in Egypt; the writer Namik Kemal in Turkey; and the liberal constitutionalists in turn-of-the-century Iran regarded the education of women as instrumental in raising the tone of the family and nation, an essential part of the struggle for political emancipation. Those who subscribed to this viewpoint included sections of the aristocracy and also members of the substantial class of state officials and intellectuals who

8 'Inas Mektebi Talebleri' – School for Girls, Balikesir, Western Anatolia, c.1890s. From the photographic archives of Sultan Abdul Hamid, Istanbul.

This would have been one of the early generation of state schools for girls established in Turkey in the second half of the nineteenth century, and is evidence that educational opportunities for girls, although still very limited, were not entirely confined to the large cities. Unusually, for school photographs, the children are posed without their teacher. They seem quite unperturbed by the camera, and for the most part look directly at it.

These school portraits, which later became part of the unthinking rituals of school life, at this time symbolized the new kinds of relationships which these girls experienced with their teachers and peers, when previously their personal contacts would have been mostly confined to their families and neighbours.

were prominent in the 1906 constitutional revolution in Iran, the Young Turk revolution in Turkey and the early nationalist groupings in the Arab world.

Although some advocates of women's right to education also wanted wider measures for women's emancipation, others placed a more restricted interpretation on the role of education. The latter group argued that the purpose of education for women was primarily to make them better wives and mothers. When the first girls' school was opened in Istanbul in 1858, the official view of its goals was very much along these lines.

> Women should be educated in the same way as men with a view to enabling them to help and comfort their husbands on whose shoulders rests the responsibility of earning the family's living. Moreover, education will greatly help women towards a better understanding of religious and secular considerations, and encourage them to obey their husbands, to refrain from going against their wishes and above all, will protect their honour.[6]

One of the earliest advocates of women's education in Lebanon, the Christian intellectual Butros Bustani, also stressed that educating women would make them more virtuous.[7]

Conservative opponents of women's education, however, took a different view of its effects. They argued that it would make women less, rather than more amenable to the wishes of men. A common complaint, which became almost a cliché, was that women who were taught to write would gain the power to communicate with men outside their household, and that this would inevitably lead to the writing of love letters and to illicit liaisons. Thus education of women was viewed as a challenge to male authority. It was also argued that to educate women was pointless because they would not make any use of it, and would simply be distracted

from their 'natural' role as wives and mothers.

Those who advocated women's education in the more radical context of a wider campaign for emancipation shared the view of the conservatives that it would pose a challenge to these aspects of male control over women's lives. The Egyptian poet and writer Malak Hifni Nasif, addressing the National Congress in Heliopolis in 1911, demanded compulsory primary education for both sexes. Nasif, whose father was a shaikh of al-Azhar University and a disciple of Qasim Amin, took a more radical and feminist view of the goals of women's education, arguing that women should be educated to further their own personal development, rather than simply to make them better at performing their traditional roles.[8]

In the late nineteenth and early twentieth century there was a gradual increase in the opportunities for women to go to school, not only with the spread of mission education but with the establishment of embryonic state education systems in a number of areas. Until after World War I the scale remained small but it marked the beginning of a change in attitude in official circles to the idea of women's education.

In Turkey, Abdul Hamid's suspicions of the role of foreign schools and his refusal to allow Muslims to attend them were accompanied by efforts to expand the public education system in Turkey and the Arab provinces of Syria, Lebanon, Palestine and Iraq. After the Young Turk revolution of 1908, the Committee of Union and Progress (CUP) further expanded the system and placed more emphasis on education for girls.

9 Calisthenics at a private teacher-training school for women in Istanbul, 1914 (AH 1332).

This school was established before World War I by the educationalist Sati' al-Husri. His family came from Aleppo in Syria and, like a number of his relatives, he entered the Ottoman civil service. During the Second Constitutional period, from 1909 until 1914, Husri campaigned within the Department of Education in Istanbul for educational reform in the Ottoman Empire. He adopted Western principles of education, and argued that it was not enough for teachers to know their subjects: they needed to be trained in teaching techniques. To this end he set up his own school to train women teachers. After World War I he and his Turkish wife Cemile moved to Syria and then to Iraq, where Husri became an ardent supporter of Arab nationalism.[2]

After Muhammad Ali's failed attempt to establish girls' schools in Egypt, Khedive Ismail made another start in the 1870s with two girls' schools: the Siyufiyya school established by Khedive Ismail's wife Tcheshme Hanum in 1873 and the Qirabiyya school founded in 1874 by the *Awqaf* (religious endowments foundation). At first these schools attracted quite a number of pupils, mostly the daughters of high officials, but after Ismail's deposition in 1879 the numbers tailed off and the two schools were subsequently amalgamated into an institute for orphans and poor girls. In 1889 it was reorganized to become the Sanniyya school, later famous as a teacher-training institute. The first state-run girls' primary school was opened in 1895.[9]

Education for women in Iran had been limited to a handful of private schools until the 1906 revolution, when women joined men in demanding a state system of female education. According to Russian sources, a meeting of women in Tehran in 1907 adopted a number of resolutions including one which called for the building of girls' schools. By 1910 there was a total of forty-one girls' schools in the whole of Iran with just over 2,100 pupils.[10]

In the period following World War I, state education for women expanded in most parts of the Middle East, so that by the 1930s primary education was quite widely available in urban areas and secondary schools were being established. In general, these state schools offered opportunities for girls from middle-class families to receive an education, though the upper classes on the whole

10 Embroidery lesson at a school for Muslim girls in Oujda, eastern Morocco, 1930s–50s.

In Morocco, as in Algeria, education for girls laid stress on the development of what were considered to be suitable manual skills.

still tended to send their children to private schools.

While ideas of education for women owed something to Western influence and to notions about 'catching up' with the West, the attitude of the European colonial powers towards education in the regions they controlled was often ambivalent. Western observers often attributed the 'degradation' of 'Islamic culture' to, among other things, the ignorance and oppressed condition of its women but the enthusiasm of Western colonial rulers for educating these women was often tempered by economic and political considerations.

Both the British and French gave some encouragement to women's education but in colonial budgets education and social services usually came low in the list of priorities. In Algeria, under French rule since 1830, the law passed in France in 1886–87 which made primary education for both sexes obligatory was applied in Algeria only at the Governor General's discretion and was not enforced on the indigenous population. The number of Arab or even Berber girls attending school grew very slowly, partly because of a strong resistance to women's education and also suspicions of the motives of the colonial authorities. The numbers of primary schools for girls also grew very slowly. From the 1890s the curriculum was revised to focus on utilitarian subjects, much of the girls' time being consumed with 'housework', and some craft schools for girls were established. Another major difficulty in expanding female education was that there was no cadre of female teachers.[11]

In Iraq, women's education got off to a slow start under Ottoman rule since the state system introduced under Abdul Hamid was very limited and there were fewer foreign or community schools than in the other Arab provinces of the empire. In Iraq's case the effect of British indirect rule under the Mandate system on education was not adverse. Some encouragement was given to establish more schools and the Arab education system expanded quite rapidly in the 1920s and 1930s, though as far as female education was concerned

11 'Ittihat ve Terakki Kiz Mektebi' – School of Union and Progress for Girls, Alexandria (Egypt). Published in Sehbal *magazine.*

The Committee of Union and Progress which took power in Turkey in 1908 stressed the importance of women's education. This was a school set up by their supporters in Egypt. Note the Western style of dress of the students.

the starting-point after World War I was very low. By 1930 there were 7,000 girls in school compared with 27,000 boys. Secondary education became available for girls only in 1929.[12]

Both in Syria under French, and Palestine under British rule, the demand for education during the Mandate period seems to have outstripped provision, particularly in the rural areas. And predictably, the provision of education for girls, though it improved, lagged far behind that for boys. The Palestinian educationalist Abdul-Latif Tibawi who worked in the Palestine Education Department under the British Mandate challenged the British official view that while there was a strong demand for the education of boys, there was little such pressure for education of girls, because of religious and social prejudices. He wrote that in 1944/45, of 400 government village schools, only forty-six were for girls, with a total roll of 3,392 pupils compared with 38,760 boys. In the towns, he added, despite the fact that the practice of secluding women still continued in some sectors of society, there were none the less two girls for every three boys attending school. He suggested that one of the main reasons for the paucity of female education in the countryside was that for the first fifteen years of the Mandate, the authorities made no provision whatsoever for the training of women teachers for rural schools.[13]

Despite the force of Tibawi's argument, there was one factor that he did not mention. That was the reluctance of peasant families to send their daughters to school, not merely out of ignorance or religious prejudice, but because girls were regarded from a young age as part of the family labour force and were needed to look after younger children or help their mothers with domestic and agricultural tasks. This has proved to be one of the major problems in promoting the spread of female education in rural areas, not just in Palestine, but in most parts of the Middle East. Even governments willing to invest much more money and effort in education than the British were in Palestine have found it difficult until quite recently to persuade parents to enrol their daughters in school and keep them there.

Higher Education and the Educational Establishment

In most parts of the Middle East access to higher education for women was gained, in principle at least, with far less of a struggle than primary or secondary education. Istanbul University formally admitted women from 1921; in 1926 Damascus University allowed women into the faculties of medicine, law and arts, despite the fact that the debate about secondary education for girls in Syria continued long after this date. When the University of Tehran opened in 1936 both sexes were admitted. At the American University of

12 *Travel pass, issued to Süreyya Ağaoğlu, Istanbul University, 1920/21.*

Süreyya Ağaoğlu was the first woman to study law at the university. She had graduated from a Turkish girls' college in 1919 and applied to the university's faculty of law. Her father, who had encouraged her education, was a professor of law, which may have helped her case. She was told that the faculty of law could not create a class for one woman – since it had not begun formally admitting women students at this time – and that she must find two other women students to enrol for the law degree. This she did and the three started their studies in the afternoons (the men's classes were in the mornings). But after six months the two classes were allowed to integrate. Süreyya Ağaoğlu's memory is that the male students behaved 'very well' towards the three women. She began practising as a lawyer in 1929 (see Chapter V, Caption 21).

Beirut, coeducation was formally introduced in 1926 but until 1951 women students had to attend a separate institution, Beirut College for Women, for their freshman (*sic*) and sophomore years (AUB followed the American university system).

At AUB's 'twin' institution, the American University in Cairo, women were first admitted in 1929 while at Cairo University, the rector, Ahmad Lutfi Sayyid, who was an advocate of women's education and was urged on by leaders of the Egyptian Feminist Union, quietly allowed qualified women to begin their studies at around the same time. He relied in doing so on the clause in the university's charter which said that it was open to all Egyptians. In fact, at both AUC and Cairo University, women had been attending talks and even giving lectures on an informal basis since the years of World War I and well-known women intellectuals of the day, such as the Lebanese writer May Ziyadeh and Malak Hifni Nasif, had delivered lectures there.

By the late 1920s, the Egyptian Feminist Union was including among its demands 'equality of men and women in higher education to be opened to all women who want it'. The reasons they gave were an interesting amalgam of the various arguments which had been made in favour of women's education:

1. It makes women better able to fill the duties of wife and mother.
2. It helps those who need work to find an honest job.
3. It helps those with natural talents to realize and profit from them.
4. It raises the general intellectual level of the country.
5. The understanding between husband and wife cannot be complete with an ill-educated wife.[14]

All this time these changes touched so small a group of women out of the whole population that although they represented a triumph for the advocates of women's education, they were not yet perceived as a serious threat to male domination of education and the professions, despite the ritual objections of conservatives.

Perhaps more influential and significant was the appearance of women of stature and determination within the education services where, because departments dealing with women's education were new, they were able to rise to positions of some authority. One of the most forceful of these women was Nabawiyya Musa, who became briefly director of Women's Public Education in Egypt in the late 1920s. Unlike many of the other early members of the Egyptian Feminist Union and women activists generally, she did not come from an upper-class background, but from a conservative middle-class family of modest means. She was the first girl to sit the state secondary-school examinations in 1907, studying at home because there were no secondary schools (apart from expensive private ones) open to women at this time. She later graduated from the Sanniyya school as a teacher.

More than any of the other early Egyptian feminists she devoted her life to the promotion of women's education, which she saw as the key to improving other aspects of women's lives. She was particularly concerned that educational opportunities still did not reach girls from poor families, both because insufficient schools were available and because of family opposition to women's education. She established a school in Alexandria which concentrated on giving an educational start to girls from poor families, encouraging them to go on to state schools. In the late 1920s, when she was in charge of women's education, the atmosphere under a liberal-minded Minister of Education favoured the development of female education, though it suffered a setback after the fall of the Wafd government in 1930.[15]

In Iran, where opposition to women's education seems to have been more ferocious, Mrs Bamdad ol-Moluk, herself one of the leading educationalists of the time, tells in her book *From Darkness into Light* of how women first ventured into educational administration. Shams ol-Haya Mansuri became the first provincial chief inspectress of girls' schools. The daughter of a liberal constitutionalist from Shiraz, she had learnt to read and write from her father and after her marriage at the age of twelve resumed her education.

When, as an adult, she moved from Tehran back to Shiraz in 1921, she found the atmosphere more liberal than in the capital, and when in 1923 the local eduction department decided to convert the Quran schools into state primary schools, there was a chronic shortage of women teachers and adminstrators for the girls' schools. Even educated upper-class women would not serve in the education department, so Shams ol-Haya and five other women joined as volunteers. They faced some violent opposition from local people, men and women, who disapproved of sending girls to school. Later Shams ol-Haya moved to the educational department

13 Cartoon of Nabawiyya Musa portraying her conflicts with the Egyptian Ministry of Education which appeared in Ruz al-Yusuf *on 18 February 1930.*

It plays on the relationship, here thrown into question, between assertiveness and maleness. (Nabawiyya Musa testified in her trial, exposing the many offences perpetrated in the Ministry of Education by Abd al-Fattah Bey Sabri and Ali Bey Umar)
– All right, enough now! Shame! You're a woman and we're men – you can't talk to us like that!
– Men are in the eyes of the beholder. Who told you I'm a woman? I'm the man and you're the woman!

The Education of a Woman Doctor

Saneya Haboub, one of the first women to practise as a doctor in Lebanon, gave the following account of her educational experience to the Lebanese novelist Hanan al-Shaykh.

Saneya was born at the turn of the century and her mother, Turkish in origin but brought up in Algeria, was from the outset determined that her daughter should receive the education she herself had been denied. So Saneya was sent at the age of two and a half years to a school run by an old woman renowned for her severe discipline. In 1907 she went on to a religious school in the Ain al-Mraise district of Beirut, and subsequently to an English school where she excelled at Arabic language – and at games, despite the fact, she says, that she was fat. At the age of twelve she got her wish to move to the American School in Beirut, but at fourteen her father told her that a Dr Bouji, whom he described as 'a good and clever man' had asked to marry her. She replied, 'As you like, father,' without really thinking of the consequences. Two and a half years later they were married, but soon her husband went off to Germany to study, and since she had not become pregnant, she decided to continue her education. It seems her husband recognized her lack of interest in the marriage and they later separated. When Saneya had completed her studies at the American School, she went on to Beirut College for Women. Although her parents encouraged her to continue her studies they faced the derision of neighbours whose opposition to the idea of educating girls extended to sending the family threatening letters.

Saneya came to the decision that she wanted to study medicine in the United States and was enrolled at the Medical College of Pennsylvania. She supported herself by working as a laboratory assistant and therefore scarcely went out and had little social life. After she graduated one of the women lecturers offered her a job at a local hospital, but she was obliged to refuse and return home because her mother was seriously ill. Back in Beirut, she decided she wanted to work as a gynaecologist after her father told her that there were many women who refused to see a doctor because doctors were all men.

When she started to practise, people at first called her a *dayyah* (midwife) which made her angry (because it implied at that time that she was unqualified – see pp. 165–6) but very soon she had more patients than she could deal with. She and Adma Abu Shadid, who graduated from medical college at almost the same time, were the first women doctors practising in Lebanon and they served as a model for other women wanting to be doctors.

She met her second husband, journalist Muhammad al-Naqqash, when he came to interview her about her work. They had two daughters.*

*Summarized from a series of articles by Hanan al-Shaykh which appeared in *Al-Nahar* supplement, Beirut, 1974–5

14 *'Maalimeh [teacher] Catibeh. Teacher at Ram Alla 1877'. A. Rosenthal & M. Martinovicz, Jerusalem.*

Catibeh (or Katibah) al-Khouri was the teacher at the Quaker mission's girls' school in Ramallah, Palestine, from about 1877 until the late 1880s. She came from Souq al-Gharb in Lebanon, where she had trained as a teacher. She was later joined at the Ramallah school by her sister. But Katibah's position as a woman working as a teacher away from her own community was not an easy one. She worked closely with the head of the Ramallah mission, Jacob Hishmeh, who came from Nazareth and had trained at the Church Missionary Society school in Jerusalem, and with his wife Jamilah. Katibah and Jamilah also ran a society for women in the district. In the 1880s, however, rumours began to circulate about a relationship between Jacob and Katibah. In 1885 he became involved in a legal dispute with the London committee of the Quakers and Katibah was subsequently dismissed from her teaching post because of the 'scandalous rumours' about an illicit relationship. She went to teach in Jerusalem, and in 1895, after Jamilah's death, she and Jacob were married.[3]

in Isfahan and subsequently became headmistress of a girls' state secondary school in Tehran.[16]

As women's teacher-training colleges were established throughout the region, more women were gradually drawn into the teaching profession, which today is considered one of the most acceptable jobs for women. But for a long time, regional imbalances remained. Lebanon, for instance, had long been exporting women teachers, begining in the late nineteenth century when religious groups such as the Quakers sent Lebanese women teachers to work in their girls' school in Ramallah, and their other village schools in Palestine.

In the 1930s, Freya Stark, visiting a girls' school in Baghdad, remarked on the number of 'Syrian teachers' there (she included Lebanese under this category). She noted that the Beiruti teachers' French clothes and city manners were both resented and imitated among their Iraqi counterparts and even among the students. Her description contains a characteristic note of condescension, but she none the less acknowledges their courage in going to work far from home:

> Among the various forms of pluck in the world, that of these little Arab teachers deserves a mention. They give themselves no airs of feminine emancipation, but at eighteen or twenty launch out alone into strange and distant cities: they find their own lodgings and make their own lives in countries where professional women are as yet unknown and quite unprovided for; and they do it with a cheerful enthusiasm which middle-aged people attribute to ignorance and youth.[17]

Education has not proved to be quite the panacea for women's problems that some of its early advocates hoped. Both in the Middle East and in other parts of the world this breakthrough, for which reformers fought, has been for the most part absorbed into existing power structures of both class and gender. Today, questions are being raised about the nature and content of education, and whether, in its present form, it does not frequently reinforce sexual and social oppression. Yet even with the benefit of hindsight, and an awareness of the difficulties and disillusionment which followed, the photographs and the stories of those early women students, graduates and teachers do reflect something of the sense of hope and enthusiasm education inspired in that era.

15 A Syrian former teacher at the Church Missionary Society school at Wad Madani, Sudan. Studio portrait, 1920s–30s.

According to the caption, her father had left Aleppo 'to get his family educated, and also that he might put a store of ready-made goods in Wad Madani'.

Chapter VIII
Campaigning Women

New Images

The twentieth century brought a wave of new images of women which contradicted many of the past assumptions both in their own societies and in the West. There were photographs which showed women addressing meetings, marching in demonstrations, attending international conferences. Pictures of this kind appeared in local newspapers and magazines and occasionally in the Western press, which otherwise rarely showed Middle Eastern women in any political context.

These new roles evoked mixed reactions from the photographers (mostly male) who took the pictures, the journalists who wrote about them, and from viewers. Some were hostile because women were portrayed as active, taking initiatives in the public eye; others, especially Westerners, regarded these manifestations of women's new assertiveness as an interesting curiosity. The woman marching in a Cairo demonstration might represent the opposite of the passive stereotype of the harem woman, but for many less informed Western observers, she still had a quality of otherness. While the image of the English suffragette demonstrating in the streets of London might seem very threatening, the sight of a Middle Eastern woman demanding her rights was usually viewed as curious rather than disturbing.

In all parts of the Middle East where active women's movements emerged, they were closely linked to two other developments: the spread of formal education for women, and the emergence of nationalism as a key political feature in the region. Both these factors affected the self-images of women campaigning for emancipation and the images others created for them. Nationalism took several forms: pan-Turkism and pan-Arabism, based on the notion of an identity of all peoples sharing the same language and culture; and specific nationalisms, which emerged from the collapse of the Ottoman Empire, based on the boundaries dictated by the Great Powers at the end of World War I.

Except in Turkey, these specific nationalist movements focused mainly on a struggle for political independence from the direct or indirect control of the Western powers. Their ideologies of popular unity allowed women as well as men to become activists and to gain respect for public political participation. It even became quite common to personify the nation in the figure of a woman, attributing to this figure heroism, patient suffering under oppression, or the use of 'feminine wiles' against the colonial ruler. But as Marina Warner points out, the use of women's bodies to represent

Justice, Liberty and Wisdom in eighteenth- and nineteenth-century Western art did not necessarily mean that women could expect either justice or liberty from society. Similarly, the embodiment of the nation in the figure of a woman did not always imply the readiness of the nation to allow women a full share in the fruits of national independence.[1] National-ism opened many doors for women's participation but very soon began to slam others.

At the same time, however, new demands being made by or on behalf of women sought to give them more individual rights and freedoms. These included the demand for educa-tion for women, and for improvements in their status within the family and marriage. Political rights and enfranchisement were usually the demands given least priority.

Most women campaigning for emancipation saw education as a crucial means of releasing women from their 'back-room' role in society. A pioneer of women's education in Iran, Dorrat ol-Ma'li Khanum, expressed this view: 'In our country there have always been numerous women who dominated men and indirectly determined the course of important events. What distresses me is the fact that they gained this influence through charm and allurement and felt no need for intelligence and rationality.'[2] A few historical examples suggest that women's political roles may have been more diverse than Dorrat ol-Ma'li's comment implies, but she was voicing a sentiment shared in reformist circles that women should be able to participate in public life as of right, rather than simply because they were exceptional indi-viduals.

It is certainly possible to find examples from the nineteenth and early twentieth centuries of women who intervened in political life. Even among poor women there were those who were not afraid to raise their voices in public. Lucie Duff Gordon wrote of Cairene women in 1863: 'The Pasha has ordered all the women of the lower classes to keep indoors while he [the Sultan] is here. Arab women are outspoken, and might shout out their grievances to the great Sultan.'[3] During strikes which took place in Turkey in the 1870s, particularly over delays in payments of workers' wages, wives, mothers and sisters joined in the protests. In 1876, during a dockworkers' strike, women armed with sticks attacked strike-breakers. In the textile industry, with a predominantly female labour force, there were nine strikes between 1872 and 1907.[4]

But though women from these classes might voice their grievances and try to oppose injustices, they were rarely able to exert power or influence as individuals. Those who from time to time were able to do so came mostly from prominent families, whether in urban-based, rural or tribal societies, and their ability to command, or to influence events beyond the family circle depended mostly on their class and status in society. As individuals, however, they were unusual because

1 Mahd-e Awliya, mother of Nasir ed-Din, Shah of Iran.

Mahd-e Awliya appears to have had a considerable, and not always benign influence on affairs of state: for example, she is said to have played a leading role in the dismissal of Nasir ed-Din's first reform-minded chief minister. Yet she was respected for her learning and intellectual acuity. The nineteenth-century Iranian chronicler Mo'ayer al-Mamalek gave the following description of her.

'She was not beautiful but was endowed with spiritual virtues; she had character and integrity and was well-versed in Persian literature, Arabic language and calligraphy. She had studied history and religion and could compose poetry. Her private library was made up mostly of these two subjects. She talked in an engaging manner and was quick-witted, using colloquialisms and stories a lot. After the death of [her husband] Muhammad Shah [in 1848] and until the arrival of the crown prince [Nasir ed-Din] from Tabriz, she took over the affairs of state like a man. Every day the ministers and statesmen would present themselves in the big hall of the palace and [Mahd-e Awliya] would discuss affairs of state with them from behind a curtain and issue orders and instructions. When the crown prince arrived at the capital and became Shah, each time mother and son would come across each other they would bow. And however much the son pleaded with his mother to stop this practice, she refused. Mahd-e Awliya ran a grand and elaborate establishment . . . Every day, about sixty or seventy of Fath Ali Shah's children and other grandee ladies would gather at her palace . . . She held her own religious ceremonies . . . On days of mourning, ladies would gather round the food table and she would then herself begin the recitation of the Quran [accompanying herself] on the *shur* [musical instrument].'[1]

2 Fatima al-Asad (Umm Kamil), 1898–1978.

Fatima al-Asad was the eldest daughter of Kamil al-Asad, one of the most powerful landowners in southern Lebanon. Fatima and her sister were brought up in the strictest seclusion. Their father, who had two wives, is remembered as having been very harsh with the women in his family. Fatima was taught to read, though not to write, by a *shaikh*, and in later life she always read a good deal.

When Fatima was twenty-six, her father died and a new phase of her life began. She married her cousin Ahmad, which secured her share of the family inheritance. At the time Ahmad was nineteen, seven years her junior, and a student at the American University of Beirut. The family's affairs, economic and political, seem to have been left largely in their hands, especially after the death of Ahmad's father Abdul Latif in 1934.

Umm Kamil, as she came to be known after the birth of her son, continued to live a secluded life but wielded great influence in political and family affairs. Her husband, initially inexperienced and, in her view, too trusting of people, came to depend on her shrewd judgement. Over the years her stature grew and she was often referred to as *Umm al-Junub* (mother of the South).

212

3 Adila Khan. C.J. Edmonds (a British political officer in Iraq), Iraqi Kurdistan, 1920s.

Adila Khan, whom Edmonds referred to as 'the Lady Adila', came from a prominent Kurdish family in northern Iraq. She was married to Osman Pasha, a leading member of the Jaf tribe of southern Kurdistan. Towards the end of the Ottoman era, he had been appointed *qaimaqam* (district governor) of the Kurdish province of Shahrizur.
'By all accounts,' Edmonds wrote, 'he was an easy-going man who was frequently absent from his post, and all effective authority gradually passed, even during his lifetime, into the hands of his wife, Adila Khan. At the time of the [British] occupation, she was already a widow, but remained the uncrowned queen of Shahrizur.'[2]
During the 1920 Iraqi uprising against the British, she was a staunch supporter of the British and was later decorated by the government. When this picture was taken in the 1920s, she exercised her influence through her son Ahmad Beg (*right*) who was nominally *qaimaqam* for the region.

they found ways of making or influencing decisions normally left in the hands of men.

To reinforce their arguments about women's inherent capabilities, feminists from time to time also searched their own history, especially that of early Islam, for examples of independent women. They looked to the heroines of that age, such as Aisha, one of the prophet Muhammad's wives, who after his death played a significant role in Meccan politics and even accompanied an army into battle during the struggles of succession which dominated the politics of the early caliphates.[5]

In Shia Islam, a heroine emerged from the party which struggled against Aisha and her allies. Zeynab, the sister of Hussain, one of the contenders for the caliphate who is regarded as one of the great martyrs of Shia Islam, is portrayed as a woman of great courage and ability, who took charge of the remnants of Hussain's followers after his death.[6]

Inherent in the references to these women was the often-repeated view held by most Muslim women involved in feminist movements that Islam was not initially unjust to women. They argued that it was the customs which had

Challenging Authority: a Babi Intellectual

Several women played a prominent part in the Babi movement, led by Mirza Ali Muhammad, known as the Bab, which emerged in the 1840s as a breakaway from orthodox Shia Islam. One of its distinguishing features was to accord more rights and freedoms to women. The fulsome praise given to these women by the Babis and their sympathizers probably owes more to their heroic status in the movement than their qualities as women. None the less, the following description, by a Babi sympathizer, of Qorrat al-Ain, one of the leading Babi intellectuals, does paint a picture of a remarkable woman, even when allowance is made for the hagiographic exaggerations.

Qorrat al-Ain was the daughter of a member of the *ulema* (Shia clergy) which probably explains why she received such an extensive religious education. She joined the Babi movement, which soon came into conflict with the Qajar regime and the orthodox religious authorities, and after a Babi attempt to assassinate Nasir ed-Din Shah, Qorrat al-Ain was executed in Tehran in about 1850, after a term of imprisonment.

She was 'the daughter of Hajji Mullah Salik, the sage of Kasvin, the erudite doctor. She, according to what is related, was skilled in diverse arts, amazed the understandings and thoughts of the most eminent masters by her eloquent dissertations on the exegesis and traditions of the perspicious [*sic*] Book [the Quran] . . . At the supreme shrines [Nejf and Kerbela in Iraq] she borrowed light on matters divine from the lamp of Kazim (Hajji Sayyid Kazim of Resht – the teacher of the Bab) and freely sacrificed her life in the way of the Bab. She discussed and disputed with the doctors and the sages, loosing her tongue to establish her doctrine. Such fame did she acquire that those people who were scholars or mystics sought to hear her speech and were eager to become acquainted with her powers of speculation and deduction. She had a brain full of tumultuous ideas and thoughts vehement and restless. In many places she triumphed over the contentious, expounded the most subtle quotations . . . In short, in elocution she was the calamity of the age, and in ratiocination the trouble of the world. Of fear and timidity there was not a trace in her heart, nor had the admonitions of the kindly-disposed any profit or fruit for her. Although she was of (such as are) damsels (meet) for the bridal bower, yet she wrested pre-eminence from stalwart men, and continued to strain the feet of steadfastness until she yielded up her life at the sentence of the mighty doctors in Tehran.'*

Ali Muhammad Shirazi, *A Traveller's Narrative to Illustrate the Episode of the Bab* ed. and trs. by E.G. Brown, Cambridge 1891, pp. 30–2

4 An Iranian painting of Rostameh, a woman who was regarded as a heroine of the early Babi movement in Iran.

She was said to be one of the leaders of the Babi uprising against the Qajar monarchy in Zinjan in the 1850s when the Shah's troops besieged the town for almost a year. The bravery of the Babi women during this siege became legendary. The style of this painting seems to owe much to Western nineteenth-century images of women as the personification of heroic virtues of justice, patriotism and wisdom – for example, the figure of Britannia common in British imperial art.[3]

evolved during later centuries which had hedged women's lives with restrictions such as seclusion, which could not necessarily be extrapolated from the original tenets of Islam.

Some women, however, sought images of capable and free women beyond the historical boundaries of Islam, going back to pre-Islamic days to seek examples of a freer, more untrammelled life for women: for instance, in some of its literature, the Egyptian Feminist Union looked to the Pharaonic era for images of independent women.

Women in the Middle East also began to act consciously to project new images. They allowed themselves to be photographed when they knew that the resulting pictures were not just to be put in a family album, but would be publicly visible. Huda Shaarawi and Saiza Nabrawi, for example, gave the press photographs of themselves when they made news by appearing unveiled in public for the first time in 1923 (see pp. 139–40).

Another, earlier example came from Iran in the period leading up to the 1906 constitutional revolution. One of Nasir ed-Din Shah's daughters, Malek-e Iran, was an ardent constitutionalist and her husband, Zahir ol-Dowleh, was head of the Okhuvat (Brotherhood – a secret society supporting constitutionalism). She is said to have attended the meetings of the society unveiled and to have spoken at them. Both she and her daughters were members of a *darvish* (Sufi) order and, according to Bamdad ol-Moluk, her daughters allowed themselves to be photographed in *darvish* costume with their faces uncovered, clearly making a political point.

The Development of Feminist Ideas

Debates about women's status had developed in the late nineteenth century in the Middle East as part of a wider discussion about the nature of society. These debates were most intense in the intellectual centres of the region: first in Istanbul, Cairo, Beirut and Tehran, but over time, they reverberated beyond these capitals. The ideas expressed varied from those of the Islamic reform movement, strongest in Turkey and Egypt, to the secular modernist ideas expounded by an intellectual circle based in Beirut.

Women began to join in these debates, both in private and through the medium of a thriving press. First in Lebanon and Egypt, then in Turkey and Iran, magazines directed at the small audience of literate women became important vehicles for spreading new ideas and attitudes and gave new confidence to those women who wrote and published them. Later, magazines appeared which directly represented the views of organized feminist groups, such as the Egyptian Feminist Union's *l'Egyptienne* (in French, directed at an international as well as an Egyptian audience – launched in 1925) and *al-Misriyya* (in Arabic – launched during the

5 *A cartoon from* Ruz al-Yusuf *in which a woman symbolizes Egypt being wooed by the British High Commissioner, published on 11 February 1930.*
'*The liberal constitutionalists' press begins to attack and wound His Eminence the High Commissioner.*
Egypt: *Why is that bunch pelting you with bricks?*
High Commissioner: *Because they see how polite I am to you.*'

This cartoon appeared during the prolonged political crisis in Egypt after King Fuad had dismissed the first Wafd (nationalist) government in 1928 and closed parliament. The British were viewed as having backed the King in this action. The liberal constitutionalist cabinet, which was in office at the time this cartoon was published, also objected to British interference. Here Egypt is portrayed in the dress of a well-to-do, respectable woman, with the star and crescent on her forehead identifying her as the symbol of the nation. She is apparently in danger of succumbing to the blandishments of the High Commissioner, a sign that Egypt – portrayed as having the weaknesses of a woman – is itself in danger.

6 *May Ziyadeh, a Lebanese writer and poet who settled in Cairo at the turn of the century and became an influential figure in literary circles.*

She espoused feminist ideas, particularly in relation to the role of women as writers and artists. In an address to a press banquet in Cairo in 1928 she gave the following analysis of how, in the history of Arabic literature, women had largely followed the intellectual and stylistic dictates of men.

'Until very recently, when an Arab woman ventured to raise her voice, she was content [merely] to follow the beaten track, reiterating whatever ideas and sentiments were in vogue, and above all, imitating the very shadow of man, her master and law-maker. With very few exceptions, our most famous women of antiquity – women whose names and deeds have come down to us over the centuries – limited themselves to elegies, verses in praise of famous men and, on occasion, epic poetry. We can sense a certain constraint in their writings, due, no doubt, to their position in society. There is almost always a concern to imitate men, to write like men, without seeking to discover their true selves and to find an adequate means of expression for that other, feminine aspect of human nature.

'However, two Egyptian women – since here I'm speaking particularly of Egypt – were more honest and natural: the first of these is the poetess Aisha Ismet Taymour . . . who died in 1902. Several of her lyrical, elegiac poems reveal an exquisite feminine sensibility. The second is the much-lamented Malak Hifni Nasif, better known under the pseudonym Bahissat al-Badiah (searcher of the desert) who died young in 1918. In her writings of social criticism a new voice is heard, expressing the anguish of modern woman and her need for social reform, education, emancipation and progress.'[4]

7 The poet Parvine Etesami was born in Tabriz in 1906. She was educated at home up to high-school level and her family then moved to Tehran where she learnt English at the American School. Her father was an intellectual who used to translate Western poetry into Farsi. He encouraged his daughter to appreciate poetry and by the age of nine she had already written her first poem.

In the 1920s she began teaching literature in Tehran and wanted to publish a book of poetry. Her father apparently accepted that she should go out to work but for fear of gossip would not allow her to publish a book of poetry while she was still unmarried. Publishing books was still not considered 'proper' for a woman at this time. In about 1934, at the age of twenty-eight, she married her cousin, mainly, it seems, in order to get her book published. She broke off the marriage after four months.

Her poetry became quite highly regarded, touching on both philosophical and religious themes, but she also wrote about aspects of women's emotional life, foreshadowing the poetry of Iran's greatest modern woman poet, Furugh Faroukhzad, who achieved enormous popularity in the 1950s and 1960s. Parvine Etesami died of typhoid at the age of thirty-five and was buried in the city of Qom.[5]

1930s). But the earliest women's magazines were created by a small number of well-educated women, most of them the product of Christian missionary schools in Lebanon.

Al-Fatat, the first magazine to be directed specifically at women, was set up in Alexandria, Egypt, in November 1892. Its founder was Hind Naufal, who came from Tripoli in Lebanon. In the first issue of the review *al-Hasna* (1909) also published in Lebanon, Georges Baz wrote the following appreciation of the early women's press and the important role of Syrian (including Lebanese) women writers in establishing it:

> Educated Syrian women soon realized that the only way for the Oriental woman to understand her rights and duties and widen the scope of her ideas is through the press – the most effective instrument after schools and the various women's associations. It is with this aim and in order to serve the public interest that we find them embarking on this course. It is only in Egypt, however, that they have seen their dream come true.[7]

Before 1910 eight more women's journals had appeared in Egypt. Though most were concerned with self-improvement and various kinds of domestic issues, they also carried from time to time articles on women's status, sometimes drawing comparisons with women's status in the West. A few also made a link between national liberation and the liberation of women.[8] In Turkey and Iran, the Young Turk revolution of 1908 and the constitutional revolution in Iran loosened the constraints previously imposed by censorship and a flood of new publications appeared, including a number of magazines and journals aimed specifically at women.

All these publications represented the aspirations of the newly literate generation of upper- and middle-class women, often from families which had been involved in political movements advocating reform. These women grasped eagerly and often eclectically at new ideas on how to view themselves and how to conduct their lives. The journals and magazines reflected this trend, mingling ideas and images drawn from the West with those from their own cultures.

Some women also longed for new forms of activity to match this ferment of ideas. Restless and impatient with their still-restricted lives, these well-to-do women in the main cities of the region began to form clubs and associations which gave them the chance to meet other like-minded women, to discuss their ideas and become involved in charitable activities. But if these developments were common ingredients of the women's movements which emerged in the first decades of the twentieth century, their specific characteristics were moulded by the wider political contexts in which they were formed, especially by the relationship of particular states with the West.

Feminism and the State: Turkey and Iran

The first women's organization in Turkey was formed in 1909, during the period of euphoria which followed the seizure of power by the Committee of Union and Progress (CUP). The Organization for the Improvement of the Status of Women was headed by Halide Edip (see p. 197). In 1913 another group was established with more radical aims – the Organization for the Rights of Women. This group initiated several campaigns, including one to give women the right to their own passports (a woman was not permitted to travel without the consent of her husband, father or brother) and, more importantly, a successful campaign to allow women to work in post offices (see also p. 163).

But the activities of these and other women's groups which emerged had little chance to develop as they were largely eclipsed by the succession of wars which engulfed Turkey from 1912 until 1922. The national need for labour swept aside prejudices against urban women working outside the home and resulted in their employment on a scale which the women's movement had not had a chance to achieve. Women worked in a variety of roles, from desk jobs to sweeping the streets and making roads. During the Turkish–Greek war of 1920–22 both urban and rural women fought in Atatürk's army. Women were also drawn into voluntary work in large numbers and the Red Crescent became the largest organization of women in the country. The Islamic Association for the Employment of Ottoman Women, founded in 1916, was also important in organizing women workers. According to Deniz Kandiyoti:

> . . . if the war effort created interest in women as workers there was no less interest in an intensification of their role as mothers and reproducers of the nation. It is interesting and significant that the Empire's first pro-natalist policies also focused on the employees of the Islamic Association for the Employment of Ottoman Women for whom mandatory marriage by the age of twenty-one for women and twenty-five for men was introduced. The Association used newspaper columns for matchmaking, provided girls with a trousseau and staged well-appointed wedding ceremonies.[9]

After the wars had ended, women's organizations were not left to campaign independently for change. The republican government of Kemal Atatürk, which came to power on a wave of patriotic fervour after World War I, rapidly took the initiative in making quite sweeping alterations in women's legal status, their freedom of movement and prospects for education and employment. Educational opportunities for women were expanded and a literacy campaign was launched. Most startling was the decision to change the personal-status law, previously based, as elsewhere in the region, on

8 Belkis Şekvet, the first woman in Turkey to fly in an aeroplane. Photograph published in a Turkish magazine, 1913.

This was part of a campaign launched by the Organization for the Rights of Women to obtain the right for women to travel without male consent. It was a publicity stunt, quite spectacular for its time, when flying was still a dangerous business, to draw attention to the fact that women, like men, were capable of physical courage and endurance.

Photographs of this kind, taken both by foreigners and Turkish photographers working for the government or for newspapers, were common in Turkey of the 1920s and 1930s. The 'new woman' was often seen, as here, in activities previously confined to men. Yet most of these photographs were less a comment on the changing divisions between male and female roles than a symbolic evocation of vigour, youth and energy in a new, regenerated Turkey.

sharia (Islamic religious) law. The new Turkish personal-status law, passed in 1926, was based on the secular Swiss code and went so far as to outlaw polygamy, a reform not achieved elsewhere in the Middle East until Tunisia's personal-status law reforms of 1956.

For urban middle- and upper-class women who gained most from the legal reforms as well as from education and employment opportunities, these changes were, as Turkey's first woman lawyer Süreyya Ağaoğlu recalls it, 'a breath of fresh air'. Halide Edip, leader of the first of the pre-war women's groups, became an ardent supporter of Atatürk as well as of the reforms. But important as these changes were, they took the initiative entirely out of the hands of women themselves, and in the view of some historians, made women instruments to be used for wider political ends. In particular, it is argued that Atatürk wanted to get rid of the remnants of the Ottoman state structure, based on religious law and precepts, and that changing women's status was a crucial part of this process.[10]

Though the reforms were certainly welcomed by women who had previously demanded change, they did not reflect the vision of those groups in the pre-war women's movement which had argued in favour of women's emancipation not from a secularist viewpoint but from the perspective of reformist Islam. Furthermore, among more conservative elements of the population, especially in the rural areas, the changes were not easily accepted. For instance, the legal protection of women's rights in marriage was often evaded by simply not marrying under civil law, but under *sharia* law. Many of the reforms also required women to take their case to court, something which was very difficult for poor and illiterate women.

Visual images of Turkish women from the 1920s and 1930s, however, reflected few of these doubts and ambiguities. The photographs which appeared in government-sponsored publications and in Western newspapers stressed women's new physical freedom, and their opportunities for

work and study. The many women who could not take full advantage of these benefits are much less in evidence. These photographs not only advertised improvements in women's lives but also symbolized the new dynamism and modernism of Turkey as a nation.

The Atatürk government not only pre-empted women's organizations by initiating reforms itself but it also changed their role. In place of the pluralistic movement of the pre-war period, reflecting a variety of ideas about women's emancipation, Atatürk established a single Turkish Women's Union which reflected Kemalist ideas. The measure of its subordination to the state was that in 1935, just after women had been given the vote in national elections and seventeen women had been returned as members of parliament, Atatürk closed the union down, saying that its task was complete. 'Liberation', it seemed, had been achieved by fiat.

In fact, the downfall of the Turkish Women's Union appeared to have been caused mainly by the one instance in which it deviated from official policy. Ironically it was also the occasion which gave it the widest publicity. In 1935 the organization played host to a conference of the International Alliance of Women, held in Istanbul, an occasion which brought the Turkish Women's Union considerable publicity in the local and international press. But during the conference, the Turkish delegates put forward a position similar to that taken by some of their European counterparts,

10 Three of the first women parliamentarians in Turkey on tour in the town of Nazilli, with officials from the municipality, 10 March 1937.

A total of seventeen women were elected as Members of Parliament in the 1935 elections. In no subsequent election, up to the present day, have as many women been returned as MPs.

220

favouring peace and disarmament. By implication, this was in opposition to the policies of the Axis powers, which were not represented at the conference. This view, however, was not endorsed by the Turkish government, which viewed the Turkish delegates' statements as allying Turkey with one side in the European political arena, while it wished to maintain a strictly neutralist position. This appears to have been the incident which triggered the demand that the Turkish Women's Union should 'dissolve' itself.[11]

None the less, the argument used publicly to justify the closure of the union – that everything necessary to women's emancipation had already been achieved in Turkey – gained some credence, even among women. It was undoubtedly one of the major reasons that, since the 1930s, Turkey has never had a strong women's movement independent of male-dominated political parties. But whatever the problems and limitations of the reforms of women's status in Turkey, they had a very considerable impact on thinking in other parts of the region, and were often held up as an example of what could be done if politicians only had the political will for change.

In Iran, the history of the women's movement has some parallels with its Turkish counterpart, particularly in the era after World War I when Reza Shah tried to initiate 'modernist' policies of social and economic reform along the lines of those implemented by Atatürk. But Iran's long experience of foreign interference in its internal affairs made the background to this period rather different from that of Turkey. Nationalist consciousness was based not so much on patriotic fervour as on anti-imperialism and resistance to foreign encroachment.

Stories of women's interventions in politics in the late nineteenth and early twentieth centuries centre on this resistance. The story is told that when Nasir ed-Din Shah signed a tobacco concession in 1890 which granted a monopoly to the British Imperial Tobacco Corporation of Persia, senior clergy and merchants organized a boycott of tobacco (this in a country where both men and women smoked). There was wide compliance with the boycott, and the women of Nasir ed-Din's harem, it is said, smashed their *qalyan* (water pipes) and refused to smoke even when asked to by Nasir ed-Din, saying that the clergy had forbidden smoking and even his command did not override that edict.[12] This story is also an indication of the clergy's ambivalent role where women were concerned. Mullahs often lent their authority to anti-imperialist actions with which more politicized women agreed, but equally members of the clergy periodically used their considerable influence to obstruct attempts to reform women's status.

It was during the constitutional revolution which began in 1906 that women first played a significant public role in politics. Many of those who became involved came from families of the intellectual and bureaucratic elites which led the revolution in opposition to the Qajar dynasty. Women joined secret societies and appeared in public demonstrations, often at considerable physical risk to themselves. Though there were men who admired their courage, there were others who were implacably opposed to women taking part in public gatherings, and sometimes resorted to physical violence against them.

The most famous incident of this period took place in 1911 when the new parliamentary government was wavering in the face of foreign pressure. Britain and Russia had divided Iran into spheres of influence under a treaty of 1907, and by 1911 the Russians were trying to prevent the parliament implementing a series of economic reforms. William Morgan Shuster, an American financial adviser brought in to assist with the reforms, observed that, 'They have a saying in Tehran that when the women take part in a *chuluk* (riot) against a cabinet of the government, the situation has become serious.' He recounted in dramatic detail the occasion when women intervened in the deliberations of the *majlis* (parliament). When rumours spread that the deputies had decided in secret session to surrender to Russia's demands, a group of women decided to act.

> Out from their walled courtyards and harems marched three hundred of that weak sex, with the flush of undying determination in their cheeks. They were clad in plain black robes with the white nets of their veils dropped over their faces. Many held pistols under their skirts or in the folds of their sleeves. Straight to the *majlis* they went and, gathered there, demanded of the President that he admit them all. What the grave deputies of the Land of the Lion and the Sun may have thought at this strange visitation is not recorded. The President consented to receive a delegation of them. In his reception hall they confronted him, and lest he and his colleagues should doubt their meaning, these cloistered Persian mothers, wives and daughters exhibited threateningly their revolvers, tore aside their veils, and confessed their decision to kill their own husbands and sons, and leave behind their own dead bodies if the Deputies wavered in their duty to uphold the liberty and dignity of the Persian people and nation.[13]

Shuster makes much of the image of these women breaking out of the harem into public view and, while the incident was undoubtedly dramatic, it is probable that many of these women had already participated in previous protests during the constitutional era and came from the stratum of educated women who were already involved to some extent in politics.

Although there were numerous photographers at work in Iran at this time, few photographs have come to light of women on public demonstrations. One Russian source claimed to have seen photographs of women with guns at barricades in the city of Tabriz, one of the main centres of the constitutional revolution. No photographs have emerged of the women's march on the *majlis*, but there is one painting of uncertain origin depicting the scene in the *majlis* in a melodramatic style which matches Shuster's narrative. It shows an unveiled woman brandishing a revolver while a group of turbaned deputies cower before her.

By the 1920s several groups had emerged to campaign for women's education and women's rights and a number of magazines and journals propagated their views. These organizations shifted the focus away from the nationalist issues which had preoccupied women activists in the era of the constitutional revolution. But as Reza Shah consolidated his power after the coup of 1921 he gradually narrowed the freedoms allowed to any independent groups, including those advocating women's rights. One of the main women's groups, the Patriotic Women's League, was dismantled by the government in 1932 for no known reason. In 1935 the Shah ordered the establishment of a government-subsidized organization entitled *Kanoon Banovan* (Ladies Centre) which concentrated on charitable works and implementing his decision that women should discard the veil (see pp. 130–1).

The more or less forcible abolition of the veil was Reza Shah's major reform in relation to women. But this symbolic gesture allowed him to duck most of the other major questions relating to women's status, especially as regards marriage, divorce and family rights. Polygamy and temporary marriage (*mut'ah*) remained. *Mut'ah* is a practice confined to Shia Islam whereby a man can very easily take a temporary 'wife' who is often little more than a servant, has few legal rights and can be repudiated without compensation. It was quite widely practised in Iran at that time. Since Reza Shah had three wives he was unlikely to be very keen on abolishing polygamy.[14] Although upper- and middle-class women certainly had more opportunities for education and even employment by the end of the 1930s when compared with previous decades, the basic reforms achieved were far less substantial that those in Turkey, while the independent women's movement had been similarly suppressed by the state.

'Independent' Feminism: Egypt

If the pace of change in women's status in Turkey and Iran was dictated mostly by the male rulers, women in Egypt had a rather different experience. During the same period, the Egyptian women's movement became the most forceful and independent of all the women's organizations in the region. None the less, male politicians still largely defined the limits of its effectiveness in changing crucial aspects of women's condition.

Nationalism, in Egypt as elsewhere in the Arab world, was the key to the legitimacy of the women's movement in the eyes of both politicians and the public. It was the resistance to the continuation of British rule during the years from 1919 to 1922 which gave women the chance to show publicly their commitment to the nationalist cause, and laid the organizational basis for the future women's movement. As in Iran, some women from families involved in nationalist politics, particularly in the newly-formed Wafd Party, played active roles in this conflict. When husbands and brothers were arrested and deported by the British, their wives and sisters were drawn into policy-making in their place. But a wider constituency of women was also attracted to the Wafdist camp. At a public meeting in Cairo in 1920 attended by about 1,000 women, a women's committee was formed within the Wafd Party, a previously unheard-of idea.[15]

But the most spectacular aspect of women's involvement in this struggle, from the point of view both of Egyptians and the outside world, was their participation in the mass street demonstrations which characterized the period. Both the uprising itself and women's participation in it attracted considerable press attention in Europe and the United States because Britain's control of Egypt was viewed as crucial to its imperial strategy. Its lines of communication with India depended on free passage through the Suez Canal.

Western photographers sent to cover these scenes of mass protest were obviously fascinated by the sight of carriage-loads of veiled women bearing anti-British placards and sometimes even addressing the crowds. The English picture magazine *The Sphere* (sister publication of the *Illustrated London News*, specializing in imperial affairs) on 31 May 1919 devoted a whole page to two large photographs of veiled Egyptian women in demonstrations, under the headline 'The New Désenchantées of Egypt', referring to Pierre Loti's novel of that name, published in 1910, which described Turkish women's discontent with their seclusion (see p. 11). The caption under one of the photographs showing a group of veiled women posed with an Egyptian flag reads,

> The stirrings behind the Mashribiyyehs of Constantinople which M. Pierre Loti discovered for the Western world appear to have communicated themselves to Cairo, where the women are beginning to claim new privileges and more freedom than has ever been known before. During the recent rioting in that city they took an active part in the proceedings, making speeches and parading in the streets with banners.[16]

But not all Western commentators took an interest in these scenes from the point of view of women's

11 Portrait of Safiya and Saad Zaghloul, on the cover of Ruz al-Yusuf, *28 December 1925.*

The caption refers to Safiya Zaghloul as *Umm al-Masriyyin* (mother of the Egyptians) and to Saad Zaghloul as the 'restorer of Egypt'. Safiya became directly involved in politics in 1919 when Saad, as leader of the Wafd Party, was deported to the Seychelles by the British, and she stepped into his place in the midst of the nationalist uprising. Though she later acquired this symbolic role in nationalist politics as the mother of the nation, she did not become closely involved in the feminist campaigns of the 1920s and 1930s. This photograph shows the Zaghlouls, as the caption says 'in their youth', as the ideal couple. But in the 1920s, this image would probably have suggested the sharing of responsibilities, for nation and family, which fitted the liberal idea that marriage should be a partnership, albeit one where the man retained final authority.

emancipation; some saw the women simply as another bunch of anti-British troublemakers. A news photographer working for the US-based INP agency wrote the following caption to one of his photographs of demonstrating women:

Egyptian women in Cairo demonstrate against the Milner Commission (22 January 1920). Egyptian women are now entering the political field. During the recent riots in Cairo many masked Egyptian women drove through the streets of the city shouting, 'Down with the Milner Commission' and waving red flags [actually the Egyptian national flag]. These women led on excited mobs and gangs of ruffians, and British soldiers were empowered to break up any such throngs and to disperse riotous gatherings.[17]

As the struggle developed, the participation of women widened beyond those directly associated with the Wafd leadership, though they continued to play a leading role in organizing women's actions. Women from the middle class, particularly teachers, writers and even actresses joined in the demonstrations. Schoolgirls went on strike, sometimes in defiance of their teachers. But it was from among women of

12 Veiled women addressing a crowd in a Cairo street, 1919. INP news agency photograph.

The women are apparently part of a street demonstration, riding in an open carriage and addressing the male onlookers. The atmosphere during the events of 1919–22 in Egypt was such that women were able to engage in public activities which previously would have been regarded as unacceptable, but which in the heat of the moment were tolerated and even welcomed.

the poorer classes, who also participated in the Cairo demonstrations, that the uprising claimed some of its martyrs. On 10 April 1919 a twenty-eight-year-old widow Shafiqa Bint Muhammad Ashmawi was killed when British troops opened fire on a crowd, and at least four other women are known to have been killed in subsequent clashes with British soldiers.[18]

Through the Wafd women's committee the range of actions taken by women was extended beyond participation in street demonstrations. During the 1922 boycott of British goods, according to Huda Shaarawi's memoirs, women withdrew their money from British banks and put it in the Egyptian national Bank Misr, something they could do independently, since Islamic law gave them control over their own property. They also organized a wider circle of women to boycott British consumer goods.[19]

The women who had become politically active during this period received something of a shock when this phase of the struggle against the British was over. Although male politicians praised the women for their dedication to the national cause, it rapidly became apparent that on general political questions, not to mention issues directly connected

13 The Wafd Women's Committee. Cover photograph of al-Musawwar, 13 March 1925.

The caption pays fulsome tribute to the contribution made by the women members of the Wafd Party to the Egyptian nationalist movement. Yet at this time, in the aftermath of the anti-British upheavals, appreciation of these women's political role had not persuaded the majority of male politicians of the need for major reforms of women's status. This committee represented mostly women of the upper class or from professional families. Note the variety of styles of dress: a few of the women are still fully veiled while the majority have discarded the veil entirely and wear hats or scarves.

with women's interests, a major part of the Wafd's male leadership was not prepared to take them seriously or consult them. This was despite the fact that some individuals, including the Wafd leader Saad Zaghloul, had frequently voiced their sympathy for the women's cause. As Lilli Doss, an Egyptian campaigner for women's rights since those years, remarks: 'The politicians were happy to have women's support while it was useful – and then they were discarded.' It was in this context that the Egyptian Feminist Union (EFU) emerged as the largest and most effective of women's groups, pursuing specific women's issues in which the Wafd showed little interest, though the EFU's leadership always retained close contacts with male sympathizers both inside and outside that party.

Huda Shaarawi resigned as president of the Wafd women's committee in 1924 after a disagreement with the leadership over an issue of nationalist policy, but she had also become impatient with their lack of concern over feminist questions. She later wrote the following eloquent and perceptive passage in her memoirs on the way men view women who play a part in public affairs in times of crisis.

14 Huda Shaarawi, leader of the Egyptian Feminist Union, in a photograph published in the May 1938 issue of the Egyptian Broadcasting Authority's magazine Radio Misriyya, which focused on the role of women in broadcasting.

Exceptional women appear at certain moments in history and are moved by special forces. Men view these women as supernatural beings and their deeds as miracles. Indeed, women are bright stars whose light penetrates dark clouds. They rise in times of trouble when the wills of men are tried. In moments of danger, when women emerge by their side, men utter no protest. Yet women's great acts and endless sacrifices do not change men's views of women. Through their arrogance, men refuse to see the capabilities of women. Faced with contradiction, they prefer to raise women out of the ordinary human plane instead of placing them on a level equal to their own. Men have singled out women of outstanding merit and put them on a pedestal to avoid recognizing the capabilities of all women. Women have felt this in their souls. Their dignity and self-esteem have been deeply touched. Women reflected on how they might elevate their status and worth in the eyes of men. They decided that the path lay in participating with men in public affairs. When they saw the way blocked, women rose up to demand their liberation, claiming their social, economic and political rights. Their leap forward was greeted with ridicule and blame,but that did not weaken their will. Their resolve led to a struggle that would have ended in war if men had not come to acknowledge the rights of women.[20]

The Egyptian Feminist Union continued to support the nationalist line but was not tied to any particular political party. In the 1920s and 1930s it concentrated on campaigning for a number of reforms: the development of women's education and the right to work; changes in the personal-status law; social reforms relating to health and family life; and, more tentatively, political suffrage. But the male legislators still defined the boundaries within which reforms could occur. The EFU and its allies had most success in the field of education and achieved some changes in attitudes to upper- and middle-class women taking jobs outside the home. They also brought about some modest improvements in conditions for the poorer strata of women who had always worked.

Most of the women who led the EFU came from the upper and middle classes, and on the whole they did not aim to challenge the overall hierarchy of social classes. None the less, the demands they made for the improvement of the education, health and legal rights of poor women could scarcely have been completely fulfilled within the existing social order. But because of the problems they encountered in implementing even limited reforms, members of the leadership often displayed considerable caution in their public pronouncements, and it is sometimes difficult to know how far this accounts for the apparent conservatism of some of their views.

In its literature, the EFU generally stressed the view that the family, at whatever level of society, was the key to a harmonious social order, and that while women's position in the family remained one of inferiority and subordination, neither the family nor society would be healthy. Saiza Nabrawi once suggested that the violent, and in her view, unnecessary political disputes among male politicians of the day had their roots in the divisions within the family caused by the inequality of men and women. The family, she concluded, is the basis of all social progress and real national development.[21]

The key to family harmony, the feminists argued, was a more equal relationship between husbands and wives. They campaigned strenuously from the mid-1920s for changes in the personal-status law, but only limited reforms were achieved. They succeeded in setting the minimum age of marriage for a woman at sixteen, and achieved minor improvements for women in the conditions for divorce, though the laws governing both divorce and inheritance remained heavily weighted in favour of men. Polygamy was practised less and less widely, but remained legal. In the 1920s and 1930s opposition to such major changes was too great, and the feminists were unable to mobilize sufficient support to push the reforms through. This was despite the fact that, in public at least, the EFU leadership was at pains to stress that women were not trying to usurp male roles. Huda Shaarawi, in her speech as president of the EFU at a public commemoration in 1928 of the death of the pro-feminist Egyptian writer Qasim Amin, was careful to spell out their compatibility, if women were given their rights:

15 'Why is it that a man is permitted to marry four women [while] a woman cannot marry four men?' asks the woman in this cover cartoon from Ruz al-Yusuf published in March 1928.

This cartoon reflects the heated debate at that time in Egypt on the question of reforming the personal-status laws as regards women. Although the practice of polygamy was even at this time on the decline, no attempts to make it illegal have succeeded in Egypt.

You will not be unaware, gentlemen, that all human beings tend instinctively to imitate their superiors. And if women – none of whose rights is recognized – seek to imitate men, this is because they see men, who are accorded their full rights, exercising greater power and enjoying more privileges in society than they do. But the day that women's rights are recognized and firmly established, and when women occupy, alongside men, their rightful position in society, you will find them clinging jealously to their natural feminine attributes, just as men cling to male qualities. The nation as a whole could not fail to benefit from this mutual understanding between men and women in every aspect of life.[22]

The EFU played a leading role, with other women's groups, in the provision of social services for women, in the absence of state provision. A considerable part of Huda Shaarawi's own personal fortune was spent on the establishment of schools and clinics. The upper-class members of the EFU also used their contacts with royalty to obtain substantial donations to their social work. Other women activists worked independently to create such services: for example in the mid-1930s Lilli Doss and two colleagues set up an innovative clinic in a popular district of Cairo to care for the numerous tuberculosis sufferers but also to provide support and practical help for their families.

Feminists also conducted campaigns to curb prostitution, drunkenness and drug taking, in which they again appealed to the imagery of the stable harmonious family. At the 1933 Conference of Muslim Women held in Tehran, an EFU delegate, Hanifa Khouri, described how the EFU was conducting a poster campaign to promote its message on the evils of drink and drugs:

> Some of these posters portray happy family life – the husband and wife drawing all the members together in a spirit of harmony; the children gathering round them, polite and well brought-up, cheerful and happy; and all living together in an atmosphere of joyous intimacy. Meanwhile other posters depict families where the husband and wife, sunk to the lowest depths through drink or opium, have reduced the disintegrating family to penury while the children, lacking all education, have grown up vicious and wild.[23]

Huda Shaarawi's campaign against licensed prostitution met with opposition during World War II. The authorities considered licensed prostitution 'necessary' (not to say lucrative) because of the large numbers of British and allied troops stationed there. In fact Cairo in this period renewed its Orientalist stereotype as the 'Ali Baba' city of pimps and belly dancers, a popular image created by troops on leave

16 A woman drinking buzah *(palm wine spirit) in a bar in a popular quarter of Cairo. Photograph published in* Al-Dunya *in 1938.*

A photograph which contrasts sharply with the usual images of women's decorum. *Al-Dunya*, as already mentioned, had a somewhat unconventional approach to the treatment of social issues. Acknowledging the fact that some women drank alcohol in public places, the story accompanying the picture reports, 'There is a need for somewhere for women to drink *buzah* in the place where they buy it, but it would not be permissible for men to be present. So the owners (of the shops) decided to admit women but to provide a separate place for them [to sit and drink their *buzah*] rather than have them drink outside the door of the shop. So they put up a sign "for women only" [visible in the photograph above the table]. The men and women are separated, but can talk together. And so we found them, with the women in their corner, drinking in peace.'

there. Only after the boom time ended, in 1949 (after Huda Shaarawi's death), was prostitution made illegal, though, of course, it did not entirely cease.

Despite its predominantly upper- and middle-class membership, the EFU's programme did not confine itself to interests of those classes. Its demands on health, education and legal status had relevance to women of all classes, and the leadership stressed the need to spread reforms beyond the privileged strata. But the movement was much less successful in mobilizing women from other classes. While it worked and campaigned on behalf of poor women, the EFU did not succeed in drawing them into the feminist ranks, and membership remained confined mostly to the urban elites.

Doraya Shafiq, a protégée of Huda Shaarawi and one of the younger generation of feminists, wrote in the 1940s of the wide gap which existed between the women of the elite, who had been most able to take advantage of the new opportunities, and the mass of poor women in Egypt who had scarcely begun to see the benefits of feminist campaigns:

> I have often reflected on the great gulf separating women of the elite from the women of the poorer classes in our society. We are like a huge machine whose cogs fail to mesh. There has been too much progress at the top of society and none at all at the bottom. Yet it is on this base that the solid foundations of any society, and particularly of female society, are laid and it is from this layer of society that the majority of mothers come. This is an issue to which we should devote the greatest attention.
>
> We are struck by a galling contrast – namely, the remarkable advances made by the women of the elite on the one hand, and the miserable condition of the rest of womankind on the other. The distance between them is so great that the elite itself is paralysed by it . . . .[24]

17 Members of the Egyptian Feminist Union, outside Huda Shaarawi's house, dressed for a visit to the royal palace, 1930s.

Because the royal women still appeared in public with a face veil which rather resembled a scarf or *fichu*, women being received at an audience with members of royalty had to wear similar attire. Upper-class women in the EFU, like Huda Shaarawi, had social connections at court, and some of the royal women played an important role in fundraising for the charitable work of the EFU and other voluntary organizations. However, both King Fuad and later King Farouq seem to have been at best ambivalent about the main issues of feminist campaigns.

230

But with all their limitations, both those imposed upon them by the prevailing political and social climate, and those created by their own views, the early Egyptian feminists did succeed in promoting a new, alternative self-image of women as active, educated and thinking for themselves. This image was scarcely thought of fifty years before when Huda Shaarawi was growing up, picking her way through a myriad of restrictions, uncertain of her ground. Even though this new image was one to which only a minority could aspire, it had altered the terms on which the debate about women's status was conducted.

Like their counterparts elsewhere in the Middle East, the activists of the EFU drew their ideas on women's status from a variety of sources. Certainly Western liberalism, and from the 1920s, the views of Western feminists, were yardsticks by which progress could be judged, particularly in the field of legal and political rights. But with a few exceptions, the Egyptian feminists had their intellectual and political roots in another tradition: the Islamic liberalism articulated by Qasim Amin and Muhammad Abdou which sought reforms within the framework of that religion and culture, arguing that

18 A women's demonstration against the British occupation of the Suez Canal zone, late 1940s.

This was a new generation of women activists on the march. These women were not part of the Egyptian Feminist Union but represented a range of political groups, from the Communist Party to the Muslim Brotherhood. Inji Aflatun (*centre, in plaid skirt and beret*) was an artist, an active leftist and an ardent feminist. To her left, the woman wearing the white *hijab* was probably a supporter of the Muslim Brotherhood which had wide popular support in the late 1940s and sought to involve women in its work, though usually in separate and subordinate roles to men. It also advocated education for women to make them better mothers.

Although the women shown here represented a spectrum of social classes and ideological goals, at this time they were still able to unite on nationalist issues, and their placards symbolize their links with both the earlier nationalist and feminist struggles. In the centre is a placard showing Huda Shaarawi, and on the right, a portrait of Umm Sabir, one of the women who was killed in the 1919 uprising.

19 *Doraya Shafiq (*centre*), with Mufida Abdul Rahman (*left, in black*) and a visiting woman lawyer from the US, Egypt, 1952.*

Mufida Abdul Rahman was one of the first practising women lawyers in Egypt (see Chapter V, Caption 21) and a leading member of the leftist women's group *al-Hisb al-Nisa'i al-Watani*, which had close connections with the *Hizb al-Amal* (Workers' Party). Doraya Shafiq, a protegée of Huda Shaarawi's, started a magazine, *Bint al-Nil* (*Daughter of the Nile*) in 1945 and in 1948 she launched a new feminist group, the Bint al-Nil Union. She came from a middle-class family in Tanta, where her father was an engineer. When she was a teenager the family moved to Alexandria. She was educated in French mission schools and largely though her own initiative and the support of Huda Shaarawi, she entered the Sorbonne in Paris as a student in 1930. On her return to Egypt she became a teacher.
In the early days of *Bint al-Nil* her ideas seem to have been quite close to those of the EFU, but by the 1950s she had begun to press strongly on a new front – to gain the vote for women. She embarked on a campaign of sit-ins and hunger strikes, but became increasingly isolated, particularly during the Nasser period when she was for a time put under house arrest. She eventually committed suicide. The vote was granted to women in 1956 but in practice was limited to those who made a formal application for this right.[6]

Islam's basic tenets need not be construed as inimical to women. While Egyptian feminists' nationalist convictions did not prevent their admiring aspects of Western culture and even imitating its styles and fashions, few had any simplistic desire to turn themselves into mirror images of Western women.

Endeavours to reinterpret Islamic thought in ways which were favourable to women were not confined to Egypt. In Beirut, one woman, Nazirah Zein ed-Din, caused a considerable stir in Muslim religious circles with a book she published in the 1920s arguing for a radical reinterpretation of the role of women under Islam. She was the daughter of the one-time head of the Lebanese court of appeals, educated, as was quite common among members of the Muslim upper classes, at missionary schools. She none the less became an intense student of Islamic thought and was encouraged by her father to publish her conclusions, which attracted very hostile polemics from some religious shaikhs.

She took the arguments that the laws of Islam and the customs which had grown up during the Islamic period were designed to control women's dangerous sexuality, and turned them on their head. She contended, among other things, that the Prophet Muhammad had basically regarded polygamy and slavery (both practised in pre-Islamic Arabia) as abuses of women's rights. However she concluded, as some male religious thinkers had done, that social conditions in Muhammad's day made it impractical to abolish these evils completely. Therefore Muhammad tempered their evil effects by the imposition of a set of rules about men's conduct towards wives and slaves – for example, the stricture that a man should not take more than one wife unless he feels able to treat all his wives equally.

But Nazirah Zein ed-Din went on to argue that what lay behind this was not the inherent weakness, inferiority or even dangerousness of women, but the violent and exploitative nature of 'man's instinctive character'. And she continued, 'What improved such inherent personality traits is religion, and it is to it that man owes the betterment of his condition.' Thus Islam protects women against the inherent dangers of man's character, rather than vice versa.[25] While this argument was unlikely to have met with wide acceptance even among like-minded women, it does suggest that in intellectual circles, women were casting round for ways to define themselves within their own cultural and religious traditions, rather than looking solely to the West in their search for new self-images.

Feminism and Nationalism

However, in those regions under colonial rule at this time – Syria, Lebanon, Palestine, and for a shorter period Iraq – the overriding preoccupation became the nationalist struggle, which, to a much greater degree than in Egypt, pushed women's issues into the background. Women became actively involved in resistance: Druze women took part in the revolt against the French in Jebel Druze (in Syria) in 1925/26; women demonstrated and confronted troops on the streets of Beirut in the early 1940s during protests against French rule. But it was in Palestine that the conflict, the violence and the eventual losses were greatest.

Nationalist opposition was directed both against Britain, as the colonial power, and against the Zionist movement, which under the aegis of the British was establishing a

20 *Young women in Nablus, Palestine, collecting donations for the nationalist cause during the Palestine rebellion, 1937/38. This photograph was published in* The Arab Woman and the Palestine Question *(al-mar'a al-arabiyya wa qadiya filastin) (The proceedings of a conference of Eastern women, Cairo, 15–18 October 1938).*

The photograph shows these young women wearing the *kufiyyeh*, the men's headdress which at this time became the symbol of Palestinian nationalism. Again, nationalist mobilization in a time of crisis made it acceptable for women to do this kind of work in public, even in this conservative town where it might otherwise have been frowned upon.

'National Home' for the Jews in Palestine. This meant the development of a separate enclave which involved immigration of Jews from Europe and settlement on the land (see pp. 29–31). The new immigrants generally shared Western views of the Arabs as 'backward natives' and either dismissed the Palestinians as irrelevant to their National Home project or viewed them with hostility because they constituted a threat to its success.

The struggle which ensued from the 1920s onwards involved women as well as men. Among the upper- and middle-class Palestinians who initially dominated the nationalist movement, the women, Muslim and Christian, largely left the struggle to their menfolk until the late 1920s. But after the establishment of the Arab Women's Executive Committee in Jerusalem in 1929 they participated in public demonstrations – still quite daring for women from more conservative families. During the six-month general strike of 1936 and the three-year-long Arab rebellion which followed it, more women were drawn into the conflict. During the strike, which centred on urban areas, the organized women's groups played a role, and even schoolgirls went on strike. During the period of the rebellion most of the fighting was in the rural areas and village women were drawn into the conflict for the first time, mostly in the classic roles women have played in wars of this kind: acting as go-betweens and messengers, smuggling arms, hiding people and generally acting to back up the men. Later still, in 1948, women also played their part in attempts at local level to stave off the final defeat which brought exile and statelessness to some 800,000 Palestinians.[26]

In these circumstances, issues of women's rights slid to the bottom of the agenda. Some women, like Matiel Mogannam, one of the leaders of the Women's Executive Committee, argued that it was virtually impossible to achieve reform of women's status under colonial rule. Referring to calls at the International Alliance of Women's conference in Istanbul in 1935 for the abolition of child marriage, she wrote:

> Any such reforms in mandated territories will have to remain unenforced for the simple reason that the authorities are reluctant to deal with matters which may arouse any objection on the part of any religious authority. This is one of the evils of the mandate system. It is therefore difficult for any women's organization in Palestine or Syria to obtain any legislative sanction for matters of which the country may be in need.[27]

The ambivalence of women's position in nationalist struggles – admired for their courage and fortitude, held up as symbols of national continuity and steadfastness, but still not accorded social, economic or political equality with men – has certainly left its legacy in the Palestinian nationalist

21 Men and women who volunteered to serve in the Red Crescent in Bethlehem during the fighting of 1947–48.

Some of these women were members of the Bethlehem Women's Union. During and after the 1948 war, Palestinian women such as these played an important role in helping refugees before agencies such as the Red Cross and later UNRWA began to provide assistance.

22 Women demonstrating against French rule in Lebanon. M. Saadé,
Official Photographer of the Lebanese Republic, Beirut, 12 November 1943.

On 11 November, the Free French administration in Lebanon had closed the
Lebanese parliament and arrested several members of the government,
including the Prime Minister, Beshara al-Khouri. The confrontation was
over French reluctance to give up the Mandate under which it had ruled
Lebanon since 1920 and Lebanese demands for political independence. The
ensuing protests by the populations of Beirut, Tripoli, Saidon and other
towns were put down with considerable brutality. In both Beirut and in
Saidon, it was reported that women were prominent among the
demonstrators.

On the morning of 12 November, some 200 women led a march first to the
British Legation where some fifty of the leading women of Beirut, a number
of them the wives of politicians, presented a petition for help addressed to
the British Prime Minister from 'The Ladies of Lebanon'. The
demonstration then proceeded to the US Legation to deliver a similar
message. The subsequent events were described in a report by the first
secretary at the Legation:

'This morning by about 12.30, an orderly crowd of from 500 to 600,
composed of approximately 200 of the leading women of the city . . . joined
by some 350 boys and miscellaneous street people, plus a delegation of
about seventy-five political and business leaders had gathered in front of the
Legation, overflowing down the front steps, into the garden and on to the
street. From time to time they were addressed in Arabic by one of their
leaders, speaking from the wall of the Legation garden; the response to the
speeches was cheers and applause from the crowd.

'Suddenly two French Army troop-carrying lorries drove up, each
containing sixteen to twenty black troops [Senegalese] and two or three
white French non-coms [non commissioned officers]. All were fully armed
with machine-guns, bayonetted rifles or drawn revolvers.

'The overflow crowd in the streets quickly dispersed into the Legation
gardens or up and down the street, under the threat of aimed and manned
machine-guns in both directions while black troops with rifles and bayonets
took up a menacing guard in front of the Legation building – without
however penetrating into the property.

'The women meantime had for the most part gathered in the garden behind
the wall, insulting and spitting (even the best of them) at the troops and
screaming that the Senegalese would shoot. No actual shot was fired near
the Legation (although Mr Gwynn said he had heard machine-guns firing
just before) . . .

'When the street itself was quite clear, although 200 or more [women] were
still inside the wall of the garden, still hissing and insulting the French, the
troops climbed back into their trucks with their machine-guns and rifles still
pointed directly at the women in the garden and at myself [standing] . . . in
the street.'[7]

movement until recent times. It has often made it difficult for women to campaign for their own rights when this means coming into conflict with the men with whom they share nationalist ideals.

In the case of Algeria, where the nationalist movement gathered momentum in the 1940s, the long years of French rule and the harshness of the struggle for independence brought this problem into even starker relief. Political radicalism in these circumstances could easily be combined with a view of women which placed them in the role of the guardians of 'traditional' Algerian culture against French attempts to crush it. As Assia Djebar, an Algerian woman novelist, put it in an interview in 1962, just after independence had been achieved:

> . . . the woman, traditionally the guardian of the past, became [under colonial rule] passive in her role. The Algerian man, at this time, was colonized in the street, in his work, obliged to speak a language that was not his own outside; he found his real life at home, in his house, with his wife. The house was still the sacred place, where the foreigner never entered.[28]

Even after independence when the need for greater rights and opportunities for women was formally acknowledged by the government, these attitudes among men, internalized during colonial rule, died hard, to women's detriment.

23 Women on an outing during the Conference of Eastern Women on Palestine, Cairo, October 1938.

This conference, organized by Huda Shaarawi of the Egyptian Feminist Union and Bahia al-Azmeh of the Syrian Woman's Union, included sixty-six delegates from five countries including Iran. For this reason Huda Shaarawi had insisted that it should be called a conference of 'Eastern' rather than Arab women. It was the first women's conference in the region to deal with a major political issue and took place at the height of the Palestine rebellion. It followed appeals from Palestinian women's groups for support in their struggle. Apart from passing motions of solidarity with the Palestinians, the conference was also a remarkable social experience for some of the women delegates who had never travelled abroad before unchaperoned, or appeared in public unveiled. And however little effect their resolutions had, it was new for women to unite across frontiers on a major political issue.

It is difficult to generalize about the achievements of women's organizations in the Middle East during this period because the conditions under which they functioned, and their immediate goals, varied considerably. With the exception of those relatively brief periods when women became involved in wider popular movements of national resistance, the number of women who were active in politics or in women's organizations of any kind remained small and generally confined to the main cities.

Nationalism had a considerable impact on the way women saw their role in politics and society and sometimes imposed limits on the extent to which women would challenge men's authority. Although there was a consensus among most women activists in different societies on their basic demands – for legal reform of women's status within the family, the right to education and to work, and better welfare provisions for poor women – there was a considerable diversity of views on wider political and social issues. By no means all these women were political radicals: only a handful of women, for example, went so far as to question the class structure of their societies.

The impact of women's organized efforts to change their lives is difficult to disentangle from those changes which were the result of social and economic developments in society as a whole. Women activists of all political persuasions were well aware of the social and economic problems which faced the majority of women, but the steps they could take to change these conditions were limited by a number of factors – political and class considerations; male hostility; the social conservatism of men and women; and frequently also by economic stringency and the obstructive policies of colonial regimes.

Where relationships between men and women were concerned, most of those who considered themselves feminists, with a few exceptions, did not fundamentally challenge the notion of the patriarchal family. Rather they were seeking ways to renegotiate the rules by which men controlled women's behaviour, and which women themselves often internalized. These rules had always been more flexible than most outsiders supposed, or than most men were prepared to admit. What at any one time appeared to be unalterable norms of behaviour in fact altered according to circumstances and were subject to wider social pressures. The way the rules were applied also varied according to the individual and the family concerned: from time to time women even risked flouting these rules, but more often they simply tested the limits of what was permitted, using whatever powers of persuasion were available to them.

On the whole women activists simply extended this process by attempting to persuade men of the value of this inherent flexibility to give women more freedom within the family. This, they argued, would promote harmony and a sense of partnership. But more importantly, women's movements took the significant step of bringing these issues openly and consciously into the public domain and gave women the experience of acting collectively outside the confines of the family to change their lives.

Afterword

Photography plays a much greater role in people's lives today than it did during the period when the pictures in this book were taken. In most cities of the Middle East, photographic studios cater to all but the poorest layers of society, turning out wedding pictures and portraits by the thousand. Photographs are used on advertising hoardings and billboards, and stalls are filled with illustrated magazines, local or foreign. Television now reaches the homes even of the poor and of those who live in remote rural areas.

The photographs in this book were taken in an age when technology was less sophisticated and when fewer people saw such pictures on a daily basis. The technology has now changed dramatically: gone are the days when photographers clamped their subjects into position in the studio and the more adventurous hauled their equipment around the countryside in a cart or on muleback. Furthermore, film, television and video have far outstripped still photography in importance and have a widespread influence on popular culture.

In theory at least, these advances in technology offer the opportunity to produce far more nuanced images than the relatively crude still cameras of the late nineteenth and early twentieth centuries were capable of doing. But how much have the resulting images, especially those of women in the Middle East, actually changed?

This book has argued that, in the century from 1850 to 1950, women and photographic images of women have often been used as symbols for concepts which have little or no relation to their identity as women or as individuals. Proponents of Orientalism, nationalism, 'westernization' and various religious ideologies have all found in women powerful metaphors for their own concerns. Women have often been used, not at their own behest, to represent ideas in debates conducted largely by men. Women certainly began to make conscious efforts to alter the terms of these debates, but their success in changing the underlying patterns of domination was limited. Thus in various forms of visual representation and in literature women appear as, for example, the 'anchor' of the family, the embodiment of motherhood, the model of probity and respectability. They may also be seen as a symbol of national redemption or progress, as sexual objects, or as the archetypal victims of war and violence.

Photography is only one of a number of forms through which these ideas may be conveyed, but it is one which has grown in importance over the years and which, because it is frequently credited with objectivity and neutrality, often disguises the patterns of symbolism and domination which underpin the images.

I have suggested that two forms of domination have been crucial in shaping the portrayal of Middle Eastern women in both photography and other visual forms. First, the domination exercised by the West over the Middle East which extended beyond political and economic control to assertions of cultural superiority and a desire to define and label so-called 'subject peoples'. Second, women were subject to forms of domination which existed within Middle Eastern societies – of one class over another, and of men over women.

Both these forms of power were reflected in perceptions of women, creating and sustaining images of how they were expected to behave and what roles they should play. During the era of direct imperial control in the Middle East, the way women from these societies were represented in the West conflicted with the dominant attitudes within the colonized society. And at times, the struggle for power between the imperial rulers and national liberation movements was symbolically embodied in a battle over the representation and status of women. Yet in other instances the two forms intertwined to create new meanings and idioms for the representation of women. Through the medium of photography, itself a Western import, came new images of women – in dress, pose and demeanour. But despite surface appearances these new images did not necessarily reflect significant changes in the underlying patterns of control exercised over women. I would argue that such power relationships were often reproduced by these visual images, though in new and different guises, and continued to shape society's views of women and their status and also women's perceptions of themselves.

Since the 1950s there have certainly been some significant changes in the way Middle Eastern women are represented. The underlying structures of domination, however, would seem to have changed much less, though this has varied from area to area; where changes have occurred, they have mostly been confined to particular social classes. To examine these changes and continuities in detail would require another book, and what follows is simply intended to suggest some common themes in the way women are represented, and how this relates to social change. While it would be unsafe to make generalizations about the roles this imagery may play in different Middle Eastern societies, the two forms of domination mentioned earlier still form a basis for discussion.

The relationship between social and political change and the persistence of cultural norms or ideas is a complex one, particularly in the way visual imagery reflects class and gender relations. It cannot always be assumed, for example, that a new political ideology, or changed economic circumstances will automatically alter relations of power and control within the family, even though it may alter outward appearances. Family photographs of successive generations, for example, may reveal considerable variations in dress and demeanour, but these may not signify any fundamental changes in relationships between family members.

Images of women may also be used in conflicting ways – as symbols of progress on the one hand, and as symbols of continuity with the cultural past on the other. Such symbols have frequently been created in reaction to representations of women imposed from outside the society, reflecting a preoccupation with the unequal relationships of power with the West.

Despite the fact that since the 1960s most of the states in the region have had formal political independence, political and economic inequalities have persisted, along with various kinds of cultural domination, and this has continued to affect the way national histories and cultures are portrayed. Women have continued to appear as symbols in a variety of guises: in the West as reflections of persistent myths about the Middle East and Islam, and in the Middle East as emblems of nationhood and cultural nationalism. Thus photographs in newspapers, television and advertising present an often puzzling mixture of representations of women, with startling images of change mingling with clichés and stereotypes reminiscent of an earlier age.

Western Images

In the Western media women have remained important as metaphors for Middle Eastern politics and culture: reviving old myths of the erotic and exotic East and reinforcing notions of a fanatical Islam. Ideas about change in Middle Eastern societies are frequently presented by visual juxtaposition, as they were, for example, in images of the 'new woman' in Turkey and Egypt in the early twentieth century.

In the 1950s and 1960s the forward march of 'modernization' was presented through images of people in the Middle East, particularly women, looking more and more 'like' Europeans or Americans in dress and demeanour. This reflected the views of certain social science theorists who saw social and political change in terms of 'take off'. This was defined by the acquisition of certain types of consumer goods, of 'modern' attitudes and political attributes such as parliamentary democracy and secular society associated with the West. The more closely the peoples of non-Western societies conformed to these Western models, it was argued, the nearer they were to achieving 'modernization'. Other social and cultural values, and considerations of class and power were largely ignored. A nation's 'progress' in this sense could thus be demonstrated, for example, by the juxtaposition of traditional modes of dress or behaviour against this new modernity. Women were particularly popular subjects in this kind of idiom which represents change as a series of sharply contrasted statements. Implicit is the assumption that the 'old' is automatically anachronistic, something to be discarded in favour of the 'new'. It thus precludes any understanding of how cultural and social ideas can persist in new forms and new images.

While few in the Western academic establishment today still credit this simplistic view of progress and modernization, the assumptions behind it still remain as popular currency in newspapers, television, films, novels and travelogues. Furthermore, events in the Middle East over the past two decades have had a considerable impact on Western views of the region: the oil boom, thirteen years of civil war in Lebanon, the Iranian revolution and the Gulf War, Western obsessions with Colonel Qaddafi's adventurism, and the appearance in a number of countries of political opposition movements based on various fundamentalist interpretations of Islam. All these events have encouraged the widely-held Western view that previous trends towards 'modernization' in the region have been eclipsed by a return to some kind of Dark Ages.

This attitude has been supported by the persistence of the Orientalist assertion that all Middle Eastern societies are basically the same – a notion which rests on a monolithic conception of Islam. According to this view, as Norman Daniels has suggested, Islamic societies are commonly characterised by a mixture of violence, cruelty, hypocrisy and lasciviousness.

Thus the turmoil in the region with its social and economic contradictions is often taken to mean that the Middle East is reverting to its 'essential character'. Although there have been some sensitive and sophisticated attempts to depict the diversity of women's experience in the Middle East, particularly on film, these productions generally speaking only reach minority audiences. For the most part the popular press, television and mass-market novels and thrillers tend to portray Middle Eastern women as veiled figures of exoticism and mystery, associated with sinister plots or dangerous fanaticism, or as the passive victims of war or male violence.

Visual imagery, particularly photography, in this vein can easily be used to assert 'facts' from which generalizations are drawn. The photograph of the veiled Saudi woman in the streets of London may be presented as documentary evidence of how Saudi women are oppressed, but it is also automatically assumed to reflect the oppression of women throughout the Middle East and Islamic culture. It echoes the earlier Orientalist rhetoric of the veil and concealment – an image of an oppressive and fanatical religion masking luxury, decadence and lasciviousness.

Over the past ten years, the Western press has carried with increasing frequency photographs of Shia women in Iran and southern Lebanon wearing the *chador* and women in Egypt wearing the *hijab*. These pictures often seem not so much intended to document a political or social phenomenon, as to 'demonstrate' in a generalized way the rise of militant Islam and religious fanaticism, a threat to the West. These images are identified with Islam itself, suggesting that they are somehow quintessential manifestations of its tenets. This is despite the fact that large numbers of Muslims do not subscribe at all to these militant movements.

A second type of photograph which recurs in the Western media presents women as victims of war and violence. Many of these pictures are indeed moving: for example, Don McCullin's powerful photographs of Palestinian women fleeing the Phalangist onslaught on Karantina in 1976; and the endless succession of photographs of women 'hysterically' mourning their dead in Lebanon, in Iran and in Iraq. In these pictures women become the embodiment of the suffering and madness of war. But they are also generally projected, quite inaccurately, as completely passive victims. For instance, in the Palestinian refugee camps, women have often been portrayed in this light, and it is only when foreigners who have lived in their midst tell the world of their strength and ability to cope in horrendous conditions that this notion is belied.

The vision of the passive, suffering woman, victim of uncontrollable circumstances, also fits a wider pattern of imagery which uses pictures of suffering women and children to draw attention to drought, famine and the ravages of war. When the subject is the Middle East, however, the surrounding text is less likely to elicit sympathy and sometimes even suggests that these people brought their troubles on themselves by their irrationality and/or religious fanaticism. Thus such women are not seen as wholly innocent victims.

Where women are portrayed as active participants in the various conflicts in the region, they rarely appear in a very positive light. The Palestinians have been subject to the sharpest dichotomies: between the 'helpless' refugee woman in her tent surrounded by children, and Leila Khaled the hijacker. Both men and women have been the subjects of these stereotypes but they are harsher and more shocking in the case of women. Recently other groups have been added to the iconography of female militancy – for example, young Shia women in Lebanon carrying guns and wearing the *chador*. These women might be regarded as heroines by their own people, but in the Western media they appear, without much attempt at explanation, as indices of fanaticism. This is all the more shocking because they are female – fanaticism being a characteristic expected of Middle Eastern males.

In all these images, the assumptions about the Middle East and its women which had been moulded in previous generations – and are evident in many of the photographs in this book – have resurfaced and are used to 'explain' current behaviour. Just as in the past, the particular documentary quality of photographs lends them an air of veracity which discourages questions about their construction or their motives. The wide screen or the video may be very far from the albumen print in technical sophistication but this does not prevent the repetition of well-worn visual clichés with little challenge to their credibility.

But it is not only in the West that visual images of women have had a powerful public impact. In the last thirty years they have played an important role in Middle Eastern societies in countering some of these Western stereotypes, while at the same time creating new kinds of images and clichés and imposing controls – at both the state and private levels – on women's lives.

In the Middle East, the media today fufil many of the same functions as they do in the West: to entertain, to sell products, and as vehicles for information, education and propaganda. Television is now probably the most powerful medium in all these roles, and it is the one where the state and its ideology generally exercise the strongest influence over the way women are portrayed. In the majority of countries in the region, close government supervision of programming is the norm, and many locally-made news, feature and educational programmes reflect an 'official' view of how women should be presented.

This clearly varies from country to country, the image of women in Saudi Arabia, for example, being very different from that presented in Egypt or Algeria. It may also change according to the differing ideologies of successive regimes. Yet there is at least one common theme – women are presented in a way which conforms with the wider values of society. Sometimes this also encompasses an effort to distance women's status and role from the kind of Western imagery discussed earlier, and also from Western ideas about the position of women in society. At other times, these images include some themes or stereotypes which are in fact drawn from the West.

In a state such as Saudi Arabia where highly conservative social values are set by the ruling elite, the prevailing imagery of women stresses probity and respectability with an overt emphasis on the need for men to exercise control over women. Any deviation from this in public would be perceived as damaging not just to the individuals concerned, but to the image of the nation and to its particular form of Islamic observance and culture, as well as the social value promoted by the dominant elite.

In other societies, images of women have also been important as symbols of new nationhood and social progress. They have even been used, from time to time, to educate and mobilize people for certain kinds of social change. For example, in post-independence Algeria and Nasser's Egypt women sometimes appeared as emblems of progress and enlightenment, emancipated to work and participate in society. This frequently entailed the use of 'modernist' and westernized images somewhat similar to those used in Turkey in the 1930s. Yet on the whole, these images of emancipation, while they might promote the idea of the progressive nation, did not challenge basic gender relations in society, particularly male domination of the family structure. Male leaderships were careful to avoid upsetting the status quo in this respect.

A more recent example of a dramatic change of women's image is the much publicized appearance of female bodyguards with Colonel Qaddafi in Libya – apparently overturning the conventional view of male and female roles. In the West this is treated as little more than a variation on the theme of the harem but it seems intended, in Libya, to symbolize the national mobilization of women even in conventionally male spheres. Yet it is unlikely to have been viewed as a challenge to male hegemony in a wider social context.

Major ideological changes obviously affect the way women are presented to promote national goals. The most obvious example is the contrast between the way women were portrayed in the media in Iran during Pahlavi rule and since the revolution. During Muhammad Reza Shah's reign women were officially promoted through largely Western imagery of 'progress', stressing middle-class values, while under the Islamic Republic they are presented as the embodiment of a particular vision of an 'Islamic society'. But in both instances, these images form an important element in the way the regimes promote and legitimize themselves. At the same time, neither kind of image necessarily reflects with any accuracy the changes or the continuities in the everyday life of women of different classes.

When regimes have wanted to stress cultural continuity, to assert difference and separateness from the West (from which many of the images of 'progress' are drawn), women have been cast as the repositories of cultural values passed down through the family. This may take the form of glorifying the 'woman of the people' and her role in the transmission of folklore and traditional crafts, many of which are now dying out.

Heroines of the past, whether from a particular national culture or from the common strands of the history of Islam, are also revived from time to time, particularly in historical film dramas, to stress the continuities of national feeling, religious inspiration or cultural values. In more recent times, women in Algeria after independence continued to be glorified for their role in the national struggle, but this did not allow them or their daughters to play a full or independent role in Algerian society. As in most other imagery of heroines, acclaim for their heroism is based on their support for male-led struggles and does not offer them the opportunity fundamentally to alter their status or challenge male hegemony. Thus heroines can be rendered 'safe' as symbols of national pride and tradition.

Governments of all political persuasions also use the media as a vehicle for social information and education campaigns, many of which are intended mainly to influence the behaviour of women, particularly on matters relating to health, nutrition and education within the family. Even in countries with radical regimes, on these issues there is generally a sense of treading a fine line between changing women's attitudes, creating models of progress and at the same time confirming the importance of women's role as childbearers and nurturers of the family. Male roles in this domain are rarely brought into question. Even those who are eager to bring about wider changes in women's lives tend to challenge male roles only in an indirect way. These media campaigns also have another dimension: for the most part they represent the efforts of bureaucrats and 'experts', whether male or female, to impose urban middle-class ideas and norms on women from other sectors of society.

However, the meanings ascribed to images of women within Middle Eastern cultures have not been confined to those promulgated by the state. This book has suggested that control of women's appearance in the public domain, whether by state directive or by the more general mechanisms of social control by family or community, has been an important aspect of the wider control exercised by men over women's lives, and one which is often encapsulated in visual forms such as photography.

In the present state of political and social flux which exists in many parts of the Middle East, this imagery reflects often conflicting currents of opinion about women's roles. It is also complicated by the uneasy relationship between images of women derived from Western cultures, which have taken on new and different connotations in the Middle East, and efforts to create images of women considered by various ideological tendencies as more appropriate to their own cultures. While certain groups of women have become very conscious of the nature of this imagery and the need to exert more control over it, generally speaking men continue to dominate the process of creating 'acceptable' public images of women, images which for the most part are internalized by women themselves.

There is a general rejection of the 'Orientalist' view of Middle Eastern women, and many people react angrily to popular Western stereotypes which are variations on the old themes of the harem and hidden sexuality. The exception seems to be a growing trend among wealthy Middle Eastern collectors to purchase nineteenth-century Orientalist paintings and photographs, including such 'exotic' images of women, and treat them at times as if they were authentic historic relics of their own culture.

But much more pervasive has been the acceptance of Western imagery of women imported particularly through advertising and fashion, and import of US and European films, television drama and soap operas. Most of the main urban centres have been opened at various times to the promoters of Western-style consumerism whether among the old upper classes and bourgeoisie or the nouveaux riches. Until the 1950s, this type of consumerism, fashion and manner of presenting women was confined to the upper echelons of society in a few cities but in the intervening years its influence has spread beyond the confines of these elites.

Women appear in this context as symbols of acquisition, whether of desirable goods, of wealth, or of sexual power, adding stereotypes of sexuality and power prevalent in many Western cultures to the images already discussed. This kind of imagery has in some instances come to signify privilege, class power and inequality. This was the case in Iran under the Shah and is very evident in Egypt since President Sadat initiated his 'opening' (*infitah*) to the West in the 1970s. It is not simply that the dispossessed cannot aspire to the jewels, cars and nightclubs which women's bodies are so often used to advertise, but it can also carry with it a rejection of imported culture. This rejection is frequently embodied in attacks on the way in which women are presented, as sexual objects and symbols of wealth, but also apparently (though not in fact) escaping from male control over their conformity to the norms of 'good behaviour'. The 'chic' woman in evening gown and jewels may thus be judged as loose, as well as privileged, so that both class and morality based on gender roles are implicit in the judgement. Sometimes the fear is also expressed that other, less privileged women could be 'led astray' by aspiring to such lifestyles.

In other contexts, however, the presentation of class differences among women may not appear so threatening to the norms of female behaviour. Take, for example, Egyptian soap operas, which are among the most popular television programmes, watched avidly in most parts of the Arab world. In these dramas, the characters present not only stereotypes of certain kinds of 'male' and 'female' behaviour, but like many soap operas in the West, also offer clear, if rather unrealistic stereotypes of men and women of different classes. Thus a *fellaha* (peasant woman) and a middle-class woman will conform to an 'ideal-type' which polarizes the image of both class and gender roles. Dress, accent and general behaviour will make these 'types' instantly recognizable, and acceptable, though they may not conform to people's everyday experience at all. Equally, images of patriarchal power, of relations between husbands and wives, fathers and daughters are easily identifiable and even conflicts between them are conducted along ritualized lines which usually reconfirm the accepted roles for each sex.

In the broader domain of feature films, while the majority do not deviate far from these norms, there have always been directors, and sometimes actors and actresses from a number of countries, particularly Egypt (which is the largest produc-er of films in the Arab world) to challenge these class and gender stereotypes. But with a few notable exceptions these films do not reach popular audiences and are seen mainly by the intelligentsia and at film festivals abroad.

Attempts to document social change in women's lives – as opposed to changes in idiom and symbolism – through photographs is thus fraught with complications. This is certainly not to say that no indications of changing status, or of changing attitudes to women can be gleaned from them, but they cannot be read according to any simple formula whereby certain changes in visual imagery are assumed to mean that there have been changes of the same magnitude in women's status or personal freedoms. The most obvious example of this is photography showing the way women dress. Earlier in the book it was suggested that there was no direct or simple way of 'reading off' class, social change or alterations in women's role from their clothing. The plasticity of this imagery is perhaps even more obvious when viewed from the vantage point of the present day. The same kinds of dress can embody a variety of social or political meanings, depending on time and context. At the same time, images which suggest dramatic changes in women's lives and freedoms may simply mask old forms of control in new guises. What is constant, however, is the significance attributed to the way women present themselves, both by their own societies and by the West. The meanings attached to their appearance may therefore have an important bearing on their own sense of identity.

Take, for example, the range of meanings, according to period, place and class, which might be ascribed to a photograph of a woman in a Middle Eastern city, walking down the street in a coat and skirt of Western cut. In a photograph from Turkey in the 1930s it would suggest what was becoming the norm for the urban middle class and might be used in official publications to demonstrate how 'modern' and progressive Turkey had become. In Egypt at the same date such attire (especially without headcovering) would suggest a woman from a liberal well-to-do family or it could mean a woman making a gesture of defiance against the norms of her class, community or family. In neither case, would it necessarily indicate what other personal, legal or social freedoms were available to her. Photographs such as these seem to imply an enormous leap from the veiling and seclusion prevalent among the upper and middle classes of earlier generations. But, as this book has argued, the changes in women's lives were often less dramatic and more complex than this transformation of appearances would suggest.

A similar photograph from the 1960s, from cities such as Cairo, Jerusalem, Tehran or Algiers would mean something different again. This style of dress, especially among young women, had become quite common throughout the middle class and would therefore not be understood in any but the most conservative milieux as a gesture of defiance. Such clothes would only invite censure if they were too revealing or attracted too much attention to the wearer. Again, such clothes would say very little about the other kinds of patriarchal control exercised over women's lives. While at this time, 'Western'-style dress was used by some regimes as an indication of modernity and liberality in regard to women, it did not necessarily have much bearing on their personal freedom.

As an indication of class, too, the lines demarcated by styles of dress have become more blurred. Access to mass-produced Western clothes in many countries, now for women as well as men, has altered consumer habits across classes. Class is now more clearly indicated by the quality of whichever style of clothing is chosen, rather than by the style itself.

At the same time, dress has continued to have strong moral and ideological connotations, some of long standing, some new. In some countries the state still intervenes directly to enforce particular styles of dress for women. In Saudi Arabia, veiling in public is still the norm, and is enforced by 'morality police' (*al-Mutawa'a*) who patrol the streets in the cities. Here veiling suggests conformity to conservative norms in regard to women's behaviour and appearance which the regime perceives as an important aspect of the social order. For the wealthy, however, this does not prevent women at home wearing, as their sisters in the Ottoman elite used to do, the latest creations from Paris or New York. In most other Gulf countries, though women's dress in public is very much under scrutiny, there is no comparable enforcement of total covering of the body or face, and styles of dress vary according to class and preference.

In Iran, under the Shah's regime, 'modernity' was equated with the styles of dress adopted by the urban middle class – which basically followed Western fashions. After the 1979 revolution a radical change in appearance was forced upon all women – the wearing of the *chador* in public. The regime was thus making a clear statement of its ideological position through the physical appearance of women. Its impact, however, also had a class dimension, since for poor urban women, wearing the *chador* had always been common practice. In contrast, for the middle classes, it represented a radical change and was accompanied by considerable limitations on their freedom to work, as well as alterations in their legal rights.

In some parts of the Arab world, changes in women's dress have had other political connotations not directly linked to the ideology of the state, or enforced by it. In a number of countries today – particularly Egypt, Jordan, the West Bank and Gaza Strip, Turkey and parts of North Africa – a new style of dress has emerged. Women are seen wearing long skirts and long-sleeved shirts or jackets with the *hijab*, a scarf which covers the forehead, hair and neck. In a sense, this manner of dress is an 'invention' of tradition. It is often presented as a return to 'traditional' dress, as an expression of religious piety and cultural continuity. Yet it is not actually the same as any past style of veiling, headcovering or dress. It has none the less developed strong political and ideological connotations. It is usually taken to suggest allegiance to one or other of the Islamic fundamentalist groups and the way the *hijab* is worn is somewhat distinct from the way older women in the popular quarters of cities wear their scarves.

This style of dress has become quite widespread in urban society and is often a clear assertion of difference, and of belonging to a particular ideological trend. In Turkey, for example, where Islamic fundamentalism has formed a persistent but certainly not dominant political force, there are some Turkish women students who wear the *hijab* to class against the wishes of their professors and of the university authorities. In urban Egypt, the *muhajjabah* (woman wearing the *hijab*) is an increasingly common sight, leading many Western observers to assume that the country is now entirely dominated by Islamic fundamentalist ideology. Yet it seems that the symbolism of this form of dress has already become more complex than a simple statement about religious fanaticism, as is often assumed.

The phenomenon also represents a wider reaction against the continuance of aspects of Western domination, political, economic and cultural, in the Middle East. In Egypt, especially since the 1970s, it is also a challenge to particular kinds of class privilege, associated with ostentatious Western-style consumerism. It is hardly an accident that the 1986 riots of the Central Security Forces (*amn markazi*) in Cairo were directed first and foremost against nightclubs on the Pyramids road. This was an attack not only on privilege but on a particular kind of lifestyle of which images of sexual licence form a part. In this way, against the image of the 'loose' women associated with this lifestyle is counterposed the image of the modest, pious and obedient woman, who at the same time respects her own culture.

Thus the way in which women dress is again a part of the definition of behaviour as well as, perhaps, ideological allegiance. Yet the motives which individual women have for choosing how to present themselves do not seem to be simple. In some milieux women are responding to social or peer-group pressure in making such decisions. Furthermore these 'Islamic' styles of dress have now also been adopted by the well-to-do and have become less austere than may have been intended. There are even, in Cairo, fashion shows which include outfits in this style.

Despite these apparent innovations in the ways women are perceived, it is scarcely less difficult to escape the connotations of these images and the power structures which lie behind them than it was in the past. Women also continue to internalize these definitions of themselves, sometimes without even being conscious of it. For those women who are aware of these forms of power and who are fighting to control their own lives, rejecting the images imposed upon them by others, society still does not offer any easy options. While it may be possible for women in the Middle East to draw some lessons from the experience of Western feminists in this respect, the paths which they follow will inevitably be different and rooted in their own history and culture.

Notes

The notes to the captions follow those to the main text.

Introduction pp. 1–35

1. Quoted in Alan Sekula, 'Traffic in Photographs', in *Photography against the Grain*, ed. Alan Sekula (Halifax, Nova Scotia: The Press of the Nova Scotia College of Art and Design, 1984), p. 82.

2. ibid., p. 78.

3. Susan Sontag, *On Photography* (Harmondsworth: Penguin, 1979); Roland Barthes, *Camera Lucida* (London: Fontana, 1984).

4. Walter Benjamin, 'The Work of Art in the Age of Mechanical Reproduction', in *Illuminations*, ed. Hannah Arendt (London: Jonathan Cape, 1970), p. 228.

5. Victor Burgin (ed.), *Thinking Photography* (London and Basingstoke: Macmillan, 1982), p. 152.

6. Quoted in Jean Sagne, 'L'Exotisme dans le portrait photographique au XIXe siècle', in *Revue de la Bibliothèque Nationale*, 1ère année, No. 1, September 1981, p. 29 (translated from the French).

7. Victor Hugo, *Les Orientales: Poèmes* (Paris: Charles Gosselin, 1829), p. ix (translated from the French).

8. Edward Said, *Orientalism* (London: Routledge & Kegan Paul, 1978), p. 177.

9. Mary J. Harper, 'Recovering the Other: Women and the Orient in Writings of Early Nineteenth-Century France', *Critical Matrix*, Vol. I, No. 3, 1985, p. 6, citing Johan d'Ivray, *L'aventure Saint-Simonienne et les femmes* (Alcan, 1928), p. 144.

10. Quoted in *The Orientalists: Delacroix to Matisse*, ed. Mary Ann Stevens (London: Royal Academy of Arts, 1984), p. 192.

11. Linda Nochlin, 'The Imaginary Orient', *Art in America*, May 1983, p. 127.

12. Edward Said, op. cit., p. 188.

13. *Flaubert in Egypt: a Sensibility on Tour*, ed. Francis Steegmuller (Boston/Toronto: Bodley Head, 1972), p. 220.

14. Gérard de Nerval, *The Women of Cairo: Scenes of Life in the Orient (Voyage en Orient)*, 2 vols (London: George Routledge & Sons, 1929), Vol. II, p. 36.

15. See Zeyneb Khanum, *A Turkish Woman's European Impressions*, ed. and trs. Grace Ellison (London: Seeley, Service & Co, 1913), p. xiii.

16. Pierre Loti, *Disenchanted (Les Désenchantées)*, trs. Clara Bell (London: Macmillan & Co., 1906).

17. J.E. Budgett Meakin, *Life in Morocco and Glimpses Beyond* (London: Chatto & Windus, 1905), p. 71.

18. S.H. Leeder, *The Veiled Mysteries of Egypt and the Religion of Islam* (London: Eveleigh Nash, 1912), p. ix.

19. Reverend Harris Jessup, *Women of the Arabs: Seventeen Years a Missionary in Syria* (New York, 1873), p. 229.

20. John Mackenzie, *Propaganda and Empire: the Manipulation of British Public Opinion, 1880–1960* (Manchester: Manchester University Press, 1984), p. 113.

21. Hilma Granqvist, *Marriage Conditions in a Palestinian Village* (Helsinki, 1931, '35); *Birth and Childhood among the Arabs: Studies in a Muhammadan Village in Palestine* (Helsinki: Söderstrom & Co., 1947); *Muslim Death and Burial: Arab Customs and Traditions Studied in a Village in Jordan* (Helsinki, 1965), Tom. 34, No. 1.
Portrait of a Palestinian Village: the Photographs of Hilma Granqvist, ed. Karen Seger (London: Third World Centre for Research and Publishing, 1981).
Winifred S. Blackman, *The Fellahin of Upper Egypt* (London: G.G. Harrap, 1927).
H.A.R. Dickson, *The Arab of the Desert: a Glimpse into Bedawin Life in Kuwait and Saudi Arabia* (London: George Allen & Unwin, 1949).
Alois Musil, *The Manners and Customs of the Rwala Bedouins* (New York/Prague: Oriental Explorations and Studies No. 6, 1928).

22. P. Lucas and J.-C. Vatin, *L'Algérie des anthropologues* (Paris: Maspero, 1982).
French women anthropologists working in Algeria also tended to concentrate on either Berber societies or Arab communities with special characteristics, such as the people of the Mzab region. For example:
Matthéa Gaudry, *La Femme chaouia de l'Aurès: étude de sociologie berbère* (Paris: 1929).
Amélie Marie Goichon, *La Vie féminine au Mzab:*

252

étude de sociologie musulmane (Paris, 1927).
Laure Lefevre-Bousquet, *Recherches sur la condition de la femme Kabyle: la coutume et l'oeuvre française* (Algiers: Imprimeries La Typo-Litho et Jules Carbonel réunies, 1939).

23. M.W. Hilton Simpson, *Among the Hill Folk of Algeria* (London: T. Fisher Unwin, 1921), p. 71.

24. Lucas and Vatin, op. cit., p. 204 (translated from the French).

25. Frantz Fanon, *A Dying Colonialism*, trs. Haakon Chevalier (London: Writers & Readers, 1980), pp. 37–8.

26. See, for example, her story 'Fellah', written in 1902 and published in the Egyptian feminist magazine *L'Egyptienne*, 1 September 1925, pp. 242 ff.

27. Gertrude Bell, *The Desert and the Sown* (London: Virago, 1985 rpt).
The Letters of Gertrude Bell, selected and edited by Lady Bell, 2 vols (London: Ernest Benn, 1927).
Gertrude Bell: from Her Personal Papers 1889–1926, ed. Elizabeth Burgoyne (London: Ernest Benn, 1958/61).
Lady Anne Isabella Noel Blunt, *A Pilgrimage to Nejd*, 2 vols (London: Frank Cass & Co, 1968).
Lady Isabel Burton, *The Inner Life of Syria, Palestine and the Holy Land: from My Private Journal*, 2 vols (London: H.S. King & Co., 1875).
Freya Stark, *Baghdad Sketches* (London: John Murray, 1937); *Seen in Hadramaut* (London: John Murray, 1938); *Letters from Syria* (London: John Murray, 1942). These are just a few of her numerous books on the Middle East.

28. Isabella Bird, *Journeys in Persia and Kurdistan*, 2 vols (London: John Murray, 1891), Vol. I, p. 253.

29. Sophia Lane Poole, *The Englishwoman in Egypt: Letters from Cairo during a Residence there in 1842, 3 and 4. Letters during 1845–6*, Second Series. 3 vols (London, 1844–46), Vol. II, pp. 74–5.

30. L.M.J. Garnett, *The Woman of Turkey and Their Folklore* (London: D. Nutt, 1890/91), Vol. II, p. 546.

31. Hubertine Auclert, *Les Femmes arabes en Algérie* (Paris, 1900), p. 49 (translated from the French).

32. Madame Rushdi Pasha (Eugènie le Brun), *Harems et musulmanes d'Egypte: Lettres* (Paris: Librairie Felix Juven, 1902); *Les Répudiées* (Paris: Librairie Felix Juven, 1908).

33. See the private correspondence of Margery Corbett Ashby in the Fawcett Library, London.

34. Huda Shaarawi, *Harem Years*, trs. and ed. with introduction by Margot Badran (London: Virago, 1986; New York: Feminist Press, 1987).

Halide Edip, *Memoirs* (New York/London: Century Co., 1926).
Emine Foat Tugay, *Three Centuries: Family Chronicles of Turkey and Egypt* (London: Oxford University Press, 1963).

35. For a detailed analysis of these intellectuals active in the Arab world, see A.H. Hourani, *Arabic Thought in the Liberal Age, 1798–1939* (Cambridge: Cambridge University Press, 1983 rpt). On the role of women in debates on their rights, see Margot Badran, 'Independent Women: a century of feminism in Egypt', paper presented at the Symposium on Arab Women: 'Old Boundaries, New Frontiers', Georgetown University, 1986.

36. Namik Kemal, 'On the Education of Women, a Draft', quoted in Emel Sönmez, 'Turkish Women in Turkish Literature of the Nineteenth Century', *Die Welt des Islams*, Leiden, NS 12, No. 1–3, 1969, p. 8.

37. A.H. Hourani, op. cit., p. 167.

38. Deniz Kandiyoti, 'From Empire to Nation State: Transformations of the Woman Question in Turkey', forthcoming in *History of Women: Changing Perceptions* (Paris, UNESCO).

39. Judith Tucker, *Women in Nineteenth Century Egypt* (Cambridge: Cambridge University Press, 1985), pp. 197–8.

40. Leila Ahmed, 'Feminism and Feminist Movements in the Middle East', in *Women and Islam*, ed. Azizah al-Hibri (Oxford: Pergamon, 1982), p. 162. On the persistence of male control over women's sexuality, see Margot Badran, 'Independent women', op. cit.

Chapter I The Development of Photography in the Middle East pp. 36–69

1. Maxime du Camp, *Le Nil, Egypte et Nubie*, quoted in Francis Steegmuller, *Flaubert and Madame Bovary* (London: Robert Hale, 1939), p. 196. My attention was drawn to the role of Hajji Ismail in Maxime du Camp's Photography by Julia Ballerini who kindly showed me her unpublished talk 'The Stillness of Hadji-Ismael'.

2. Quoted in *Photography: Essays and Images*, ed. Beaumont Newhall (London: Secker & Warburg, 1981), p. 112.

3. Roland Barthes, op. cit., p. 80.

4. Volume I on Syria was published in Paris in 1866.

5. Saadia and Lakhdar, *L'Alienation et la résistance de la famille algérienne* (Lausanne, 1961), p. 121. Quoted in Lucas and Vatin, op. cit., p. 246 (translated from the French).

6. Frank Staff, *The Picture Postcard and Its Origins* (London: Lutterworth Press, 1979), p. 87.

7. Lucie Duff Gordon, *Letters from Egypt* (London: Virago, 1983), p. 57.

8. Quoted in 'A Legacy of Light', *Aramco Magazine*, Nov.–Dec. 1983, p. 23.

9. Ritchie Thomas, 'Bonfils and Son: Egypt, Greece and the Levant 1867–1894', *History of Photography* Vol. III, No. 1, Jan. 1979, pp. 41 and 45.

10. Lucie Duff Gordon, op. cit., p. 21.

11. Quoted in *British Journal of Photography*, Vol. IX, 1862, p. 49.

12. E. Chantre, *Recherches anthropologiques dans l'Afrique orientale – Egypte* (Lyon, 1904), p. xvi (translated from the French).

13. Quoted in the brochure of the Albert Kahn Museum, 'Au-dela d'un Jardin – Albert Kahn', p. 9 (translated from the French).

14. Jennifer Scarce, 'Isfahan in Camera: Nineteenth-century Persia through the Photographs of Ernest Hoeltzer', *Art and Archaeology Research Papers*, April 1976.

15. Tom Hopkinson, *Picture Post 1938–1950* (London: Chatto & Windus, 1984 rpt) [p. 6].

16. D.J. Miller, 'The Craftsman's Art: Armenians and the Growth of Photography in the Near East (1856–1981)', M.A. Thesis, American University of Beirut, Beirut, Lebanon, August 1981.

17. Umm Kulthoum, 'Memoirs' in *Middle Eastern Women Speak*, ed. E.W. Fernea and B. Bezirgan (Austin, Texas/London: University of Texas Press, 1978), p. 145.

18. Quoted in Frederick Wakeman Jr., 'Lost China', *New York Review of Books*, 8 Feb. 1979.

19. Nicholas Monti, 'Images to Fuel an Empire', *Aperture* No. 94, Spring 1984, p. 8.

20. *The Photographic News*, 10 Jan. 1890, p. 27.

21. Janet Quinn Tassel, 'Dragomans, Skeikhs and Moon-faced Beauties', *Art News* No. 79, Dec. 1980, p. 109.

22. W.H. Barbrook, 'Algeria and Tunis as a Field for Photography', *The Camera*, 1 Dec. 1886, p. 181.

23. See the photograph on p. 123 of Malek Alloula's *The Colonial Harem* (Minneapolis: University of Minnesota Press, 1986; Manchester: Manchester University Press, 1987).

Notes to captions in Chapter I

1. Published as plate 4b in *Voyages au Soudan oriental, dans l'Afrique septentrionale et dans l'Asie Mineure, executés de 1847 à 1854 . . . Atlas des vues pittoresques, scènes de mouers, types de végétation remarquables, etc . . .* (Paris: Borrani, 1852–58).

2. Mary Ann Stevens (ed): *The Orientalists,* op. cit., p. 118.

3. Published in Ernest Chantre, *Recherches Anthropologiques*, op. cit., p. 183.

4. Published diary: Elizabeth Burgoyne (ed): *Gertrude Bell, from Her Personal Papers*, op. cit., Vol. I, p. 292. Unpublished Diary in the Gertrude Bell Archive, Department of Archaeology, Newcastle-upon-Tyne.

5. Engraving published in Jane Dieulafoy, *La Perse, la Chaldée et la Susiane* (Paris: 1887), narrative on p. 122.

Chapter II The Seen, the Unseen and the Imagined: Private and Public Lives pp. 70–91

1. Zeyneb Khanum, op. cit., p. xvi.

2. Nabia Abbott, 'Women' in *Mid-East: World Center: Yesterday, Today and Tomorrow*, ed. Ruth Nanda Anshen (New York: Science of Culture Series, Vol. 7, 1956), p. 203.

3. For a detailed description of life in Turkish palace harems, see N. Penzer, *The Harem* (London: Spring Books, 1965). For a general overview of Western ideas about the harem and its imagery, see Annabelle d'Huart and Nadia Tazi, *Harems* (Paris: Chene/ Hachette, 1980).

4. Fatima Mernissi, *Beyond the Veil* (London: Al Saqi Books, 1985), p. 19. For further discussions of women and sexuality in the Middle East, see F. Sabbah, *Women in the Muslim Unconscious* (New York: Pergamon Press, 1984); A. Boudhiba, *Islam and Sexuality* (London: Routledge & Kegan Paul, 1985). For details on *hbel shitan*, see Lawrence Rosen, 'The Negotiation of Reality: Male–Female Relations in Sefrou, Morocco', in *Women in the Muslim World*, ed. Lois Beck and Nikki Keddie (Cambridge, Mass./ London: Harvard University Press, 1982), pp. 566–7 and footnote 3, referring to observations by Kenneth Brown.

5. Marina Warner, *Alone of All Her Sex: the Myths and Cult of the Virgin Mary* (London: Weidenfeld & Nicolson, 1976).

6. Madame Rushdi Pasha, *Harems . . .* , op.cit., p. 2 (translated from the French).

7. E.W. Lane, *An Account of the Manners and Customs of the Modern Egyptians, Written in Egypt during the Years 1833–35* (London: Gardner, 1895), p. 188.

8. Jane Dieulafoy, *La Perse, la Chaldée et la Susiane*, op. cit., p. 36 (translated from the French).

9. Harriet Martineau, *Eastern Life, Present and Past*, 3 vols (London, 1848).
Elia Sykes, *Persia and Its People* (London: Methuen & Co., 1910); *Through Persia on a Sidesaddle* (London: A.D. Innes & Co., 1898).
Sophia Lane Poole, op. cit.
Isabel Burton, op. cit.
Isabella Bird, op. cit.
Lady Anne Blunt, op. cit.
For a discussion of Western women's visits to harems, see Margot Badran, 'Huda Shaarawi and the Liberation of Egyptian Women', D.Phil. Thesis, St Antony's College, Oxford, 1977, pp. 29–31.

10. Sophia Lane Poole, op. cit., Vol. II, p. 74.

11. Harriet Martineau, op. cit., Vol. II, p. 167.

12. L.M.J. Garnett, *Turkish Life in Town and Country* (London: George Newnes, 1904), p. 51.

13. Zeyneb Khanum, op. cit., fp. 192.

14. Dorina L. Neave, *Twenty-six Years on the Bosphorus* (London: Grayson & Grayson, 1933), p. 67.

15. Margot Badran, 'Huda Shaarawi . . .', op.cit., p. 36.

16. For changes in urban women's lives in Egypt, see Margot Badran, ibid., Chapter II. For a description of women's position in a more conservative urban milieu in the early twentieth century, see A. Jaussen, *Coutumes Palestiniennes I: Naplouse et son district* (Paris: Geuthner, 1927).

17. A.M. Goichon, 'La Femme de la moyenne bourgeoisie fasiya', *Revue des Etudes Islamiques*, Vol. III, 1929, pp. 64–5.

18. For example, Huda Shaarawi, op. cit., and Halide Edip, op. cit.

19. Bamdad ol-Moluk, *From Darkness into Light: Women's Emancipation in Iran*, ed. and trs. F.R.C. Bagley (Smithdown, NY: Exposition Press, 1977), pp. 7–8.

20. Public speech at the commemoration of the death of Qasim Amin, 4 May 1928. Quoted in *L'Egyptienne*, June 1928, p. 14 (translated from the French).

21. For discussions of control of women's appearance and visibility, and the question of public and private space in the Middle East, see:
Nora Seni, 'Ville ottomane et représentation du corps

féminin', *Les Temps Modernes* No. 456–7, July/August 1984, pp. 66 ff.
Roxan A. Dusen, 'The Study of Women in the Middle East: Some Thoughts', *MESA Bulletin*, Vol. X, No. 2, 1976, pp. 1 ff.
Cynthia Nelson, 'Public and Private Politics: Women in the Middle Eastern World', *American Ethnologist*, Vol. I, No. 3, August 1984, pp. 551 ff.

Notes to captions in Chapter II

1. Malek Alloula, *The Colonial Harem*, op. cit., p. 24.

2. *Gertrude Bell, from Her Personal Papers*, Vol. I, op. cit., pp. 299–300.

3. Information from Bahija Rashid, Cairo.

4. Published in Huda Shaarawi, *Harem Years*, op. cit., Part II.

5. Margot Badran, 'Huda Shaarawi . . .', op. cit., p. 101.

6. Information from Ali Razavi.

7. Hilma Granqvist, *Muslim Death and Burial*, op. cit., p. 150.

Chapter III Family Portraits pp. 92–117

1. Julia Hirsh, *Family Photographs: Content, Meaning and Effect* (New York/London: Oxford University Press, 1981), pp. 82–3.

2. Pierre Bourdieu et al, *Un Art Moyen* (Paris: Le Sens Commun, 1965), p. 41.

3. Sophia Lane Poole, op. cit., Vol III, pp. 55 ff.

4. Huda Shaarawi, op. cit., pp. 52–60.

5. Nadia Farraq, 'Al-Muqtataf 1876–1900: Journalism in Syria and Egypt', D.Phil. Thesis, University of Oxford, 1969.

6. Madame Rushdi Pasha, *Harems* . . . op. cit., p. 62 (translated from the French).

7. Kazim Daghestani, *Etude Sociologique sur la famille musulmane contemporaine en Syrie* (Paris, 1932), p. 138 (translated from the French).

8. Halide Edip, op. cit., pp. 144–5.

9. Madame Rushdi Pasha, *Harems* . . . op. cit., pp. 220 ff (translated from the French).

10. Malek Alloula, *The Colonial Harem*, op. cit., p. 39.

11. See for example Winifred Blackman's only published photograph of a husband and wife together,

entitled 'Husband and Jealous Wife' in *The Fellahin of Upper Egypt*, op. cit., p. 39.

12. Cromer Papers, PRO/FO 633/14, Cromer to F. Graham, 14 Oct. 1910, f. 128. Quoted in Judith Tucker, op. cit., p. 117.

13. A.M. Goichon, 'La Femme de la moyenne bourgeoisie fasiya', op. cit., p. 26 (translated from the French).

14. E.R.J. Owen, *The Middle East in the World Economy 1800–1914* (London: Methuen, 1981), p. 244.

15. Roland Barthes, op. cit., p. 85.

Notes to captions in Chapter III

1. Snouk Hurgronje, *Mecca in the Latter Part of the Nineteenth Century* (Leiden: E.J. Brill; London: Luzac & Co, 1931).

2. Information from Nada Andraous, interview with the author 1986.

3. For a similar story of a Circassian woman coming to Egypt and marrying into upper-class Egyptian society at this time, see Huda Shaarawi's account of her mother, Iqbal Hanum, in *Harem Years*, op. cit., pp. 25–6.

4. Information from Aziza Galal, interview with the author 1986.

5. For a more detailed account of proceedings in a Cairo divorce court at the turn of the century, see Madame Rushdi Pasha (Eugènie le Brun), *Les Répudiées*, op. cit.

6. Freya Stark, *Beyond Euphrates*, op. cit., p. 141.

7. For a full description of the ritual see Winifred Blackman, *The Fellahin of Upper Egypt*, op. cit., pp. 102–3.

8. For examples of emigration to the United States around the same time, see the histories of two families from Ramallah, Palestine, in Sarah Graham-Brown, *Palestinians and Their Society, a Photographic Essay 1880–1946* (London: Quartet Books, 1980), pp. 150–1.

Chapter IV Dressing the Part pp. 118–43

1. Shelagh Weir and Widad Kawar, 'Costumes and Wedding Customs in Bayt Dajan', *Palestine Exploration Quarterly*, No. 107, 1975, p. 47.

2. *Les Costumes populaires de la Turquie en 1873. Publié sous le patronage de la Commission Imperiale Ottomane pour l'Exposition Universelle de Vienne. Texte par son Excellence Hamdy Bey et Marie de*
Launay (Constantinople, 1873). Introduction (translated from the French).

3. Jeanne Jouin, 'Le Costume féminin dans l'Islam Syro-Palestinien', *Revue des Etudes Islamiques*, Vol. 8, 1934, pp. 497–8 (translated from the French).

4. ibid., p. 481 (translated from the French).

5. E.R.J. Owen, op. cit., p. 261.

6. Wilfrid Sparroy, *Persian Children of the Royal Family: the Narrative of an English Tutor at the Court of H.I.H. Zillu's-Sultan* (London/New York: John Lane, 1902), p. 228.

7. Isabella Bird, *Journeys in Persia and Kurdistan*, op. cit., Vol. I, p. 264.

8. Nora Seni, op. cit., pp. 66 ff.

9. L.M.J. Garnett, *The Women of Turkey . . .*, op. cit., Vol. II, p. 15.

10. Quoted in Deniz Kandiyoti, op. cit.

11. *L'Egyptienne*, 1 Sept. 1925, p. 142 (translated from the French).

12. For more details see Eliz Sanassarian, *The Women's Rights Movement in Iran* (New York: Praeger, 1982); Henri Massé, 'Le Dévoilement des Iraniennes', *Revue des Etudes Islamiques*, Vol. IX, 1935, pp. 411 ff.

13. *The Sphere*, London, 22 August 1925, p. 22.

14. 'The Transformation of Turkey', *National Geographic Magazine*, Vol. LXXV, Jan. 1939, fp. 16.

15. Jeanne Jouin, 'Iconographie de la mariée citadine dans l'Islam nord-africain', *Revue des Etudes Islamiques*, Vol. V, 1931, pp. 313 ff.

16. Kazim Daghestani, op. cit., p. 130.

17. Hamid M. Ammar, *Growing up in an Egyptian Village* (London: Routledge & Kegan Paul, 1954), p. 97.

18. From an oral history collected by Kitty Warnock, West Bank, 1985.

19. On veiling of women in urban society, see Margot Badran, 'Huda Shaarawi', op. cit., p. 7.

20. Gérard de Nerval, op. cit., Vol. I, pp. 2–3.

21. Malek Alloula, op. cit., p. 14.

22. Marina Warner, *Monuments and Maidens: the Allegory of the Female Form* (London: Weidenfeld & Nicolson, 1985), p. 295.

23. Frantz Fanon, op. cit., p. 42.

24. Margot Badran, 'The Feminist Vision of Three Turn-of-the-century Egyptian Women'. Paper given at

the British Society of Middle Eastern Studies conference, London 1986.

Notes to captions in Chapter IV

1. For the Maronite practice of wearing the *tantur*, see W.M. Thomson, *The Land and the Book*, (London: T. Nelson & Sons, 1980), pp. 73–4. Thomson described the wearers of the *tantur* as 'horned ladies'.

2. Freya Stark, *Seen in Hadramaut*, op. cit., p. x.

3. Emile Marmorstein, 'The Veil in Judaism and Islam', *Journal of Jewish Studies*, Vol. II, 1954, pp. 1–11.

4. Ella Sykes, *Persia and Its People*, op. cit., p. 198.

5. For more examples from this series of photographs, see Y. Papetti, B. de Freminville, F. Valier and S. Tisseron, *La Passion des étoffes chez un neuro-psychiatre: G.G. de Clérambault (1872–1934)*, (Paris: Solin, 1981). The authors argue that de Clérambault himself had an obsession with women's clothing just as much as did the women he studied.

6. This photograph appears in Malek Alloula, *The Colonial Harem*, op. cit., p. 126.

7. Wilfrid Sparroy, *Persian Children of the Royal Family*, op. cit., p. 179.

Chapter V Working Women pp. 144–69

1. Hilma Granqvist, *Birth and Childhood . . .*, op. cit., p. 158.

2. Matthéa Gaudry, op. cit., *avant-propos* (translated from the French).

3. H.D. Ammar, op. cit., p. 50.

4. Hilma Granqvist, *Marriage Conditions . . .* op. cit., p. 293.

5. ibid., p. 210.

6. Afaf Lutfi al-Sayyid Marsot, 'The Revolutionary Gentlewoman in Egypt' in *Women in the Muslim World*, ed. Beck and Keddie, op. cit., p. 265.

7. For a detailed account of female domestic slavery in Egypt in the nineteenth century, see Judith Tucker, op. cit., pp. 164 ff.; on slavery in the Ottoman Empire generally, see E.R. Toledano, *The Ottoman Slave Trade and Its Suppression 1840–1890* (Princeton, N.J.: Princeton University Press, 1982).

8. For instance, see Budgett Meakin, op. cit., pp. 105 ff.

9. Judith Tucker, op. cit., p. 46.

10. A.M. Goichon, 'La Femme . . .' op. cit., p. 58 (translated from the French); and on the control of property by women in Egypt, see Judith Tucker, *passim*, and Margot Badran, 'Huda Shaarawi', op. cit., p. 82.

11. Judith Tucker, op. cit., p. 87.

12. Samir Khalaf, *Persistence and Change in Nineteenth Century Lebanon* (Beirut: American University of Beirut, 1979), p. 134.

13. Judith Tucker, op. cit., pp. 40–1.

14. ibid., p. 90.

15. Deniz Kandiyoti, op. cit.

16. For example, Zafer Toprak, historian at Boğaziçi University, Istanbul, interview with the author, 1986.

17. Demetra Brown [Vaka], *The Unveiled Ladies of Stamboul* (New York/Boston: Houghton Mifflin Co., 1923), pp. 32 ff.

18. Naguib Bey Mahfouz, *The History of Medical Education in Egypt* (Cairo: Government Press, 1935), p. 72.

Notes to captions in Chapter V

1. Granqvist, *Birth and Childhood*, op. cit., p. 157.

2. Information from Ali Razavi, London.

3. Account summarized from A.C. Edwards, *The Persian Carpet* (London: Gerald Duckworth, 1953).

4. E.R.J. Owen, *The Middle East and the World Economy*, op. cit., p. 158.

5. Interview with Süreyya Ağaoğlu, 1986; Margot Badran, 'Huda Shaarawi . . .', op. cit., Chapter 10, p. 367.

Chapter VI Women in the Public Eye pp. 170–91

1. For a number of examples of this type of studio photography, see Malek Alloula, op. cit., pp. 85 ff.

2. Lane, op. cit., p. 384.

3. Frank Edward Johnson, 'Here and There in North Africa', *National Geographic Magazine*, Vol. XXV No. 1, Jan. 1914, p. 13.

4. Vanessa Maher, 'Women and Social Change in Morocco' in *Women in the Muslim World*, op. cit., pp. 111–13.

5. Lucie Duff Gordon, op. cit., p. 20.

6. Georg Moritz Ebers, *Egypt, Descriptive, Historical and Picturesque*, trs. Clara Bell, 2 vols (London: Cassell & Co., 1983), Vol. II, pp. 312–14.

7. Judith Tucker, op. cit., p. 152.

8. ibid, pp. 151–3.

9. Eugenia Popescu-Judetz, '*Koçek* and *Cengi* in Turkish Culture', *Dance Studies*, Vol. VI, 1982, pp. 53–6.

10. Huda Shaarawi, op. cit., p. 42.

11. C.J. Edmonds, *Kurds, Turks and Arabs* (London: Oxford University Press, 1957), p. 234.

12. Madame Rushdi Pasha, *Harems . . .*, op. cit., p. 78 (translated from the French).

13. John Allwood, *The Great Exhibitions* (London: Studio Vista, 1977), pp. 89–92; Pierre Nora, *Les Lieux de Mémoire* (Paris: Gallimard, 1984), pp. 562–4; Burton Benedict, *The Anthropology of the World's Fairs* (London: Scholar Press, 1983), p. 77.

14. Umm Kulthoum, 'Memoirs', op. cit., p. 155.

15. Nermin Menemencioğlu, 'The Ottoman Theatre 1839–1923'. Paper given at a symposium on the Turkish theatre at the School for Oriental and African Studies, London University, March 1983.

16. Published in *Mai Ziadeh wa 'Alam Asriha: asa'il makhtutah lam tunshur 1912–1940* (Mai Ziadeh and her times: unpublished letters) (Beirut: Mu'assasat Naufal, 1982), p. 328 (translated from the Arabic).

17. Umm Kulthoum, 'Memoirs', op. cit., *passim*.

Notes to captions in Chapter VI

1. M.W. Hilton Simpson, *Among the Hillfolk of Algeria*, op. cit., p. 103.

2. Georg Moritz Ebers, op. cit., Vol. II, p. 312.

3. Information from Ali Razavi.

4. Information from Virginia Danielson.

5. Jacques Berque, *Egypt: Imperialism and Revolution* (London: Faber & Faber, 1972), pp. 350–1.

6. Information from Virginia Danielson; Jacques Berque, op. cit.

7. Margot Badran, 'Huda Shaarawi . . .', op. cit.

8. Information from Virginia Danielson; Ali Jihad Racy, 'The Record Industry and Egyptian Traditional Music 1904–34', *Ethnomusicology*, 1976, pp. 23–48.

9. Information from Virginia Danielson.

Chapter VII The Spread of Education pp. 192–209

1. Zeyneb Khanum, op. cit., p. 97.

2. Huda Shaarawi, op. cit., p. 40.

3. *The Daughters of Syria: a Narrative of the Efforts of Mrs Bowen Thompson for the Evangelization of the Syrian females*, ed. H.B. Tristam (London: Seeley, Jackson & Halliday, 1872), pp. 213–14.

4. Mary Mills Patrick, *A Bosporus Adventure* (Stanford University/London: Stanford University Press and Oxford University Press, 1934).

5. ibid., p. 228.

6. Quoted in Emel Sönmez, op. cit., p. 25.

7. Nadia Farraq, 'Al-Muqtataf . . .' op. cit.

8. Margot Badran, 'The feminist vision . . .' op. cit.

9. Margot Badran, 'Huda Shaarawi', op. cit., pp. 19–20; Henri Laoust, 'Introduction à une étude de l'enseignement arabe en Egypte', *Revue des Etudes Islamiques*, Vol. VII, 1933, pp. 30 ff.

10. 'The Feminist Movement in Persia', *Central Asian Review*, Vol. VII, 1959, p. 75.

11. Y. Knibiehler and R. Goutalier, *La Femme au Temps de Colonies* (Paris: Stock, 1985), p. 233; D.C. Gordon, *Women of Algeria: an Essay on Change* (Cambridge, Mass: Harvard University Press, 1968), pp. 39–45.

12. S. Longrigg and F. Stoakes, *Iraq* (London: Ernest Benn, 1958), p. 173.

13. A.L. Tibawi, *Arab Education in Mandatory Palestine* (London: Oxford University Press, 1956), pp. 228–9.

14. From a summary of the EFU's aims given in a speech by Mrs Ihsan Ahmad, published in *L'Egyptienne*, May 1928, pp. 18 ff (translated from the French).

15. Margot Badran, 'Huda Shaarawi . . .', op. cit., p. 259; 'Feminist vision . . .' op. cit.

16. Bamdad ol-Moluk, op. cit., pp. 183–4.

17. Freya Stark, *Baghdad Sketches*, op. cit., p. 98.

Notes to captions in Chapter VII

1. Yvonne Knibiehler and Regine Goutalier, *La Femme au temps des colonies*, op. cit., p. 235.

2. W. Cleveland, *Sati' al-Husri: the Making of an Arab Nationalist* (Princeton, 1971).

3. H.J. Turtle, *Quaker Service in the Middle East* (London: Friends' Council, 1975), pp. 22 ff.

Chapter VIII Campaigning Women pp. 210–38

1. Marina Warner, *Monuments and Maidens*, op. cit., Pt. II.

2. Quoted in Bamdad ol-Moluk, op. cit., pp. 48–9.

3. Lucie Duff Gordon, op. cit., pp. 52–3.

4. *Tanzimat'tan Cumhuriyete Türkiye Ansiklopedisi*, (Istanbul: Iletişim Yayenlari, 1986), Vol. IV, pp. 867–74.

5. For an account of Aisha's role, see Nabia Abbott, *Aisha, Beloved of Muhammad* (London: Al Saqi Books, 1985).

6. For an account of Zeynab's role, see Farah Azari, 'Islam's Appeal to Women in Iran: Illusions and Reality' in *Women of Iran: the Conflict with Fundamentalist Islam*, ed. Farah Azari (London: Ithaca Press, 1983), pp. 24–6.

7. K.T. Khairallah, *La Syrie* (Paris, 1912), p. 87.

8. Margot Badran, 'Huda Shaarawi . . .', op. cit., p. 191; Phillipe de Tarazi, *Tarikh as-sahafat al-arabiyya* (History of the Arabic Press), 4 Vols (Beirut: 1913–33).

9. Deniz Kandiyoti, op. cit.

10. ibid.

11. Zafer Toprak, 'The 1935 International Feminism Congress and Peace' (in Turkish), *Dusun*, special issue on 'Women and Society', March 1986.

12. Bamdad ol-Moluk, op. cit., p. 9; Nikki R. Keddie, *Religion and Rebellion in Iran: the Iranian Tobacco Protest of 1891–2* (London: Frank Cass, 1966), pp. 96.

13. William Morgan Shuster, *The Strangling of Persia* (London: T. Fisher Unwin, 1912), pp. 186 & 188.

14. For an account of the limited gains made by the Iranian women's movement during this period, see Eliz Sanassarian, op. cit.

15. The section on Egyptian feminism draws heavily on the work of Margot Badran, particularly on 'Huda Shaarawi . . .', op. cit., Chapters IV and V. See also 'Independent women . . .' op. cit.

16. *The Sphere*, London, 31 May 1919, p. 181.

17. From the day books of photographic captions in the UPI/Bettman Archives, New York. For a detailed description of one such major demonstration from the women's point of view, see Huda Shaarawi, *Harem Years*, op. cit., pp. 112–14.

18. Margot Badran, 'Huda Shaarawi . . .', op. cit., p. 125.

19. Huda Shaarawi, op. cit., p. 125.

20. ibid., p. 131.

21. *L'Egyptienne*, July 1928, p. 3.

22. ibid, June 1928, p. 11 (translated from the French).

23. 'Deuxième congrès musulman général des femmes d'Orient à Teheran, Nov./Dec. 1932', *Revue des Etudes Islamiques*, Vol. VII, 1933, p. 45 (translated from the French).

24. Doria Shafik (Ragai), *La Femme nouvelle en Egypte* (Cairo 1944), p. 75 (translated from the French).

25. Nazirah Zein ed-Din, 'Removing the Veil and Veiling. Lectures and Reflections towards Women's Liberation and Social Reform in the Muslim World' (Beirut, 1928), trs. in *Women and Islam*, ed. Azizah al-Hibri, op. cit., pp. 221–6.

26. See Rosemary Sayegh, *Palestinians: from Peasants to Revolutionaries* (London: Zed Books, 1979) for oral histories from this period.

27. Matiel E.T. Mogannam, *The Arab Woman and the Palestine Question* (London: Herbert Joseph, 1937), pp. 54–5.

28. Quoted in D.C. Gordon, op. cit., p. 47.

Notes to captions in Chapter VIII

1. From the memoirs of Mo'ayer al-Mamalik: *Rajal-e 'Asr-e Nasiri* (The Notables of the Naseri era), (Tehran: Nashr-e Tarikh, 1361/1982), pp. 233–5 (translated from the Persian).

2. C.J. Edmonds, *Kurds, Turks and Arabs*, op. cit., p. 50.

3. Robert G. Watson, *A History of Persia from the Beginning of the Tenth Century to 1858, with a Review of the Principal Events which Led to the Establishment of the Kajak Dynasty* (London: 1866), p. 388.

4. Extract from an address to the Tenth Press Banquet, Cairo 1928, published in *L'Egyptienne*, November 1928, p. 39 (translated from the French).

5. *Zanan Sokhanvar*, ed. Ali Akbar Moshir Sahini, 3 Vols (Teheran: Elmi, 1335), Vol. I.

6. For details of Mufida Abdul Rahman's career see Margot Badran, 'Huda Shaarawi . . .'; Cynthia Nelson, 'The voices of Doria Shafik: Feminist consciousness in Egypt from 1940–1960', Centre d'études et de documentation économique, juridique et sociale, Institut Français d'Archéologie Orientale: Colloque – 'D'un Orient à l'Autre', Cairo, 1985.

7. PRO FO 226/241, File 7.

Bibliography

Abbott, Nabia, *Aisha, Beloved of Muhammad* (London: Al Saqi Books, 1985) rpt.
— , *Two Queens of Baghdad: Mother and Wife of Harun al-Rashid* (London: Al Saqi Books, 1986) rpt.
— , 'Women' in Ruth Nanda Anshen (ed.), *Mid East: World Center: Yesterday, Today and Tomorrow* (New York: Science of Culture Series, Vol. 7, 1956).

Abou, Selim, *Liban déraciné: immigrés dans l'autre Amerique* (Paris: 1978).

Afshar, Iraj, 'Some remarks on the early history of photography in Iran' in E. Bosworth and C. Hildenbrand (eds.), *Qajar Iran: Political, Social and Cultural Change: Studies Presented to Professor L.P. Elwell-Sutton* (Edinburgh: Edinburgh University Press, 1983).

Ali Muhammad *Shirazi* (calling himself al-Bab), *A Traveller's Narrative Written to Illustrate the Episode of the Bab* ed. and trs. by E.G. Browne, 2 vols. (Cambridge: Cambridge University Press, 1891).

Alloula, Malek, *The Colonial Harem* (Minneapolis: University of Minnesota Press, 1986; Manchester: Manchester University Press, 1987).

Allwood, John, *The Great Exhibitions* (London: Studio Vista, 1977).

Amin, Qasim, *Tahrir al-mar'a* (The Emancipation of Women), (Cairo: 1899).
— , *Al-mar'a al-jadida* (The New Woman), (Cairo: 1901).

Ammar, Hamid M., *Growing up in an Egyptian Village* (London: Routledge Kegan Paul, 1954).

Auclert, Hubertine, *Les femmes arabes en Algérie* (Paris: 1900).

Azari, Farah (ed.), *Women of Iran: the Conflict with Fundamentalist Islam* (London: Ithaca Press, 1983).

al-Azm, Sadiq Jalal, 'Orientalism and Orientalism in reverse' in *Forbidden Agendas: Intolerance and Defiance in the Middle East* (London: Al Saqi Books, 1984).

Badran, Margot, 'Huda Shaarawi and the Liberation of Egyptian Women', D. Phil Thesis, St Antony's College, Oxford, 1977.
— , 'The feminist vision of three turn of the century Egyptian women', paper given at the British Society of Middle Eastern Studies Conference, London, 1986.
— , 'Independent women: a century of feminism in Egypt', paper presented at the Symposium on Arab Women – 'Old Boundaries, New Frontiers' – Georgetown University, Washington DC, 1986.
— , 'Dual Liberations: Feminism and nationalism in Egypt 1870s–1920s', *Feminist Issues*, Fall 1987.

Barthes, Roland, *Camera Lucida* (London: Fontana, 1984).

Beck, Lois & Nikki Keddie, *Women in the Muslim World* (Cambridge, Mass./London: Harvard University Press, 1982).

Bell, Gertrude, *The Desert and the Sown* (London: Virago, 1985) rpt.
— , *Letters*, selected and edited by Lady Bell. 2 vols. (London: Ernest Benn, 1927).
— , *Gertrude Bell, from Her Personal Papers, 1889–1926* ed. Elizabeth Burgoyne, 2 vols. (London: Ernest Benn, 1958/1961).

Benedict, Burton, *The Anthropology of the World's Fairs* (London: Scholar Press, 1983).

Benjamin, Walter, 'The work of art in the age of mechanical reproduction', in Hannah Arendt (ed.), *Illuminations* (London: Jonathan Cape, 1970).

Berger, John, *About Looking* (London: Writers and Readers, 1980).
— & Jean Mohr, *Another Way of Telling* (London: Writers and Readers, 1982).

Berque, Jacques, *Egypt, Imperialism and Revolution* (London: Faber & Faber, 1972).

Bird, Isabella, *Journeys in Persia and Kurdistan*, 2 vols. (London: John Murray, 1891).

Blackman, Winifred S., *The Fellahin of Upper Egypt* (London: G.G. Harrap, 1927).
— , 'An Englishwoman in Upper Egypt', *The Wide World Magazine*, January–March 1924.

Blunt, Lady Anne Isabella Noel, *A Pilgrimage to Nejd*, 2 vols. (London: John Murray, 1881).

Boudhiba, A., *Islam and Sexuality* (London: Routledge Kegan Paul, 1985).

Bourdieu, Pierre et al, *Un Art Moyen: essai sur les usages sociaux de la photographie* (Paris: Le Sens Commun, 1965).

Brown, Demetra (Vaka), *The Unveiled Ladies of Stamboul* (New York/Boston: Houghton Mifflin Co., 1923).

Burgin, Victor (ed.), *Thinking Photography* (London/ Basingstoke: Macmillan, 1982).

Burton, Lady Isabel, *The Inner Life of Syria, Palestine and the Holy Land: from My Private Journal*, 2 vols. (London: H.S. King & Co., 1875).

Chaliand, G. and Y. Ternon, *The Armenians: from Genocide to Resistance* (London: Zed Press, 1983).

Chantre, Ernest, *Recherches anthropologiques dans l'Afrique orientale – Egypte* (Lyon: 1904).

Cleveland, W.L., *The Making of an Arab Nationalist: Ottomanism and Arabism in the Life and Thought of Sati' al-Husri* (Princeton: Princeton University Press, 1971).

al-Daghestani, Kazim, *Etude sociologique sur la famille musulmane contemporaine en Syrie* (Paris: Leroux, 1932).

'Deuxième congrès musulman général des femmes d'Orient à Teheran, Nov/Dec 1932', *Revue des Etudes Islamiques*, Vol. VII, 1933.

d'Huart, A. and N. Tazi, *Harems* (Paris: Chène/ Hachette, 1980).

Dickson, H.A.R., *The Arab of the Desert: a Glimpse into Bedawin Life in Kuwait and Saudi Arabia* (London: George Allen & Unwin, 1949).

Dieulafoy, Jane, *La Perse, la Chaldée et la Susiane* (Paris: 1887).

Duff Gordon, Lucie, *Letters from Egypt* (London: Virago, 1983) rpt.

Dusen, Roxan A., 'The study of women in the Middle East: some thoughts', *MESA Bulletin*, Vol. X, No. 2, 1976.

'Early photography in Egypt', *Creative Camera*, No. 186, Dec. 1979.

Ebers, Georg Moritz, *Egypt, Descriptive, Historical and Picturesque*, 2 vols. (London: Cassell & Co., 1883).

Edip, Halide, *Memoirs* (New York/London: Century Co., 1926).

Edmonds, C.J., *Kurds, Turks and Arabs* (London: Oxford University Press, 1957).

Edwards, A.C., *The Persian Carpet* (London: Gerald Duckworth, 1953).

Fanon, Frantz, *A Dying Colonialism* (London: Writers and Readers, 1980).
— *Black Skin, White Masks* (London: Pluto Press, 1986).

Farraq, Nadia, 'Al-Muqtataf 1876–1900: journalism in Syria and Egypt', D. Phil. Thesis, University of Oxford, 1969.

'The feminist movement in Persia', *Central Asia Review* (London) Vol. VII, 1959.

Fernea, E.W. and B. Bezirgan (eds.), *Middle Eastern Women Speak* (Austin, Texas/London: University of Texas Press, 1978).

Garnett, L.M.J., *Turkish Life in Town and Country* (London: George Newnes, 1904).
— , *The Women of Turkey and Their Folklore*, 2 vols. (London: D. Nutt, 1890–91).

Gaudry, M., *La femme chaouia de l'Aurès: étude de sociologie berbère* (Paris: 1929).

Gavin, Carney, 'Bonfils and the early photography of the Near East', *Harvard Library Bulletin*, Vol. XXVI, No. 4 Oct 1978.

Gellner, Ernest and C.A. Micaud (eds.), *Arabs and Berbers: from Tribe to Nation in North Africa* (London: Duckworth, 1973).

Gernsheim, Helmut, *The Origins of Photography* (New York: Thames & Hudson, 1982).

Goichon, A.M., *La vie féminine du Mzab: étude de sociologie musulmane* (Paris: 1927).
— , 'La femme de la moyenne bourgeoisie fasiya', *Revue des Etudes Islamiques*, Vol. III, 1929.

Gordon, D.C., *Women of Algeria: an Essay on Change* (Cambridge, Mass.: Harvard University Press, 1968).

Graham-Brown, S., *Palestinians and Their Society: a Photographic Essay 1880–1946* (London: Quartet Books, 1980).

— , 'Orientalism in colour', *MERIP Reports*, No. 125/126, July–Sept. 1984.

Granqvist, Hilma, *Marriage Conditions in a Palestinian Village*, 2 vols. (Helsingfors: Societas Scientiarum Fennica. Commentationes Humanarum Litterarum, Vol. III, No. 8 and Vol. VI, No. 8, 1931 and 1935).

— , *Birth and Childhood among the Arabs: Studies in a Muhammadan Village in Palestine* (Helsingfors: Soderstrom & Co., 1947).

— , *Muslim Death and Burial: Arab Customs and Traditions Studies in a Village in Jordan* (Helsingfors: Societas Scientiarum Fennica. Commentationes Humanarum Litterarum, Vol. XXXIV, No. 1, 1965).

Hamdy Bey, Ahmed and Marie de Launay, *Les costumes populaires de la Turquie en 1873. Publié sous le patronage de la Commission Imperiale Ottomane pour l'Exposition Universelle de Vienne* (Constantinople: 1873).

Hamouda, Naziha, 'Rural women in the Aurès: a poetry in context', *Oral History Journal*, Vol. 13, No. 1, Spring 1985.

Harper, Mary J., 'Recovering the Other: Women and the Orient in writings of early nineteenth century France', *Critical Matrix*, Vol. I, No. 3, 1985.

al-Hibri, Azizah (ed.), *Women and Islam* (Oxford: Pergamon Press, 1982).

Hilton Simpson, M.W., *Among the Hill Folk of Algeria: Journeys among the Shawia of the Aurès Mountains* (London: T. Fisher Unwin, 1921).

Hirsh, Julia, *Family Photographs: Content, Meaning and Effect* (New York/London: Oxford University Press, 1981).

Hobsbawm, Eric and Terence Ranger (eds.), *The Invention of Tradition* (Cambridge: Cambridge University Press, 1984).

Hopkinson, Tom, *Picture Post 1938–1950* (London: Chatto & Windus, 1984).

Hourani, A.H., *Arabic Thought in the Liberal Age 1798–1939* (Cambridge: Cambridge University Press, 1983) rpt.

Hugo, Victor, *Les Orientales: Poèmes* (Paris: Charles Gosselin, 1829).

Hurgronje, Snouk, *Mecca in the Latter Part of the 19th Century* (translation of Vol. II of *Mecca* [The Hague: 1888]) (Leiden: E.J. Brill/London: Luzac & Co, 1931).

Jaussen, A., *Coutumes palestiniennes I: Naplouse et son district* (Paris: Geuthner, 1927).

Jessup, Rev. Harris, *Women of the Arabs: Seventeen Years a Missionary in Syria* (New York: 1873).

Jouin, Jeanne, 'Le costume féminin dans l'Islam syro-palestinien', *Revue des Etudes Islamiques*, Vol. VIII, 1934.

— , 'Iconographie de la mariée citadine dans l'Islam nord africain', *Revue des Etudes Islamiques*, Vol. V, 1931.

Jullian, Philippe, *The Orientalists: European Painters of Eastern Scenes* (Oxford: Phaidon, 1977).

Kandiyoti, Deniz, 'From Empire to Nation State: transformations of the Woman Question in Turkey', forthcoming in *History of Women: Changing Perceptions* (Paris: UNESCO).

— , 'Women as metaphor: the Turkish novel from the Tanzimat to the Republic', in Kenneth Brown et al (eds.), *The State, Urban Crisis and Social Movements in the Middle East and North Africa* (Paris: L'Harmattan, 1987).

Keddie, Nikki, *Religion and Rebellion in Iran: the Iranian Tobacco Protest of 1891–2* (London: Frank Cass, 1966).

Khairallah, K.T., *La Syrie: la vie sociale et litteraire* (Paris: 1912).

Khalaf, Samir, *Persistence and Change in Nineteenth-century Lebanon* (Beirut: American University of Beirut, 1979).

Knibiehler, Yvonne and Regine Goutalier, *La Femme au temps des colonies* (Paris: Editions Stock, 1985).

Lacouture, J. and S., *Egypt in Transition* (London: Methuen & Co., 1958).

Lane, E.W., *An Account of the Manners and Customs of the Modern Egyptians, Written in Egypt during the Years 1833–35* (London: Gardner, 1985).

Laoust, Henri, 'Introduction à une étude de l'enseignement arabe en Egypte', *Revue des Etudes Islamiques*, Vol. VII, 1933.

Lebedeva, O.S., *De l'emancipation de la femme musulmane* (Lisieux, 1900).

Leeder, S.H., *The Veiled Mysteries of Egypt and the Religion of Islam* (London: Evaleigh Nash, 1912).

Lefevre-Bousquet, Laure, *Recherches sur la condition de la femme Kabyle: la coutume et l'oeuvre française* (Algiers: Imprimeries La Typo-Litho et Jules Carbonel réunies, 1939).

Lloyd, Jill, 'Old photographs, vanished peoples and stolen potatoes', *Art Monthly* (UK), No. 83, Feb. 1985.

Longrigg, S. and F. Stoakes, *Iraq* (London: Ernest Benn, 1958).

Lortet, Louis, *La Syrie d'aujourd'hui: voyages dans la Phénicie, le Liban et la Judée 1875–1880* (Paris: 1884).

Loti, Pierre, *Disenchanted* (*Les Désenchantées – roman des harems turcs contemporains*) (London: Macmillan & Co., 1905).

Lucas, P. and J-C Vatin, *L'Algérie des anthropologues* (Paris: Maspero, 1982).

Mackenzie, John, *Propaganda and Empire: the Manipulation of British Public Opinion 1800–1960* (Manchester: Manchester University Press, 1984).

Mahfouz, Naguib Bey, *The History of Medical Education in Egypt* (Cairo: Government Press, 1935).

Al-mar'a al-arabiya wa qadia filastin. Al- mu'tamar al-nisai al-sharqi al-mun'aqad fi'l Qahira min 15 ila 18 Oktober 1938. (Arab women and the Palestine situation. The conference of Eastern women held in Cairo from 15 to 18 October, 1938). Proceedings of the conference published in Arabic (Cairo, ?1938).

Marmorstein, E., 'The Veil in Judaism and Islam', *Journal of Jewish Studies*, Vol. V, No. 2, 1954.

Martineau, Harriet, *Eastern Life, Present and Past*, 3 vols. (London: 1848).

Massé, Henri, 'Le dévoilement des Iraniennes', *Revue des Etudes Islamiques*, Vol. IX, 1935.

Mazas, P., 'La Semaine sociale de Beyrouth: les droits de la femme', *En Terre d'Islam*, No. 23, 1948.

Meakin, J.E. Budgett, *Life in Morocco and Glimpses Beyond* (London: Chatto & Windus, 1905).

Menemencioğlu, Nermin, 'The Ottoman Theatre 1839–1923', paper given at a symposium on the Turkish Theatre at the School for Oriental and African Studies, London University, March 1983.

Mernissi, Fatima, *Beyond the Veil* (London: Al Saqi Books, 1985).

Miller, Dickinson Jenkins, 'The craftsman's art: Armenians and the growth of photography in the Near East 1856–1981'. MA Thesis, American University of Beirut, August 1981.

ol-Moluk, Mrs Bamdad Badr, *From Darkness into Light: Women's Emancipation in Iran*, ed. and trs. F.R.C. Bagley (Smithtown, NY: Exposition Press, 1977).

Mogannam, M.E.T., *The Arab Woman and the Palestine Problem* (London: Herbert Joseph, 1937).

Montgomery, H.B., *Western Women in Eastern Lands: an Outline Study of Fifty Years of Women's Work in Foreign Missions* (New York: Macmillan Co., 1910).

Monti, Nicholas, 'Images to Fuel an Empire', *Aperture*, No. 94, 1984.

Musil, Alois, *The Manners and Customs of the Rwalla Bedouins* (New York/Prague: Oriental Explorations and Studies, No. 6, 1928).

Nasir al-Din Shah, *Diary of HM Shah of Persia during his Tours through Europe in 1873* (London: 1874).

Neave, Dorina L., *Twenty-six Years on the Bosphorus* (London: Grayson & Grayson, 1933).

Nelson, Cynthia, 'Public and private politics: women in the Middle Eastern world', *American Ethnologist*, Vol. 1, No. 3, August 1984.
— , 'The Voices of Doria Shafik: feminist consciousness in Egypt from 1940–1960', Centre d'études et de documentation économique, juridique et sociale, Institut Français d'Archéologie Orientale: Colloque 'D'un Orient à L'Autre' Cairo 1985.

Nerval, Gerard de, *Women of Cairo: Scenes of Life in the Orient (Voyage en Orient)*, 2 vols. (London: George Routledge & Sons, 1929)

Newhall, Beaumont (ed.), *Photography: Essays and Images* (London: Secker & Warburg, 1981).

Nochlin, Linda, 'The Imaginary Orient', *Art in America*, May 1983.

Nora, Pierre, *Les Lieux de Mémoire* (Paris: Gallimard, 1984).

Owen, E.R.J., *The Middle East in the World Economy 1800–1914* (London: Methuen, 1981).
— , *Cotton and the Egyptian Economy 1820–1914: a Study of Trade and Development* (Oxford: Clarendon Press, 1969).

Patrick, Mary Mills, *A Bosporus Adventure: Istanbul – Constantinople Women's College 1871–1924* (Stanford University: Stanford University Press/London: Oxford University Press, 1934).

Penzer, N.M., *The Harem* (London: Spring Books, 1965) rpt.

Poole, Sophia Lane, *The Englishwoman in Egypt: Letters from Cairo during a Residence There in 1842, 3 and 4. Letters during 1845–6*, Second Series. 3 vols. (London: 1844–46).

Racy, Ali Jihad, 'The record industry and Egyptian traditional music 1904–34', *Ethnomusicology*, 1976.

Ramsay, W.M., *The Revolution in Constantinople and Turkey, with Episodes and Photographs by Lady Ramsay* (London: Hodder & Stoughton, 1909).

Reiter, R.R. (ed.), *Towards an Anthropology of Women* (New York: Monthly Review Press, 1975).

Rosenthal, D.A., *Orientalism: the Near East in French Painting 1800–1880* (Rochester NY: Memorial Art Gallery of the University of Rochester, 1982).

Rushdi Pasha, Madame (Eugènie le Brun), *Harems et musulmanes d'Egypte: Lettres* (Paris: Librairie Félix Juven, 1902).
— , *Les Répudiées* (Paris: Librairie Félix Juven, 1908).

Sabbah, F., *Women in the Muslim Unconscious* (New York: Pergamon Press, 1984).

Sagne, Jean, 'L'exotisme dans le portrait photographique au XIX siècle', *Revue de la Bibliothèque Nationale*, 1ère année, No. 1, Sept. 1981.

Said, Edward, *Orientalism* (London: Routledge & Kegan Paul, 1978).

Sanassarian, Eliz, *The Women's Rights Movement in Iran* (New York: Praeger, 1982).

Sayegh, Rosemary, *Palestinians: from Peasants to Revolutionaries* (London: Zed Press, 1979).

Scarce, Jennifer, 'Isfahan in camera: nineteenth-century Persia through the photographs of Ernest Hoeltzer', *Art and Archeology Research Papers*, April 1976.

Seger, Karen (ed.), *Portrait of a Palestinian Village: the Photographs of Hilma Granqvist* (London: Third World Centre for Research and Publishing, 1981).

Sekula, Allan (ed.), *Photography against the Grain* (Halifax: the Press of the Nova Scotia College of Art and Design, 1984).

Seni, Nora, 'Ville ottomane et representation du corps féminin', *Les Temps Modernes*, No. 456–7, July/August 1984.

Shaarawi, Huda, *Harem Years*, ed. and trs. with introduction by Margot Badran (London: Virago, 1986; New York: Feminist Press, 1987).

Shafik, Doria (Ragai), 'Egyptian feminism', *Middle East Affairs*, Vol. III, no. 8–9 (Aug.–Sept. 1952).
— , *La femme nouvelle en Egypte* (Cairo: 1941).

Shuster, W.M., *The Strangling of Persia* (London: T. Fisher Unwin, 1912).

Smith, Pamela Ann, *Palestine and the Palestinians 1976–1983* (London: Croom Helm, 1984).

Sönmez, Emel, 'Turkish women in Turkish literature of the nineteenth century', *Die Welt des Islams* (Leiden), NS Vol. 12, No. 1–3, 1969.

Sontag, Susan, *On Photography* (Harmondsworth: Penguin, 1979).

Sparroy, Wilfrid, *Persian Children of the Royal Family: the Narrative of an English Tutor at the Court of H.I.H. Zillu's-Sultan* (London/New York: John Lane, 1902).

Stark, Freya, *The Southern Gates of Arabia* (London: John Murray, 1936).
— , *Baghdad Sketches* (London: John Murray, 1937).
— , *Seen in the Hadramaut* (London: John Murray, 1938).
— , *Letters from Syria* (London: John Murray, 1942).
— , *Beyond Euphrates: Autobiography 1928–1933* (London: John Murray, 1951).

Steegmuller, Francis (ed.), *Flaubert in Egypt: a Sensibility on Tour* (Boston/Toronto: Bodley Head, 1972).
— , *Flaubert and Madame Bovary* (London: Robert Hale, 1939).

Stevens, Mary Ann (ed.), *The Orientalists: Delacroix to Matisse* (London: Royal Academy of Arts, 1984).

Sykes, Ella, *Through Persia on a Sidesaddle* (London: A.D. Innes & Co., 1898).

— ,*Persia and Its People* (London: Methuen & Co., 1910).

Tarazi, Phillipe de, *Tarikh as-sahafat al-arabiyya* (History of the Arabic Press) 4 vols. (Beirut: 1913–33).

Tassel, Janet Quinn, 'Dragomans, Sheikhs and Moon-faced Beauties', *Art News*, No. 79, Dec. 1980.

Thomas, Alan, *Time in a Frame: Photography and the Nineteenth-century Mind* (New York: Schocken, 1977).

Thompson, Mrs Bowen (Smith, S.E.), *Daughters of Syria: a Narrative of the Efforts of Mrs Bowen Thompson for the Evangelisation of the Syrian Females* (London: Seeley, Jackson & Halliday, 1872).

Thomson, W.M., *The Land and the Book, or Biblical Illustrations Drawn from the Manners and Customs, the Scenes and Scenery, of the Holy Land* (London: T. Nelson & Sons, 1879).

Tibawi, A.L., *Arab Education in Mandatory Palestine* (London: Luzac & Co., 1956).

Toledano, E.R., *The Ottoman Slave Trade and Its Suppression 1840–1890* (Princeton N.J.: Princeton University Press, 1982).

Toprak, Zafer, 'The 1935 International Feminism Congress and Peace' (in Turkish), *Dusun*, special issue on 'Women and Society', March 1986.

Trémaux, Pierre, *Voyages au Sudan oriental, dans l'Afrique septentrionale et dans l'Asie Mineure, executés de 1847 à 1854 . . . Atlas des vues pittoresques, scènes de moeurs, types de végétation remarquables*, Ser. 3 (Paris: 1863).

Tucker, Judith, *Women in Nineteenth-century Egypt* (Cambridge: Cambridge University Press, 1985).

Tugay, Emine Foat, *Three Centuries: Family Chronicles of Turkey and Egypt* (London: Oxford University Press, 1963).

Warner, Marina, *Alone of All Her Sex: the Myths and Cults of the Virgin Mary* (London: Weidenfeld & Nicolson, 1976).

— , *Monuments and Maidens: the Allegory of the Female Form* (London: Weidenfeld & Nicolson, 1985).

Watson, Robert G., *A History of Persia from the Beginning of the Tenth Century to . . . 1858, with a Review of the Principle Events which Led to the Establishment of the Kajar Dynasty* (London: 1866).

Weir, S. & W. Kawar, 'Costumes and wedding customs in Bayt Dajan', *Palestine Exploration Quarterly*, No. 107, 1975.

Zeyneb Khanum, *A Turkish Woman's European Impressions*, ed. and trs. by Grace Ellison (London: Seeley, Service & Co, 1913).

Photographic Credits

Photographs from family collections have been credited to the person from whom they were obtained

Introduction

1 Gernsheim Collection, University of Texas at Austin
2 Hotz Collection, Universitetsbibliotek, Leiden
3 New York Public Library
4 New York Public Library
5 Imperial War Museum, London
6 Church Missionary Society Archives, University of Birmingham
7 *Illustrated London News* Picture Library
8 Blackman Collection, Department of Archaeology, University of Liverpool
9 Granqvist Collection, Palestine Exploration Fund, London
10 Engin Çizgen, Istanbul, private collection

Chapter I

1 Library of Congress, Washington
2 Pitt Rivers Museum, University of Oxford
3 Daniel Wolf Inc., New York
4 Malek Alloula, Paris, private collection
6 Prentenkabinet, Kunsthistorisch Institut der Rijksuniversiteit te Leiden, Holland
7 Boston Public Library
9 Jacques Fivel Collection, New York
10 Bibliothèque Nationale, Paris
11 Badr al-Hajj, London, private collection
13 Lyons Collection, Middle East Centre, St Antony's College, Oxford
14 Badr al-Hajj, London, private collection
15 British Library, London
16 Palestine Exploration Fund, London
17 Gertrude Bell Photographic Archive, Department of Archaeology, University of Newcastle-upon-Tyne
18 Archives of Albert Kahn, Paris
19 British Library, London
20 Musée des Arts Decoratifs, Paris
21 Royal Geographical Society, London
22 Abdul Hamid Archive, Istanbul University
23 British Library, London
24 Engin Çizgen, Istanbul, private collection
26 Collection Roger-Viollet, Paris
27 Société de Géographie, Paris

28 Palestine Exploration Fund, London
29 Badr al-Hajj, London, private collection
30 Museum voor Volkenkunde, Rotterdam
33 Granqvist Collection, Palestine Exploration Fund, London
34 Berna Tunali, Istanbul, private collection

Chapter II

2 Foreign and Commonwealth Library, London
3 Universitetsbibliothek, Leiden
4 Malek Alloula, Paris, private collection
5 Henry Balfour Collection, Pitt Rivers Museum, University of Oxford
6 Library of Congress, Washington
7 Freya Stark Collection, Middle East Centre, St Antony's College, Oxford
8 Library of Congress, Washington
9 Bibliothèque Nationale, Paris
10 Gertrude Bell Photographic Archive, Department of Archaeology, University of Newcastle-upon-Tyne
11 Henry Balfour Collection, Pitt Rivers Museum, University of Oxford
12 Bahija Rashid, Cairo, private collection
13 German Archaeological Institute, Istanbul
14 Engin Çizgen, Istanbul, private collection
15 Hawa Idriss, Cairo, private collection
16 Armstrong Collection, Middle East Centre, St Antony's College, Oxford
17 Library of Congress, Washington
18 Collection Roger-Viollet, Paris
19 British Library, London
20 Daniel Wolf Inc., New York
21 Fouad Debbas, Paris, private collection
22 Sykes Collection, Middle East Centre, St Antony's College, Oxford
23 Granqvist Collection, Palestine Exploration Fund, London
24 Royal Anthropological Institute, London
25 Blackman Collection, Department of Archaeology, University of Liverpool
26 New York Public Library
27 Museum voor Volkenkunde, Rotterdam
28 Freya Stark Collection, Middle East Centre, St Antony's College, Oxford

Chapter III

1 Engin Gargar, Istanbul, private collection
2 Archives of the Armenian Patriarchate, Jerusalem
3 Badr al-Hajj, London, private collection
4 Hurgronje Collection, Univesitetsbibliotek, Leiden
5 Nada Andraous, London, private collection
6–10 Saad Kamil, Cairo, private collection
11 Berna Tunali, Istanbul, private collection
12 Aziza Galal, Cairo, private collection
15 Mehrez family, Cairo, private collection
16 Reem Saad, Cairo, private collection
17 Library of Congress, Washington
18 Badr al-Hajj, London, private collection
19 Freya Stark Collection, Middle East Centre, St Antony's College, Oxford
20 Library of Congress, Washington
21 Maynard Owen Williams, National Geographic Society, Washington
22 New York Public Library
23 Department of Archaeology, University of Liverpool
24 Archives of the Armenian Patriarchate, Jerusalem
25 Süreyya Ağaoğlu, Istanbul, private collection
26 Engin Gargar, Istanbul, private collection
27 Cecil Hourani, London, private collection
28 Serene Shahid, London, private collection
29–31 Tashdjian family, London, private collection

Chapter IV

1 Photothèque, Musée de l'Homme, Paris
2 Trustees of the Victoria & Albert Museum, London
3 Archives of the Armenian Patriarchate, Jerusalem
4 Library of Congress, Washington
5 Library of Congress, Washington
6 Freya Stark Collection, Middle East Centre, St Antony's College, Oxford
7 Imperial War Museum, London
8 British Library, London
9 Bibliothèque Nationale, Paris
10 Sykes Collection, Middle East Centre, St Antony's College, Oxford
12 *Illustrated London News* Picture Library, London
13 Library of Congress, Washington
15 Reem Saad, Cairo, private collection
16a–b Photothèque, Musée de l'Homme, Paris
17 Musée des Arts Decoratifs, Paris
18 Malek Alloula, Paris, private collection
19 Royal Commonwealth Society, London
21 Archives of the Armenian Patriarchate, Jerusalem
22 Tarif al-Khalidi, Oxford, private collection
24 Photothèque, Musée de l'Homme, Paris
25 British Library, London
26 Société de Géographie, Paris

Chapter V

1 Granqvist Collection, Palestine Exploration Fund, London
2 Matson Collection, Library of Congress, Washington
3 Royal Anthropological Institute, London
4 Library of Congress, Washington
5 Granqvist Collection, Palestine Exploration Fund, London
6 Tweedy Collection, Middle East Centre, Oxford
7 Freya Stark Collection, Middle East Centre, Oxford
8 Middle East Centre, St Antony's College, Oxford
9 Palestine Exploration Fund, London
10 Imperial War Museum, London
11 Middle East Centre, St Antony's College, Oxford
12 Royal Geographical Society, London
13 Fouad Debbas, Paris, private collection
14 Archives of Albert Kahn, Paris
15 Middle East Centre, St Antony's College, Oxford
17 Royal Anthropological Institute, London
20 Middle East Centre, St Antony's College, Oxford
21 Süreyya Ağaoğlu, Istanbul, private collection
22 Library of the Wellcome Institute for the History of Medicine, London
23 Blackman Collection, Department of Archaeology, University of Liverpool
24 Library of Congress, Washington
25 Cecil Hourani, London, private collection

Chapter VI

1 Nadim Shehadi, Oxford, Private collection
4 Library of Congress, Washington
5 Royal Anthropological Institute, London
6 British Library, London
7 Coghill Collection, Middle East Centre, St Antony's College, Oxford
8 Blackman Collection, Department of Archaeology, University of Liverpool
9 Sykes Collection, Middle East Centre, St Antony's College, Oxford
10 Société de Géographie, Paris
11 *Illustrated London News* Picture Library, London
14 Archives of Ruz al-Yusuf, Cairo

Chapter VII

1 Tomris Uyar, Istanbul, private collection
2 Museum voor Volkenkunde, Rotterdam
3 Archives of the Armenian Patriarchate, Jerusalem
4 New York Public Library
5 New York Public Library

6 Mehmet and Nouran Isvan, Istanbul, private collection

7 Archive of the American College for Girls, Robert College, Istanbul

8 Abdul Hamid Archive, Istanbul University

9 Mehmet and Nouran Isvan, Istanbul, private collection

10 Photothèque, Musée de l'Homme, Paris

12 Süreyya Ağaoğlu, Istanbul, private collection

14 Fouad Debbas, Paris, private collection

15 Church Missionary Society Archives, University of Birmingham

Chapter VIII

1 *Fehrest Album Halai Ketab Khaneh Saltanati* (1978), Tehran Imperial Museum

2 Amira al-Asad, Beirut, private collection

3 Edmonds Collection, Middle East Centre, St Antony's College, Oxford

6 Huda Shaarawi Association, Cairo

9 Owen Tweedy Collection, Middle East Centre, St Antony's College, Oxford

10 Library of Congress, Washington

12 BBC Hulton Picture Library, London

17 Bahija Rashid, Cairo, private collection

19 Saad Kamil, Cairo, private collection

21 Rita Giacaman, Ramallah, private collection

22 Middle East Centre, St Antony's College, Oxford

23 Aziz al-Azmeh, Exeter, private collection

Index